TRUTH AND ILLUSION:

THE POLITICS OF SPIRITUALITY

AND HOW

ONE PERSON'S LIE

IS

ANOTHER ONE'S TRUTH

REV. CAROL E. RICHARDSON

HIGHEST HARMONY HEALING & COACHING
ROCKVILLE, MARYLAND

Truth and Illusion:

The Politics of Spirituality and

How One Person's Lie is Another One's Truth

Copyright 2017 Rev. Carol E. Richardson

Highest Harmony Healing & Coaching
Rockville, Maryland

ISBN: 978-0-692-88672-4

Cover Art by Davonne Flanagan

Cover Art Copyright for the yin-yang earth image:
<ahref='http://www.123rf.com/profile_mnsanthoshkumar'>mnsanthoshkumar / 123RF Stock Photo</a>

To all my clients:

I have learned so much by working with you.

Thank you.

I am so grateful that you have been, and many still remain, a part of my life.

I love you all very much.

Thank you for showing me the Divine in you!

Love and Light,

Carol "Anandi"

CONTENTS

Introduction   6

Part I: Contemplating Truth

Chapter One: What Is Truth?   23

Chapter Two: Spiritual Worldviews and the Politics of Knowing the "Truth"   83

Chapter Three: Intellect, Intuition, and Illusion   115

Part II: Inner Ways of Knowing Truth

Chapter Four: Cultivating Wisdom – The Inner Path to Truth   134

Chapter Five: Your Intuitive Self – The Chakra System and Subtle Energy   166

Part III: The Chakra System as a Path to Truth

Chapter Six: Seven Spiritual Worldviews – Why We Think So Differently From Each Other   189

Chapter Seven: The Root Chakra – Worldview, Values, and "Truths"   205

Chapter Eight: The Sacral Chakra – Worldview, Values, and "Truths"   222

Chapter Nine: The Solar Plexus Chakra – Worldview, Values, and "Truths"   244

Chapter Ten: The Heart Chakra – Worldview, Values, and "Truths"   263

Chapter Eleven: The Throat Chakra –
    Worldview, Values, and "Truths"   277

Chapter Twelve: The Brow Chakra – Worldview,
    Values, and "Truths"   297

Chapter Thirteen: The Crown Chakra –
    Worldview, Values, and Truth   309

Chapter Fourteen: Truth as Wisdom to Heal
    Humanity – a Universal Dharma   322

INTRODUCTION

*"Human knowledge and skills alone
cannot lead humanity
to a happy and dignified life.
Humanity has every reason to place
the proclaimers of high moral standards and values
above the discoverers of objective truth."
– Albert Einstein*[1]

Age after age, humanity has struggled with the question, "What is truth?" along with correlated questions such as, "Is this true or false?" and "How can we know for certain what is true?" In the 21st Century, these questions have grown ironically more complicated. While the digital age has significantly increased our access to information and our ability to spread information, the internet and all forms of publicly accessible media have also made it increasingly easy and common to spread what is now euphemistically referred to as "misinformation."

The urgently pressing question humanity faces is: how do we distinguish lies from truth, especially in a digital world, where events, opinions, and misinformation can "go viral" literally around the globe within 60 seconds?

To make matters more complicated, both politicians and media too often reflect the "truths" that moneyed

---

[1] Quote accessed here on September 12, 2016:
http://www.higherperspectives.com/albert-einstein-quotes-1406166918.html
and also here: https://en.wikiquote.org/wiki/Albert_Einstein where it has been attributed to: "written statement (September 1937), p. 70."

interests who can afford the advertising want the populace to hear. Moreover, the political practice of calling one's opponent a liar seems to have peaked during the 2016 presidential campaign season, while giving one's own version of "truth" which did not always match online fact-checking became commonplace in American politics.

To many of us, particularly since the election, the "misinformation" has become quite obvious as we read our news through more reliable, independent online sources. We can depend on sources which are not commercially supported by advertisements in order to gain some access to at least a better sense of truth. We must seek out such greed-free sources of information rather than "truth" or "news" reported for the sake of increased revenues, as we seek to overcome media bias in our quest for the truths of everyday events.

Yet, millions of people access their "news" reports primarily through television and radio news shows which sometimes do not offer such rigorous fact-checking. As a result, the United States in particular and the world in general recently became overwhelmed with dueling versions of truth and illusion during the presidential election of 2016. Unfortunately, the dueling versions of truth and illusion have, since the election, begun to include the entirely illusory category of "alternative facts."

Moreover, this tendency to refer to opponents as liars or to accuse opponents without a shred of evidence has created less trust and even more hostility among human beings, in political as well as social spheres.

The lack of trust and overt hostility create further challenges to accessing "truth." In an atmosphere of social media image projections and illusions, defensiveness reigns, one-up-man-ship rules, and truth may be left at the bottom of the heap.

In the meantime, we wonder how we can trust each other, or how people of opposing political views can even trust their candidates. Many of us may have wondered how we can even trust our own candidates! Post-election 2016, many of us wonder if we will ever be able to trust our elected officials, including our president, to speak the truth.

If you have ever wondered, like me, how people with opposing political views can manage to believe what they believe, trust whom they trust, and value what they value, then please join me in a quest for understanding how we can think, believe, trust, and value so differently from each other that we arrive at different versions of the "truth."

We may have found ourselves wondering if those who differ with us politically are less intelligent or less well-educated. However, clearly there are intelligent, well-educated people on both sides of most issues. Or, we may have wondered if people whose views are diametrically opposed to ours just don't care about other people, or don't have a high sense of morality. Again, clearly most people operate from a sense of seeking to accomplish what seems to them to be a greater good not just for themselves but for society or for our country.

We have to ask: If differing political versions of truth and illusion don't arise from sheer virtue or from sheer intelligence, what does give rise to these different views? Is it mere conditioning via the media and previous generations in our families?

Of course, the media and our families have very strong effects on us. One example is the famous dictum that babies are not born prejudiced. Clearly, in America, prejudice is still not only common, but still helps win elections.

Specifically, the media and our families can affect our values, biases, prejudices, worldview, religious views, sense of morality, and basic knowledge levels, as well as our openness to learning new information. Beyond this, we either have the ability to think paradigmatically, or we don't. In other words, we either have the ability to question our own basis for thinking we know what we think we know, or we don't. We can either step outside our worldview and understand how others see things, or we cannot.

While most human beings have been challenged to see something from a different perspective, especially from someone else's perspective, I wonder how much of humanity has ever been challenged to think about the fact that our worldviews and paradigms of reality shape our ability to perceive what is actually "out there," and therefore, what is actually "true."

Until we are self-aware enough to know why we see reality the way we do, and aware enough to know that other people's worldviews or paradigms render a different sense of "truth," we may not be able to access anything but an extremely limited sense of truth. This book invites us to see different worldviews in order to understand ourselves and others, especially with regard to how and why we perceive anything as true or false.

The bottom line is that political lies and "truths" represent deeper underlying spiritual worldviews that often lead to bias depending on individual stages of spiritual development. I state this claim not from the perspective of any one religion, but from a synthesis of Eastern and Western understandings of human nature. By spiritual worldviews, I include both materialism and atheism, because these also express ways of viewing the intangibles of life, culture, humanity, and the universe.

> If differing political versions of truth and illusion don't arise from sheer virtue or sheer intelligence, what does give rise to these different views?
>
> . . . Political lies and "truths" represent deeper underlying spiritual worldviews that often lead to bias depending on individual stages of spiritual development.

Spirituality, at its root, consists of the essential, intangible qualities of life and the universe. Spirituality here is also understood as our awareness and expression of values relating to the ethics of human relationships, personal morality, and the meaning of life. As such, spirituality is part of human nature, whether one is an atheist, a materialist, or a very religious human being. You might argue with me that I am speaking of philosophy, to which I would reply that I see philosophy as a form of spirituality, for philosophy entails rational reflection on the essences of things and on the fundamental nature of reality.

We all have spiritual worldviews, whether we are aware of our spiritual worldview or not. In fact, our spiritual worldviews largely determine our sense of what it means to be human, what is true, and what is false. Therefore, in order to understand how one person's lie is another one's truth, we will look at two different models of human spiritual worldviews. The first offers highly insightful information, and yet does not offer a developmental view of humanity. Only a developmental understanding of spiritual worldviews can explain how human beings can evolve in our ability to access, understand, and live the "Truth."

To this end, I offer a holistic understanding of humanity's struggles with truth and illusion, including the diametric opposition of understandings of "truth" in Western political spheres. This holistic understanding arises first by combining aspects of Western psychology with Eastern understandings of human development. Secondly, this holistic understanding derives from harmonizing 10 major dualities of human thought and culture. Third, our model for understanding how we understand "truth" combines spiritual worldviews with the dualities to explore how the various combinations affect our view of truth and illusion. Lastly, we will look at two false dichotomies in order to understand truth more fully.

Our first task in this book is to ask what is truth and how can we find it. Our second task is to look at combining and harmonizing dualistic thinking in order to stop limiting our search for truth. Our third task is to understand spiritual worldviews in order to see how our human interactions are often politicized by our spiritual worldviews. Our fourth task is to seek to understand ourselves and our quest for truth developmentally.

The specific Western concepts that I include have a Western scientific basis to them. These Western concepts are: intellectual and scientific understandings of human nature; the concepts of world views; psychological development from concrete thinking to abstract thinking; moral development; and emotional learning and development.

Please know that my own views were strictly Western for the first 37 years of my life, and, perhaps like you, I had no familiarity with and little inclination to accept Eastern concepts of reality. However, I have come to understand the contributions that much of Eastern philosophy makes to a greater, more expansive recognition of truths about life.

Please join me in considering these Eastern concepts, as unfamiliar as they may be, as a way of expanding our quest for truth.

The specific Eastern concepts that I include have an Eastern scientific basis to them. I will explain what I mean by Eastern science later in this book. The Eastern concepts are: intuitive understandings of human nature; the yoga philosophy of human development along the chakra system of the body; the chakra system of the body which expresses the subtle energies[2] of human beings; and the spiritual evolution of the human soul.

I am well aware that many Americans do not know anything about yoga philosophy or the chakra system of the body (please compare with acupuncture as having practical applications and validity), so I will explain in some detail the ways that we can understand and connect this Eastern way of seeing human beings with our day-to-day experience around the world, including in the United States.

I am also well aware that many people do not believe in the science of subtle energy and the chakra system of the body. I invite you to keep reading as though you are beginning an adventure or a rollercoaster of truth and illusion to see if, together, we can throw out whatever limited thinking has not yet led us to a full discovery of truth. By considering new paradigms and worldviews,

---

[2] Subtle energies and spiritual energies are essentially synonymous, for subtle energies are in effect "intangibles,"
or spiritual aspects of reality because they go beyond material aspects of reality, and exist, in essence, ethereally.

we may discover some new ways of thinking that actually make sense.

If you're tempted to stop reading right here, I invite you to consider that our adventurous quest for truth is designed to create not only greater understanding, but also to lead us to peace and prosperity on a broader, and even global basis.

To connect the dots of truth, peace, and prosperity on a global scale, our initial plan is to combine Western and Eastern approaches. What happens when we combine these two approaches? We can finally arrive at an understanding of why one person's lie can be another person's truth.

Essentially, then, what we are seeking to understand is how a person's orientation toward life, or our worldview, either opens up or limits our sense of what can be true.

First, please allow me to give a personal example of my own evolution in experiencing and perceiving truth in order to portray, in part, the limits we sometimes place on "truth" based on our current understanding of reality.

To understand where I came from in my lifelong exploration of what is "true," it helps to know that I was raised by two highly intelligent parents, both of whom had Ivy League graduate degrees (meaning they were serious intellectuals). I was also raised in a religious worldview, since my parents were Christian missionaries for eleven years - the first five years of my life.

The whole time I was growing up, I was exposed to this sometimes confusing interplay of scientifically-oriented worldviews espoused by my parents, along with highly moral Christian worldviews that they lived out in order to serve and empower others in the name of Christ. My parents' overt goal was not so much conversion as it was serving others and honoring Christ.

On top of this juxtaposition of science and religion, I was exposed to multiple cultural and religious worldviews, as we traveled back-and-forth between Africa and the United States the whole time I was growing up. I experienced vast cultural differences as we lived in the Democratic Republic of the Congo (where I was born), my mom's hometown in west Texas, a suburb of New York City, Dar-es-Salaam, Tanzania in East Africa, where I attended a British International School, the Ivory Coast in West Africa, where I attended a French private school, and then Chevy Chase, Maryland, a highly privileged community right outside of Washington, DC.

I went into culture shock when we moved to Chevy Chase. I could not believe the materialism and competitiveness I saw in American culture. By the time we moved there, at age 11, I had a lot of experience in analyzing and contrasting cultural values. It was easy for me to become aware of the biases as well as the cultural and geographic ignorance of the highly intelligent kids with whom I attended fifth grade in Chevy Chase, even though the neighborhood was also extremely well-educated as a rule (then and now.)

In contrast to my first 11 years of life in which we moved every one or two years, we lived in Chevy Chase for six whole years in a row. Chevy Chase became the first stable home and culture that I experienced growing up. I adapted somewhat to this culture, at least enough to do well in school.

Just before the years in Chevy Chase, though, I had experienced French history lessons at the French private school my siblings and I attended in the Ivory Coast. I remember that, at the time, it seemed as though both the Americans and the French claimed to have invented the same things, which, in my ten-year-old mind, included cars and airplanes. I decided back then that one of the two countries or cultures was lying, even in textbooks. Perhaps I misunderstood what I had been taught, but my general impression was very real that two cultures provided clashing information in their schools based on nationalistic bias. I think my father had also taught me about propaganda, as put out by the American government overseas, and other nations as well.

So, at a very young age, I developed the ability to question what I was taught, to compare cultures, to think critically from outside the worldview surrounding me, and to think for myself. What a gift I received from this international childhood!

After living in Chevy Chase, we moved back to Kinshasa, the capital city of the Congo, when I was sixteen and going into eleventh grade. I went into culture shock again. I witnessed starving people. I hung out with missionary kids again. I was both spiritual and religious, but I was not convinced that miracles were real, even though I wanted to believe they are.

When the other missionary people asked us all to pray for a student who developed throat cancer, I felt guilty because I did not believe in miracles. I felt even guiltier when he died. I felt horrendously guilty when I was asked to read a scripture at his memorial service, and I thought I would never confess this guilt to anyone – but here it is: I did not believe he would be miraculously cured of throat cancer, and he wasn't. At the time, I wondered if it was my fault he died.

Mostly, moving from Chevy Chase back to the Congo and going into culture shock again gave rise to my keen desire to be able to explain life, the universe, and everything. In other words, I desired to know the Truth.

In college, I became a psychology major with a focus on hard scientific data and none of the "fluffy" psychology, Jungian or otherwise. I spent a few years being an agnostic, until a psychology professor taught us a few forms of meditation, and meditation led me back to believing in God again. But I still loved science and doubted miracles.

A couple of years out of college, I ended up studying for a master's degree in public health. During that time period, I got married and gave birth to two children. At the age of 28, I was widowed when my 34-year-old husband died suddenly of a cerebral aneurysm, leaving me with a 7-month-old son and a 22-month-old daughter.

After I had watched my husband lie brain dead in the hospital for almost a week, his death did nothing to encourage me to believe in miracles. Nonetheless, I turned to God. Somehow, I believed that God loved me anyway, and I wanted to help other people believe that God loves them even when they go through tough times. That is when I experienced my "call to ministry," because I felt so motivated to help other people experience God's love.

Despite the lack of miracles, my late husband's death and the time surrounding it did give rise to some spiritual experiences, even some mystical ones, such as I had never experienced before. I did not really know how to make sense of them at the time, and I believe I did not even share some of them with anyone else at the time, since most people around me were not inclined to mystical experiences.

Interestingly, my grandmother had once shared with me a mystical experience she had when her father died and she was only ten years old, in 1912. My grandmother apparently was out on her front porch when she saw her deceased father ride by on a carriage, and as he passed by, he turned and looked at her, and then turned forward again, and drove on. She never shared this experience with anyone until she told me when I was in college. Gradually, as a minister, I discovered that people do often have mystical experiences of loved ones after they die. Because of our culture's disdain for mystical experiences, as though they require being "crazy" instead of rational, many people never share their experiences publicly.

After being widowed, I completed my master's degree in public health (another scientific degree), by the grace of God and with the significant help of two other people. Immediately after completing the degree, I moved to Tennessee to study theology at Vanderbilt University Divinity School. At Vanderbilt, I fell in love with the combination of science and theology! After graduating in December 1993, I began my career of serving churches, but I still doubted miracles.

In 1996, I was given a copy of *Autobiography of a Yogi* by Paramahansa Yogananda. I tried to read the book, *but there were literally too many miracles for me to believe it was real, so I stopped reading it!* This presented a dilemma, because these were the actual stories of this holy man's life, so how could the stories be untrue?

My left brain worldview led me only to trust Western scientific understandings of reality. Miracles, for me, in 1996, were therefore not "true" or real in any rational sense. I had two scientifically based degrees, and I could not wrap my mind around how these mystical, almost magical stories of Yogananda's could be true.

Then I realized that, by not believing that Yogananda was telling the truth, I was not practicing multicultural respect. Having grown up in multiple countries, I knew the importance of multicultural respect, so I decided to begin to read *Autobiography of a Yogi* again, practicing multicultural respect, and believing that Yogananda was somehow speaking *his truth* and that *his truth* was somehow in the direction of "the truth."

I was aware that this approach might require me to shift my understanding of the true nature of the universe a complete 180 degrees from my current understanding. Despite my reluctance to allow that shift, I read the book, and indeed, the book began to shift my perspective.

What helped the book shift my perspective was, in part, that I had begun spiritual practices, particularly Raja Yoga meditation, which enabled the shift. Eastern forms of meditation along with beginning to experience "energy healing,"[3] began to open up and energize the more intuitive aspects of my brain. I became more open to considering that my rational mind could not know everything there is to know about life and the universe!

What I have discovered, then, through *Autobiography of a Yogi*, as well as through two decades of meditating and practicing energy healing, is that our left brains only perceive part of reality, while our right brains perceive other aspects of reality, which, to our left brains, do not even appear "real," let alone "true." Whether we call these aspects of reality other dimensions or other planes of existence doesn't matter, as long as we begin to understand that, just because we don't have rational explanations for these other aspects of reality does not make them fantasy.

---

[3] One of the most common forms of energy healing in the United States is Reiki. My initial exposure, experience, and training came from a practice called "Natural Spiritual Healing," taught as a four-week course by the Self-Realization Meditation Healing Centre in Somerset, England. I will explain more about subtle energy and healing later in the book.

The opposite of rational is irrational, but philosophy also offers the concept of a-rationality, which refers to that which is beyond the rational, without necessarily being against rationality. Mystical experiences are a-rational. Much of what we experience in life is a-rational.

From my own experience, I can testify that the combination of my left-brain dominance and limiting my worldview only to that of Western science also limited what I could believe. By limiting what I allowed myself to believe, I also limited what I could experience as being true.

Changing my understanding, and meditating, enabled more of a right brain awareness of "truth" to develop. As my right brain began to contribute more to my awareness of what I was experiencing in life, my worldview expanded, my "truth" changed, and my ability to understand other human beings and empathize with them has only grown ever since.

> My one hope is that this book will grant us all greater understanding, and therefore respect, for one another and our perhaps unique experiences of "truth."

My one hope is that this book will grant us all greater understanding, and therefore respect, for one another and our perhaps unique experiences of "truth." I also hope that this book will lead many of us to a greater openness to perceiving some universal truths or values, and that these universal truths or values will empower us to get along peacefully, and to live well together with the rest of life on this beautiful planet.

CHAPTER ONE

What Is Truth?

"The truth will set you free. But not until it is finished with you."
— David Foster Wallace, *Infinite Jest*

Long ago, Jesus Christ expressed the idea that the truth will "make us free." The Roman Governor, Pontius Pilate, responded to Jesus' references to truth with the infamous, seemingly jaded, rhetorical query, "What is truth?"

Along with Pilate, we might believe that truth is at best often elusive, and that attempting to get a majority of humans to agree on any given truth may be utterly futile, *especially* when it comes to either politics or spirituality.

I would like to suggest that we have been, for the most part, operating with limited models for how to access and verify truth. The kinds of truths we need more fully to understand are scientific as well as spiritual,

> I would like to suggest that we have been, for the most part, operating with limited models for how to access and verify truth. The kinds of truths we need to understand are scientific as well as spiritual, political, communal, and global. We need more fully to understand ourselves, one another, and this universe.

political, communal, and global. We need to understand ourselves, one another, and this universe.

For about five hundred years, we have increasingly understood the world from a particular scientific paradigm in the West. The Western scientific paradigm has been focused on the physical and measurable aspects of reality, and has used a predominantly left-brain approach to understanding virtually everything.[4] This Western approach has led to helpful observations and theories of humanity and our world on many levels: physically, psychologically, biologically, chemically, medically, and so on.

For thousands of years, in the Eastern hemisphere, a more holistic science has developed, based more on right brain forms of "knowing" and observing through experience, while measuring or sensing subtle energies and their correlated outcomes in addition to measuring physical processes and their correlated outcomes.

This holistic Eastern science has developed systems of study leading to practical applications for the greater health of humanity, as in Traditional Chinese Medicine, acupuncture, yoga, Reiki, and Tai Chi. This holistic Eastern science has also identified subtle energies that course through human bodies. Through this understanding of subtle energy, Eastern holistic sciences have explained the development of human health as well as the nature of what it means to be

---

[4] Another way of saying this is: So, Western science has entailed mainly left-brain analyses of tangible measurements of physical objects as well as of observable events, including mental events to the degree they can be observed or expressed in objectively measurable ways.

human, including our spirituality. The philosophies of yoga offer a prime example of this comprehensive view of human health and wellness.

If, as human beings around the globe, we would like to move beyond our current limits of understanding truth and illusion, humanity probably needs to combine these Eastern and Western approaches in order to understand ourselves and the universe more fully. We also need to use both sides of our brain to engage in fully knowing ourselves and understanding our world. One side or the other of the globe, and one side or the other of the brain does not constitute a comprehensive enough way of exploring what is true.

If we can accomplish this engagement of Eastern and Western, left brain and right brain understandings of human nature, perhaps we can merge the Western Age of Enlightenment of the Intellect with the Eastern Spiritual Enlightenment in order to attain a fully Holistic Enlightenment which leads humanity to understand one another more fully. If we can understand one another better, perhaps we can discover truths that enable us to live peacefully together while maintaining the health of our home, the Earth.

We also need to combine northern and southern hemispheric views of truth on this earth, since many northern cultures have been dominating, exploiting, and wiping out the cultures and cultural values of so many southern cultures around the globe. Ironically and by contrast to the northern cultures, the southern hemispheric cultures tend to value cooperation rather than competition and domination.

In fact, the northern cultures have tended to see themselves as "civilized," meaning that they have "tamed" (dominated) anything and everyone that has any sort of "uncontrollable" "wild" streak. This tendency to control other life forms, from turning wild places into small gardens and wild animals into domestic animals, has often spread to seeking to control other human beings who have been seen as "savage," that is, not willing to be controlled and dominated by the "civilized" cultures. The southern hemisphere cultures have too often been included in this "savage" category, especially people of color.

Listening to northern and southern hemispheric views becomes really important then, to enable us to understand different values and views on truth, including what it means to be "civilized."

Combining these triple hemispheric views – north, south, East, West, left and right brain - is the only way we will be able to understand each other, let alone the universe. From any one hemisphere of the brain or of the earth – north/south and east/west, our understanding of truth can be fantastic, comprehensive on some level, and instructive for life. Yet, until we combine this triple-hemisphere duality into one whole and comprehensive approach, we will continually tend to portray life, the universe, humanity, and spiritual truths in somewhat limited, and therefore potentially distorted, as well as potentially destructive ways.

As humans, we tend to see the world through one side of each duality, and this one-sided perspective limits our thinking, our believing, and our openness to perceiving truth beyond our own assumptions, misconceptions, prejudices, and overt biases. To access truth, we have to be able to see the "truths" of both sides of each duality. To get at truth, we also have to question everything, and throw out our assumptions and prejudgments.

Overcoming all human dualities by unifying them will, in fact, be necessary in order for us to obtain a balanced, universal, and more harmonious view of "Truth." In all, we will consider ten dualities, and discuss two false dichotomies.

The first three dualities we have already listed: East – West, North – South, and left brain – right brain.

I would especially like to emphasize a fourth duality to consider as we contemplate truth. This fourth duality is the duality of masculine and feminine. This duality is so vital to review because androcentrism[5] and patriarchy have dominated our reasoning, our philosophies, our consideration of possible topics worth exploring, our portrayals of history, and our politics.

Moreover, patriarchy has largely defined reality and what it means to be human. Patriarchy has generally defined what it means to be human in ways that have neglected the experiences of girls and women. Patriarchy has often disdained more feminine, nurturing, and cooperative values that are nonetheless

---

[5] Androcentrism is the tendency to see everything from a man's perspective rather than a woman's. This tends to limit experiences of empathy and also to tends to tell stories that shape our view of what is important as well as of what it means to be human merely from men's perspectives, with no consideration of women's input into what is important or what it means to be human.

inherent and essential aspects of being human. By neglecting feminine ways of being, knowing, doing, perceiving, and valuing, patriarchy has also skewed our understanding of "truth."[6]

> **Patriarchy has often disdained more feminine, nurturing, and cooperative values that are nonetheless inherent and essential aspects of being human. By neglecting feminine ways of being, knowing, doing, perceiving, and valuing, patriarchy has also skewed our understanding of "truth."**

For about 5,000 years, patriarchy and patriarchal religions have dominated the worldviews of most of humanity. The time to shift this balance is now, so that we can attain more holistic understandings of truth.

While this fourth duality, masculine and feminine, may seem separate from the two-hemisphere split of the brain and of human culture on the earth, in many ways, the right brain invites more feminine ways of knowing and experiencing reality. Moreover, women tend to

---

[6] One of the most important books I believe I have ever read, and which helped me understand not just women's but also human ways of knowing is entitled *Women's Ways of Knowing,* by Belenky, et al, . In this book, I learned about human ways of knowing, and found an understanding of human knowing which, I believe, explains how Jesus Christ related to other human beings, i.e., as a "connected knower," and as a "principled knower," which ways of knowing, when put together, very much balance feminine and masculine ways of knowing.

process information more holistically, engaging both sides of the brain.[7]

So, maybe women tend to get closer to the truth automatically! That is, in part, a joke, of course. The part that is not a joke is the importance of using both sides of the brain to process information, which apparently women's brains are better designed to do, combining both analytical (intellectual) knowing with intuitive knowing by the very structure of our brains.

It is alright for women's brains to be better at something. Men typically have bigger brains, and are generally wired to be better at other things, including motor skills.

Throughout our quest for truth, we will return to the influence of feminine and masculine perceptions of what is real, what matters, and who gets to decide these things.

A fifth duality needs to be discussed, especially as American political decision-making has been experienced by many as less democratic and less serving the needs of the poor and middle class for many years. By this, I do mean that the 1% seems to have way too much power relative to the 99%, and the middle class is seriously shrinking. This is called plutocracy,

---

[7] "Male brains have more connections within hemispheres to optimize motor skills, whereas female brains are more connected between hemispheres to combine analytical and intuitive thinking," according to Scientific American online, as quoted in "How Men's Brains Are Wired Differently than Women's," by Tanya Lewis, LiveScience on December 2, 2013, accessed on September 9, 2016, here: http://www.scientificamerican.com/article/how-mens-brains-are-wired-differently-than-women/

or more broadly, oligarchy, that is, the rule of the elite, which in this case consists of the wealthy elite ruling this country. I remember America from over 40 years ago, and from what I can see, many Americans have lost ground in that time.

In fact, Princeton and Northwestern Universities conducted research on almost 1,800 US policy decisions enacted between 1988 and 2002 and actually found that the United States has measurably become more of an oligarchy than a democracy, because a majority of the 1,800 policy decisions overrode the popular vote in favor of the wealthy elites.[8]

> **Democracy in America has often become an illusion, and government of, for, and by the wealthy has often become the truth.**

Based on this research, we could arguably conclude that we no longer live in a democracy, for democracy in America has too often become an illusion, and government of, for, and by the wealthy has too often become the truth. In fact, this research was conducted in 2012, and from my observations, this trend has only grown exponentially worse since then.

Now, I realize that many of us among the 99% may feel discouraged reading that information, and many of us

---

[8] Zachary Davies Boren, *The Telegraph*, "Major Study Finds the US is an Oligarchy," April 16, 2014, *Business Insider online*, accessed on September 17, 2016, here: http://www.businessinsider.com/major-study-finds-that-the-us-is-an-oligarchy-2014-4

may even feel jaded, especially after the recent election. If you're part of the 1%, I do wonder how you feel, and I welcome the opportunity to ask you.

Clearly wealth disparities reflect a politically relevant and crucial duality to consider when we ask questions of "what is true?" and "what is illusion?" We have to conclude that overcoming the duality of rich and poor must occur in order to access "Truth." Otherwise, the wealthy will continue to have the power to define truth, values, and what "works" for us, while the majority of us will remain trapped in the illusion of democracy, spoon-fed other people's versions of what is "real."

> **We have to conclude that overcoming the duality of rich and poor must occur in order to access "Truth." Otherwise, the wealthy will continue to have the power to define truth, values, and what "works" for us, while the majority of us will remain trapped in the illusion of democracy, spoon-fed other people's versions of what is "real."**

Let us bring some hope to the forefront as we commit to overcoming the main, significant human dualities as both a means of discovering what we can know, and as a means for seeking truth together. This commitment to including both sides of all main cultural dualities will bring us a broader, more cooperative and hopeful view of how we can access truth.

Before we further discuss how we can access truth, let us ask, like Pilate, but hopefully with a less jaded attitude: what is truth?

Of course, we can all begin by agreeing that there are facts that are objectively verifiable, and the measurement of those facts is replicable by others, and that certain events, sometimes even mental ones, now with CT scans and MRI's, are observable and quantifiable. We have managed to measure so many different aspects of the universe, from the quantum level to the universal level of gravitational waves, the speed of light, and so on.

There are also relative truths. Einstein did teach us about relativity, so that we know that sounds have different pitches, and galaxies shine different colors, depending on whether they are approaching us or moving away from us. These are relative truths based on the relativity of the curve of space-time. Two trees that appear small and spaced together for someone at a far distance will appear big and spaced far apart to someone standing much closer. Both perspectives are true, based on the physical realities of space-time.

There are also personal truths that are relative. Very basic sorts of physical truths can differ from person-to-person, such as peanuts can kill one person to peanuts can provide a good source of protein and other nutrients for another person. More subjective personal truths can also be relative, such as a certain statement sounding hostile to one person while sounding neutral to another person. So it is that we all have varying senses and experiences of the "truth" outside ourselves, as well as inside ourselves.

Some truly challenging situations can result from these differences of perception, as in the cases of police officers shooting innocent African-Americans. What is logical and defensive to one is racist to another. Can both be true? Perhaps. Is one more true than the other? Probably, because *if truth has any value for human life*, then truth will teach us that black lives matter, innocent lives matter, and we definitely need to learn how to protect the innocent people of this world, especially innocent black people, because apparently we don't yet know how to do that very well.

When it comes down to how we live with one another, truth matters, and so our ability to perceive truth matters very much, especially when human life is at stake. Truth matters, just as life matters, for life often depends on truth.

At the opposite end of the human spectrum of truth and illusion, there is denial. Denial certainly blocks our awareness of truth. Denial is a common human escape from truth caused by inward emotional pain that we have not yet learned how to handle. Usually, such immense emotional pain develops from repeated emotional pain through childhood, and often later in life as well.

Denial is like an addiction, in that it creates an escape from having to deal with some aspect of truth, or "reality." Denial also happens when we are presented with a truth that causes cognitive dissonance because it conflicts with the beliefs and understandings we already have.

This started to happen with me in the example I gave in the introduction, so that I began from a place of denial about the possibility of miracles, even as recounted by a very holy and reliable witness, because they seemed to defy the logic with which I viewed the world at the time. However, the thought of changing my worldview to include miracles was not extremely painful to me either emotionally or mentally, so I decided to open myself to the idea that miracles might be possible.

Denial tends to happen in the absence of cognitive clarity, and one finds oneself in a state of mental and/or emotional confusion. If the confusion is strong enough, and therefore "painful" enough, it will drive us to seek what we already "know" from experience, whether that is the truth or not.

I was recently working with a client who clearly experiences a lot of cognitive confusion, driven mostly by a childhood filled with various forms of extreme abuse, leading to emotional confusion. While the client is capable of thinking with perfect cognitive clarity at many points, she nonetheless exhibits cognitive confusion relative to her own coping behaviors and her religious views, sometimes choosing her family's strict religious values even when they seem in conflict with her own emotional choices. Specifically, her emotional needs once led her into a partnership with a woman, but her religious views led her to campaign against same-sex marriage. Because of her history of abuse, she seems to have denied the authenticity and moral value of her own emotional needs in relationships.

Denial of new ideas can happen when a new idea causes not only conflict with our existing understandings and beliefs, but that idea also creates very strong or even severe emotional pain when we consider changing our original understandings and beliefs. If the inner emotional pain and cognitive dissonance combined are really strong, we go into denial, even in the face of solid evidence for the truth.

One example of this that I have actually encountered was with a clergy colleague. While I now lead interfaith meditation circles, I used to serve traditional churches in a Christian denomination that values freedom of belief. Because of this freedom of belief, church members and ministers alike can have varying and even conflicting beliefs and understandings of the Christian faith, of God, of the Bible, of the universe, and of life.

I once had a discussion with a clergy colleague who had been theologically trained in a very conservative school, and who believed the Bible is literally true and inerrant. This view means that, despite conflicting statements in the Bible, and despite the lack of scientific and historical underpinnings for many claims, *every* statement in the Bible is somehow "true."

In this discussion, I discovered that my colleague believed that the Bible shows that the earth (and the universe as well), is only some 6,000 years old. I objected that this could not possibly be true, because we can see stars that are more than 6,000 light years away. My colleague claimed that God had created the universe in a way that the light was already reaching us at the moment of creation.

Now, this claim makes no sense to me in any way, scientifically or spiritually speaking. But apparently, to my colleague, it would have been more painful to perceive Biblical teachings as primarily metaphorical and to question the "truths" of the Bible rather than literally accept every statement of the Bible as completely, unerringly true and of God. Believing that the Bible is inerrant is apparently less painful for many people than believing that God could not have been advocating violence, the rape of women, slavery, and the killing of babies.[9]

Without either the ability to perceive the Bible's lack of scientific knowledge when it was written, or the ability to perceive the cultural influences in the Bible, one is left believing every word as though literally God spoke and managed to get human beings to write without human interpretation in the process.[10] Yet, any literary analysis of the Bible will see many signs of human redaction, or editing in the "original" texts, let alone interpretation during translation. Numerous Biblical

---

[9] The book of Genesis contains a story in which some strangers who were invited to stay overnight wanted to have sex with men, but since that was considered wrong, the host offered his daughter who was violently raped by multiple men and left for dead. Psalm 137:9 refers to dashing one's enemy's infants against a stone.

[10] While I am familiar with the process of channeling Divine inspiration, I also am familiar with perceiving signs of our human ego, such as human desires, personal biases, and cultural influences in religious and spiritual writings, including my own.

texts give great evidence of interpretation on the part of the "original" male writers of the Bible, in part because patriarchy is implicit throughout the Bible.

One can question the Bible's perfection and still hear the voice of God speaking through different human beings who recorded their experiences of God and of God's teachings in the Bible. Indeed, allowing for scientific and academic questioning of the Bible empowers us to be able to cherish more metaphorical understandings of Biblical statements, rather than needing them to mean some literal "truth." When we need and look for literal truths, we often miss the deeper, beautiful, and richly symbolic metaphorical meanings which may well teach great spiritual truths.

As one of my former professors at Vanderbilt University Divinity School explained, "all religious language is metaphorical language."[11]

One might apply this questioning perspective to the texts of all religions, if one is open to the possibility that messages in holy texts are both human and divine. The perfection of a human being is rare indeed, and so, those few who attain this divine perfection may be said to teach Truth, whether through the spoken word or through written words.[12] Yet, our ability to perceive anyone else as perfected in Spirit depends on our own

---

[11] For this concept, I am indebted to Dr. Sallie McFague, her courses, and her book, *Metaphorical Theology*.

[12] Or other ways; true Masters often teach by example. I just spent part of an afternoon learning from an Indian Sufi Master, Taoshobuddha.

level of perfection, so naturally we have differences of opinions on this spiritual aspect of truth!

In addition to inquiring as to the spiritual integrity of religious truths, it seems to me that truth must also somehow make sense. Intellectually and intuitively, truth must have explanatory value for making sense of our lives and for explaining what we experience in this universe. I am a philosophical pragmatist when it comes to the value of truth.

Earlier, we looked at denial as an obstacle to truth when it arises out of a degree of inner emotional pain. Let us look at another underlying root of denial: fear. I find this fascinating that fear and emotional pain can cause denial, because long ago in some of my studies (possibly pastoral care and counseling), I learned that underneath all anger lies either fear or hurt.

Anger and denial seem to go together. At the very least, when we are in a state of denial, our sense of truth can cause pain to others, and lead others to feel angry, frustrated, or powerless! We quite naturally also feel angry more easily when we are out of alignment with truth. Denial gives rise to anger because we are hurting our own selves by denying the truth. The cycle of pain continues to spread outward with denial, blocking access to truth between and among human beings in families, communities, nations, as well as around the globe.

Considering fear as an element of blocking our access to truth leads us to the recognition that a sixth duality must be considered in our quest for truth over illusion.

This duality is that of fear vs. love. Fear and love are energetic opposites: we cannot simultaneously be feeling fear and unconditional love.

Clearly, love is associated with the Divine. Fear has also been, in some religious understandings, associated with the Divine, but when has fear ever led to truth?

Fear results in a stress response in the brain. Fear results from perceived threats and stress and the resulting fight-flight-freeze-or-fold response. This brain response arises from the adrenal glands, the hypothalamus, and the pituitary gland, along with the amygdala. The adrenal-hypothalamus-pituitary gland connections are called the HPA Axis. This HPA Axis responds to stress (read fear), by triggering the sympathetic nervous system, the seat of the fight-flight-freeze-fold response.

In this state of fear, our amygdala tends to perceive everything as a threat.[13] So, literally, in the brain's amygdala, if we have been repeatedly stressed or traumatized, fear begets more fear, and perceptions of what is "out there" become distorted by the fear that everything is a threat to our wellbeing.

---

[13] I am indebted to Congressman Tim Ryan's book, *A Mindful Nation*, (New York: Hay House, 2012), pp. 52-55, for bringing this concept to my attention.

The experiences of police officers offer a perfect example of this. I cannot personally imagine how difficult it must be to be a police officer. As a clergy person, I know that it is possible to participate in "ride-alongs," so I have contemplated how I would maintain calm instead of fear, but so far, I have chosen just to admire the fact that police officers face potentially life-threatening situations every day, and I have not yet joined them.

> **In this state of fear, our amygdala tends to perceive everything as a threat ...**
>
> **... fear begets more fear, and perceptions of what is "out there" become distorted by the fear that everything is a threat to our wellbeing.**

However, the relevant note here is that, when police officers face potentially dangerous situations, the most important thing for them to do is precisely to remain calm. Otherwise, if a police officer gives in to fear, their brain chemistry changes and the amygdala begins to perceive everything as a threat.

Granted, remaining calm may seem super-challenging in police work, but if police officers will remain calm, their brains are more likely to detect what is not a threat as well as what may be a very *real* threat. If police officers will remain calm, they will be better able to perceive innocent black people for who they really are, and avoid shooting them.

Yes, I am saying that fear and an overly-stressed amygdala lead, in part, to our crisis of police shootings. However, I am also saying that police officers themselves are more likely to remain safe if they remain calm.

When we are calm and able to maintain that state of calm, our amygdala calms down and the prefrontal cortex part of our brain can become active. The prefrontal cortex leads us to be more open to perceiving what is actually out there, without perceiving everything as a threat.[14]

Literally, then, feeling calm and loving can help us perceive truth outside of us more easily and accurately than can being in a state of fear and defensiveness. In sports, this calm state is often referred to as being "in the zone." Many spiritual people would express it as "living in the flow." From the primary perspective of consciousness alone, it may be referred to as "flow state."

This may seem obvious to state, but generally speaking, love helps us feel calmer. Feeling calm means that the feeling of love is prevailing over the feeling of fear. Perhaps we can conclude that remaining in a calm *and loving* state can lead us to engaging parts of the brain that perceive things as they are, rather than as we fear they may be.

Mindfulness meditation and other forms of meditation can help us learn to remain calm even in stressful situations, so that we can perceive, think, and act from a state of love rather than a state of fear. If we would like our brains to operate more efficiently and effectively so that we can perceive objectively and respond wisely,

---

[14] Ibid, pp. 76-77.

then we need to learn to calm our fears. "There is no fear in love, but perfect love casts out fear."[15]

Fear can actually throw off our perceptions of "true" events by activating the amygdala, which perceives everything as a threat. So, when we are presented with alternative views of reality that bring us into a state of fear, the same pattern of denial may result, because we fear the possible outcome of that view of "truth" too much.

Fear may therefore be said to block our openness to and awareness of truth.

Love may be said to open us up to perceiving a larger, more accurate, as well as more universal awareness of truth. Love that is alive with non-attachment to gaining certain outcomes (love that is unconditional), may enable us to be more open to perceiving and to contemplating what exists outside of us.

> **Fear may therefore be said to block our openness to and awareness of truth.**
>
> **Love may be said to open us up to perceiving a larger, more accurate, as well as more universal awareness of truth.**

We can surmise that our sense of truth and its relation to life on a larger scale may well be determined by the

---

[15] 1 John 4:18.

level of fear or the level of love with which we live our lives.

In addition to overcoming the dualities of humanity, we also need to consider relative truths and objective truths. Sometimes, "truth" is relative. Of course, sometimes truth is objectively verifiable, as in the case of facts which we can confirm, observe, or measure. Which nature of "truth" we find ourselves experiencing depends on the kind of "truth" we are considering.

Human, social, and cultural truths can certainly be relative. One person may indeed find one approach to life to be more helpful than an approach that is helpful to someone else. For example, many children thrive in Montessori schools, while some may benefit more from traditionally structured schools. Or at least, some parents may prefer one over the other!

Some "truths" are of course objectively verifiable, like the effects of gravity or the spread of viral infections from one person to another. It is helpful when we are able to agree on these truths, including how many light years away a star is and how its light actually reached the earth. If we cannot agree on objectively verifiable truths, we tend to have inherent conflict in our relationships, and we tend to spread "misinformation" to others.

For example, the current lack of respect in America for the scientific evidence for climate change and its deleterious effects on humanity and the planet represents this kind of conflict among humans. I found it refreshing to spend time in France in late 2015, right before the International Climate Conference. In France, I was able to hear commentaries and read exhibits that represent the fact that, in France, unlike in the United States, no one seems to question the reality of climate change, because they understand that it has been scientifically measured and verified over and over again in numerous ways.

> **If factual evidence cannot yet help us agree on truth, what hope is there for humanity?**

Since then, I have realized that climate denial in our American culture appears completely irrelevant to truth as evidenced by repeatedly measured and verifiable facts related to climate change (here, as facts, let's just list the progressively warming global air temperatures, warming ocean water temperatures, melting ice caps, rising sea levels, bleaching coral reefs, and increased storms, to name a few).[16]

We might claim that denial of climate change or global warming is a form of denial so strong, that it causes what could be termed almost a complete disregard for truth. The potential negative consequences for such misinformation have been, and continue to be, enormous for the survival of human beings as well as all virtually all species on this planet. In fact, we are witnessing these changes now, according to many scientists, as the flow of the jet stream has changed,

---

[16] Here's a website that is both scientific and federal government-based: http://climate.nasa.gov/evidence/

wildfires have become rampant in the western United States, and storms, droughts, and flooding have increasingly devastated communities worldwide.

If factual evidence cannot yet help us agree on truth, what hope is there for humanity? Could it be that love and fear determine almost unconscious levels of denial or curiosity that then shape our abilities to perceive even objectively verifiable truths?

Clearly, our spiritual worldviews determine a lot of our sense of truth. By "spiritual worldviews," I do not only refer to religious perspectives on life, but also the theories from which we look at life, such as materialism or scientific determinism. Our spiritual worldviews do not only arise from our religious training or the lack of it, but also from our own levels of intellectual, emotional and spiritual development.

Generally, views such as "I am right and you are so wrong that you either deserve to die or to go to hell," or "My religion is right and your religion is wrong," reflect a certain level of emotional, mental, and spiritual development. This view of "my religion is right and yours is so wrong that you must die or go to hell," tends to reflect the worldview of any single religion when understood extremely literally and from a place of fear.

A spiritual worldview which is more emotionally, mentally, and spiritually holistic rather than dualistic tends to reach a more inclusive, harmonious, and universal spiritual understanding of the world's religions and of humanity in general.

Since most of us human beings have far more experience living and thinking dualistically rather than holistically, only a call to greater spiritual, emotional, and intellectual growth by all of us can lead us together to a more comprehensive sense of truth. Moreover, I call all of us to grow in our ability to respect one another's religious and spiritual world views, unless those views actually cause harm to other people or call for some form of damnation of others, or cause indiscriminate destruction of life on earth.

Again, I also invite us to consider that patriarchy has dominated the world's religions for 5,000 years, while matriarchal religions were common before that. A balanced view of religion and spirituality is likely to cause less harm to women and the planet, because both have been seen as less important in the male dominant religions, generally speaking.[17]

For instance, let us consider the hierarchy of relationships as seen in the classical Christian paradigm. By "classical Christian paradigm," or classical Christianity, I refer not to Jesus' teachings, but to Western theological views developed after the installation of a male hierarchy of priests.[18] According to classical Christianity, there is a distinct and dominating order or hierarchy of being in this universe:

---

[17] I am aware that in Judaism, patriarchal as it may often be, there are beautiful concepts such as Shalom and Tikkun Olam, which speak to the wellbeing of not only all of humanity, but also all of creation. I pray we may all together move in the direction of Shalom and Tikkun Olam!

[18] I could go on and on with regard to this subject, although it is not germane here. My main New Testament paper was on Jesus and the role of women in the Gospel of John. For his time, Jesus personally treated women very well.

God

Angels

Man

Woman

Animals

Earth

Given that this hierarchy also includes the biased idea that the top three are more spiritual, and the bottom three are more physical (women were perceived as more physical because we tend to menstruate, have babies, and breastfeed), and given that the spiritual is prioritized over the physical, then a certain value system arises that skews one's sense of truth towards favoring spirit and male beings over female bodies and earthly beings. This can lead to values such as the acceptance of domestic violence and rape, as well as believing that a woman and her body only count for childbearing, such that abortion is out of the question even if it would save a woman's life.[19] Another example would be that what happens to the earth does not matter, because it is seen as physical but not spiritual.

---

[19] Please understand that I respect a view in which abortion is considered murdering a child, but I personally draw the line at forcing a woman to die to give birth to a child when saving a woman's life through abortion is an option. I also respect women's individual rights to choose based on their own belief system, rather than on the beliefs of others, because, again, we all have a different understanding of "truth." As long as a human life can be saved, nurtured, and supported, I advocate for saving life, nurturing life, and supporting life – both mother and child.

Because of such extreme and potentially harmful views, I again invite us to seek truth from a perspective that balances all human dualities, with feminine and masculine qualities topping the list in order to overcome tendencies towards domination. After all, if we dominate someone else, we reject their truth outright. If we reject the truths of others without looking for the seed of truth in them, how can we arrive at a universal truth?

For example, with the above hierarchy of being, surely it is possible to conceive of very different relationships between each aspect of being, with no domination implied. When I teach meditation classes, I actually invite students to reconfigure the relationships between each aspect of being to reflect their own understandings, using small cards. Quite a variety of views have resulted, many of which I have found very refreshing for reaching a healthy and happy sense of "truth" for all of humanity and the planet. One cooperative version, for instance, places all of the cards in a circle, so that God, humanity, animals and earth are all equally valued. In this sense, spirit exists in all aspects of being, such that everything and everyone is imbued with potential sacredness.[20]

There are, in all, ten dualities that we need to consider in our quest for truth.

The next, or seventh duality is intellect and intuition. We will devote a whole chapter to that, so we will return

---

[20] As my friend and neighbor, Saqiba, who is Muslim tells me, "Trees worship Allah."

to overcoming and harmonizing this duality later. Here, I would like to express that my experience writing this book is one of a beautiful blend of intuition and intellect, for neither of which do I take credit. In fact, I find it humorous and humbling that I depend so much on a third word that begins with "in" to be able to write this text: the internet. The internet strikes me as being the perfect metaphor for the blend of intellect and intuition – that which informs, as well as that which connects the knower and the known. The internet offers, albeit a flawed, example of the source of information, the information itself, and that which connects the knower as well as the learner with all of it. On the internet, we experience a taste of the interconnections of all levels of life: the known, the source, the knower, the learner, and the very web of knowing itself.

Indeed, the internet represents the very interconnectedness of conscious knowing and the truths that we know through a universal "web of knowing." Truths upon which we agree arise from our collective web of knowing as well as from our individual knowing which informs that web. More broadly, doesn't the web of knowing include all life? Doesn't truth then include all life?

Could Truth be a web of knowing in and of itself? Or is the web of knowing that which knows truth? Or is the web of knowing both the truth and all that knows the truth as well as the source of truth? What if everything in the universe is part of this web of knowing?

If Truth is a web of knowing, including both the knowers and the known, is Truth somehow alive? If Truth is alive, is Truth Life itself? Is Truth the Source of the knowers and the known? Is Truth therefore the Source of everything, as the web of knowers, known, and source of both knowers and the known?

Is Truth a way of knowing?

For now, let us suggest that Truth is not only the known, but indeed a way of knowing; a way of knowing which includes both the parts, and the whole, and perhaps becomes somehow greater than the sum of all the parts. That would make Truth a universal Gestalt; that is, an organized, unified whole that is other than or more than the sum of the parts of this known universe.[21]

I suggest we leave these questions open-ended for the moment, and return to overcoming dualities, in order to find the whole "truth." If truth is a way of knowing as well as what is known, then my suggestion is that we overcome these dualities by finding the whole or Gestalt that they express together.

The eighth duality that faces us in the media with great frequency is the duality of civility and incivility. Being civil has to do with being a citizen, and as such, entails not only the recognition of equal rights, but also behaviors relating to being a citizen. The behaviors

---

[21] For my description of Gestalt, I am indebted to these sites:
https://www.google.com/search?q=gestalt&rlz=1C1JZAP_enUS706US706&oq=gestalt&aqs=chrome..69i57j0l5.2485j0j7&sourceid=chrome&ie=UTF-8 and
https://en.wikipedia.org/wiki/Gestalt_psychology and
http://www.dictionary.com/browse/gestalt

relating to being a citizen cannot be thought of as only individual, for a citizen is part of a whole.[22]

Being a citizen requires working for the greater good of the whole together, whether that work includes voting or creating policies for the good of the whole, or being a "public servant." One cannot be a citizen without being a citizen of something larger which is organized for the good of the citizens. The common good is an inherent truth in the nature of being a citizen, therefore of being civil. This civility includes both our language and our actions, especially as expressed publicly and towards others.

As described so beautifully on Wikipedia, "Civility is the action of working together productively to reach a common goal, and often with beneficent purposes."[23] Please notice how perfectly positive this statement is; there is no room for profane desecration of such pure positivity. Civility entails the best of the collective positive nature of humanity.

By contrast, incivility does not serve the greater good, and does not respect others as equal citizens. Incivility seems to rule our interactions daily in American life, not only in politics, but also in religion.

If we cannot attain some sense of "we all belong to something greater," that is, we are citizens on this planet, or souls who are all part of divinity, how can we

---

[22] I am indebted to Wikipedia for ideas on this subject. Not all ideas expressed here come from this site, but I found it helpful: https://en.wikipedia.org/wiki/Civility

[23] Ibid.

ever open ourselves up to a full quest for truth? If anyone is left out, the truth cannot be served, for truth, if it is truth, will encompass everyone.

No one can be left out of the circle of truth.

Therefore, in the quest for truth, civility is called for in the sense of respecting others as equals, and in the sense of respecting that everyone equally belongs together in this shared experience of "truth," and also in the sense that all of us need to cooperate to find a larger truth that engenders peace and wellbeing for all of us. If we cannot engender civility, cooperation, peace, and wellbeing for all, then we cannot find a truth worth finding.

This duality of civility and incivility represents a larger duality: the sacred and the profane. By profanity, I mean far more than just vulgar language; rather, I refer to irreverence or contempt which denies outright the good in what is at least partly sacred, such as another human being. Profanity and disrespect have no place in civil society, because they shut down and close the door on the full potential of others to contribute to a larger view of truth which benefits the common good.

Listening is the only way to truth; for if we do not listen with respect for what truth we can hear from one another, we cannot serve truth. What is more sacred than serving Truth?

Surely our quest for truth requires civil discourse, not in the name of platitudes and acquiescence to a common view, but to enlarge our voices for truth. How can the truth serve the greater good if not all voices are even heard? Civil discourse respects the voices and views of others, and without this respect, we silence opposition. Silencing opposition through disrespect is merely another attempt at domination. Speaking up and objecting civilly is a powerful way to speak one's truth, but it loses its natural and spiritual power if one's objections are spoken with disrespect, for then all view of the greater good is lost.[24]

> **It turns out that the ancient teachings "Know Thyself" and "To Thine Own Self Be True" just may form the foundation of or starting point in our quest for truth.**

Again, how can we seek truth that offers anything less than a greater good for all? For if truth serves us, then it must serve us all. If we are to find a truth to serve, it must be worthy of us all.

Indeed, we can go one step further to express what is entailed in this duality of civility and incivility, and that is to suggest that really, this duality represents a larger duality of acceptance and hatred. When we accept one another as equals, we have no need to hate one another, unless we fear one

---

[24] I am grateful that I know of one institution which actually not only teaches, but also requires civil discourse in all its affairs: St. John's College in Annapolis, Maryland. Known as "The Great Books School," St. John's has a remarkable curriculum, but its pedagogical method is stellar: students are required to listen and to speak with respect. Not even disrespectful gestures such as vehement head-shaking are allowed. My son attended St. John's College, and I believe it transformed him into an even more remarkable, more self-aware, and more considerate human being. May all schools incorporate such learning!

another. Hatred belies our own inner fears, including being left out of the greater good ourselves.

Only by fearing being left out of the greater good do we hate others enough to leave them out of the greater good.

Being aware of hatred is part of our quest, for inside each of us, we tend to have fears, and often anger and hatred, for we often feel threatened and unsafe in life. Only by becoming more internally aware of the truth that is going on inside us can we avoid denial and speak truth. Only by knowing ourselves truthfully can we contribute to a greater sense of truth which serves the greater good.

It turns out that the ancient teachings "Know Thyself" and "To Thine Own Self Be True" just may form the foundation of or starting point in our quest for truth. Without self-knowledge, our quest for truth has only a partial and shaky foundation. We need to cultivate true self-awareness in order to be able to perceive a greater good worthy of the service of truth.

For a truth that serves the greatest possible good, we need to be aware of the voices of all living beings, because doesn't everything that lives contribute to the truth of what is?

What is this greater good which truth serves? Life.

Life is our common greater good. In this sense, we are all citizens of life. For a truth that serves the greatest possible good, we need to be aware of the voices of all living beings, because doesn't everything that lives contribute to the truth of what is?

Let us harmonize ourselves with life, through acceptance and civility, in the name of opening up our quest for a universal Truth.

As we consider harmonizing ourselves with life, we need to consider a ninth duality: materialism and spiritualism. By "spiritualism," I am not referring to any particular doctrine or practice such as the living contacting the dead. Rather, spiritualism here, as the opposite of materialism, refers to the idea that spirit is distinct from matter. In this duality, for materialism, spirit does not matter, and for spiritualism, the material world does not matter.[25]

The duality of materialism and spiritualism can only be healed by a spirituality which entails a union of the two. Most of this book will discuss, and even emphasize, spirituality as the union or harmonization of matter and spirit.

Material wellbeing without consideration of spiritual wellbeing is so often seen as the basis for life in the West. In the East, traditionally, our energetic wellbeing, or the life energy in us, or our spiritual energy, is generally seen as the source of wellbeing in life.

An emphasis on material wellbeing often comes from a sense of separation: the idea that we are individuals and that we live as physical bodies, without any actual

---

[25] Yes, of course these are "double-entendres."

spirit infusing us or nature, or living beings in general. The physical is seen as either just material, or as separate from spirit if there is a belief in spirit. There is often a tendency to view us as separate individuals, or as separate collectives, for there is little to unite human beings in a materialistic worldview. In a materialistic worldview, there is much that divides humanity.

One form of materialism that does seem to have the capacity to unite humanity is entertainment. Perhaps, in our materialistic age, that is one reason why entertainment is so popular in its many forms, because it fills our mostly subconscious longing for connection with one another and with something larger than ourselves in life.

Traditions that emphasize the interconnectedness of life tend to have more holistic visions of wellbeing. This generally stems from spiritual understandings that emphasize spiritual presence as existing everywhere, in everyone, and in everything, or at least in all life.

Interestingly, most of these traditions also emphasize breath as a form of spiritual presence or focus. In Judaism, the word *ruach* refers to: the breath of God, the wind of God, or the Spirit of God. One of the elements in the multi-faceted meaning of the word Aloha is breath.

Often, breath and subtle or spiritual energy are tied together around the world. Prana is a word in Sanskrit, used in yoga to refer to the life force energy which can enter our bodies with each breath. Buddhism focuses on the breath as a way of achieving mindful awareness.

"Chi" and "Qi" as in Tai Chi and Qi Gong both refer to this life force.

Of course, breath, wind, spirit, and energy all flow, and so they are not limited as separate beings. From these various traditions, our wellbeing is tied to this Ruach/prana/aloha/chi/qi which flows with spirit in all life.

That flow of spirit in all life is generally also seen as being present in all things that exist. Therefore, we are connected by spirit. Life is understood as spirit, and spirit is understood as life. Consequently, as we consider truth, we can no longer separate ourselves from spirit, wellbeing, one another, life on earth, or the earth itself. In this view, material wellbeing flows from spirit, and is not seen as separate from it.

There are spiritual traditions, as we will see below, that do consider spirit separate. As an example, spiritualism in which matter and spirit are separate and only spirit receives priority. Such separation of being tends to lead us to individualism and individual wellbeing rather than global and universal wellbeing. That priority of individualism over against the universal would constitute the other side of the duality of material and spiritual.

To make this duality whole, we have to conceive of the unity of matter and spirit. There is no better way to arrive at truth, for dividing ourselves between matter and spirit limits and divides truth. Therefore, matter and spirit unified must speak to a greater truth than either of them can when considered separately or antagonistically.

Finally, the tenth and last duality we shall consider here in our quest for truth is that of individualism vs. collectivism, or the way we live life as human beings both individually and together within our social contexts.

For our quest for truth, I would suggest that individualism be understood as: the prioritizing of the liberty, rights, and interests of the individual over against the common or collective rights and interests of society. Individualism is also the belief that it is indeed possible to prioritize individual interests separately from collective interests and vice versa.[26]

For the purposes of our duality as it challenges human understandings of truth, collectivism may be understood as: centralization of social, political, and economic control for the primary good of society as over against the primary good of the individual.[27]

However, these views, as expressed above, are extreme, and only those who are wrapped up in dualistic thinking are likely to choose one over the other in some complete and exclusive fashion.

---

[26] For some elements of this definition, though not all, I am indebted to: http://www.dictionary.com/browse/individualism?s=t accessed September 22, 2016.

[27] I am indebted to two sites providing food for thought from which I derived this half of the duality: http://www.dictionary.com/browse/collectivism?s=t and https://www.theobjectivestandard.com/issues/2012-spring/individualism-collectivism/ accessed September 22, 2016.

As an example, one online blogger launches into a discussion of this issue with the clear aim of a one-sided choice, overtly expressing the idea that "facts" will make the decision, as though such a human endeavor can be reduced to mere objectivity. In the process of taking sides, this writer evidences multiple additional dualisms such as patriarchal sexism (evident in his gender-exclusive, male only language), uncivil language when describing opposing views, philosophical dualism as inherent in his thinking, one-sided historical analysis, and political one-sidedness as well.[28]

Quite helpfully, though, this blogger misunderstands a couple of quotes about collectivism, and this misunderstanding actually points us to a way of harmonizing this duality.

First, the blogger quotes A. Maurice Low, "What is Socialism? III: An Explanation of 'The Rights' Men Enjoy in a State of Civilized Society," *The North American Review,* written in 1913. I would object to the gender-exclusive use of the term "men" here, rather than "individuals," except that, in 1913, women in America did not yet have the right to vote, and I am sure that we

---

[28] Craig Biddle, "Individualism vs. Collectivism: Our Choice, Our Future," *The Objective Standard; Reason, Egoism, and Capitalism,* Vol. 7, No. 1, 2016. Accessed here: https://www.theobjectivestandard.com/issues/2012-spring/individualism-collectivism/ on September 22, 2016.

did not have all the other rights men had a hundred years ago, either.

While that latter observation on my part may seem off-topic, I would suggest that overlooking the duality of sexism is, and historically has been, a huge part of the problem causing humans to devolve our ideas into illusion rather than elevating them to truth.

As Low wrote in 1913: "Man has no rights except those which society permits him to enjoy. From the day of his birth until the day of his death society allows him to enjoy certain so-called rights and deprives him of others; not . . . because society desires especially to favor or oppress the individual, but because its own preservation, welfare, and happiness are the prime considerations."[29]

> **Overlooking the duality of sexism is, and historically has been, a huge part of the problem causing humans to devolve our ideas into illusion rather than elevating them to truth.**

The blogger seems to think that this statement so threatens individual rights, that he objects entirely to any notion of collectivism, but does it? In an age of

---

[29] A. Maurice Low, A. Maurice Low, "What is Socialism? III: An Explanation of 'The Rights' Men Enjoy in a State of Civilized Society," *The North American Review*, vol. 197, no. 688 (March 1913), p. 406. I am grateful to Craig Biddle for including this and numerous helpful quotes on his site: https://www.theobjectivestandard.com/issues/2012-spring/individualism-collectivism/ accessed September 22, 2016.

terrorist attacks by individuals wearing bombs, can we really believe that the rights of an individual trump the rights of society?

Or does the blogger, possibly, like our president, seemingly so dismiss those whose ideas of individual religious rights and individual sovereignty are so different than his that he would send them out of the country (our society) for whatever reason – race, religion, or country of origin?

I apologize if I am committing any errors of offense or errors against the truth by associating this issue with a blogger whom I do not know, for perhaps he views all of us as having equal worth and value as individuals in this society, despite his male-only language in his article. (I am actually grateful to this man for his expressing his views so clearly, and giving us both a foundation of concerns to consider as well as an extreme view to seek to balance.)

If we believe in the importance of individualism to an extreme, we could conclude that a person's individual right to live out his or her religious ideals entitles him or her to commit acts of terror – for what is to stop someone from doing so in a setting of complete individualistic determinism?

This would be the society of the lone wolves, which doesn't even work for wolves, because the lone wolf evades the pack. This individualistic pattern is typical of adolescent males of various species: human, wolf, and dolphins. Adolescent males in isolation from the "pack" in all three species also tend to become violent with one another. Is that the model we would truly choose? Apparently many of us would, as we seek to protect our "individual gun rights."

Either one has the right to do whatever one desires if the individual is sovereign, or there is collectivism, or there is indeed something in-between.

Virtually any mother knows that when her second child gets old enough to pick up a popular toy or to do something the older child also wants to do, both children are going to have to learn to take turns. That is just the reality of living with each other unless we want to start killing each other at age 1-1/2 over our "individual rights."

What family actually succeeds in raising children based completely on the sovereignty of the individual? On the other hand, what family actually succeeds in raising children who are anything but rebellious if they are raised through sheer collectivism without any individual freedom of expression or any individual rights? Even with infants, we have to offer them choices or we face continual tantrums, until they would perhaps feel so abused and neglected that they might lose all individual will and sense of voice. How human is that?

Perhaps, then, we can reasonably and practically conclude that both individual rights and the good of society need to be taken into consideration for human harmony as well as for our mutual discovery of "truth." My observation of the United States of America is that we continually seek to balance both individual rights with the common good of all Americans, and sometimes, we succeed. On some issues, we continue to fail.

Why do we fail? I would suggest that fear leading to an over-emphasis on individualism as well as fear and greed stemming from rampant materialism can explain most of our failure to balance individual rights with the common good of all Americans. For this trend, I lay responsibility squarely at the feet of a combination of capitalism and materialistic worldviews, the values of both of which have pervaded our culture to such an extent that none of us seem immune to these values. Capitalism, individualism, patriarchy, and materialism have formed a seemingly self-perpetuating and cohesive base for greed and lack of consideration for the wellbeing of others.

> **I propose that we employ the feminine side of the gender duality, specifically maternal wisdom, in order to bring enough balance to begin to discover the truth about human relationships in their most effective forms.**

By itself, individualism lived out-of-balance can lead to a lack of ability to consider all sides of an issue for the sake of everyone's inclusion in the quest for truth. Collectivism, if it includes continual domination of individuals, would also silence some people's voices for truth. There has to be an in-between.

I propose that we employ the feminine side of the gender duality, specifically maternal wisdom, in order to bring enough balance to begin to discover the truth about human relationships in their most effective forms.

What loving mother who is effective in her parenting does not listen to both or all of her children when they have a disagreement? What effective mother does not include all her children and support each one in their individual needs as much as possible when she is making decisions? Surely, we mothers, in our fallible humanity, fail to do so at times, but our overall goal as mothers tends to be to hear all sides and to love all our children according to their individual needs. Except perhaps when we are too exhausted!

If we bring in the maternal wisdom, we can see that individual voices can be included and balanced within a healthy family system, but sometimes, we do have to take turns and just not get our way. That is the art of compromise, which seems to have been largely lost in American politics of late.

Let's return to our helpful blogger for this discussion of individualism and collectivism. He also quotes John Dewey from Dewey's "The Ethics of Democracy:" "Society in its unified and structural character is the fact of the case; the non-social individual is an abstraction arrived at by imagining what man would be if all his human qualities were taken away. Society, as a real whole, is the normal order, and the mass as an aggregate of isolated units is the fiction."[30]

What Dewey seems to be saying is "no man is an island," and that we are inherently social animals, mostly incapable of living in complete isolation from other human beings. Therefore, society consists of both individuals *and* our interactions, not just individuals existing in isolation. *Our interactions shape our world* as much or more than do our individual choices.

However, the blogger seemingly misunderstands this quote, by responding: "According to collectivism, the group or society *is* metaphysically real—and the individual is a mere abstraction, a fiction. This, of course, is ridiculous, but there you have it."[31]

However, Dewey did not claim that the individual is a fiction. What Dewey claimed was a fiction is the idea that society is made of *isolated* individuals who are like an aggregated material. If we can picture a set of isolated individuals making up society, we would be like just so many bricks stuck together with mortar, where the mortar would keep us from interacting. No, Dewey's emphasis is on the interactive nature of individuals, rather than the isolationism of individuals.

---

[30] John Dewey, "The Ethics of Democracy," in *The Early Works of John Dewey, Volume 1, 1882–1898: Early Essays and Leibniz's New Essays, 1882–1888*, edited by Jo Ann Boydston and George E. Axetell (Carbondale, IL: Southern Illinois University Press, 2008), p. 232, as accessed here: https://www.theobjectivestandard.com/issues/2012-spring/individualism-collectivism/ on September 22, 2016.
[31] Biddle, Ibid.

Again, any mother knows that her children are going to interact, and that they do not live like solitary animals confined to their rooms all the time (until perhaps they are teenagers, but that is just a phase!). Generally, children seek out companionship, unless they live among abusive or neglectful family members. Organizing what kinds of activities children can engage in together and as a family is an important aspect of healthy parenting.

Like a happy and healthy family, society depends on healthy interactions among people. Healthy interactions leave room for some individual rights, as well as a balance of what's good for the group. Not to understand this political necessity is not to understand basic human psychology and to have no idea how to parent. No healthy parent is going to go to the kind of extreme Ayn Rand seems to visualize (as again quoted by our helpful blogger) when vehemently objecting to the phrase "the greatest good for the greatest number."[32]

Rather, in a healthy family, there is a common sense of the good: everyone gets to eat, sleep somewhere decent, have some privacy, have some sense of voice as to the common good, as well as some individual rights, all balanced by not emptying the family bank account or setting the house on fire. Families quite naturally balance individual rights such as having your own

---

[32] Biddle, Ibid.

space with the common good of maintaining a roof over everyone's head.

In healthy family systems, there is a balance and happy harmony between what is good for the individual, and what is good for the family. Society is just an extension of this concept on a larger, and granted, much more complicated scale.

If we do not lean in the direction of complete individualism or complete collectivism, what are we seeking in our quest for humanity's truth on a social, national, and even global scale?

I literally could find no words in English that I thought were adequate to express a balance of individualism and collectivism. Is this an example of Western cultural bias in action? Perhaps there is such a word, but it currently has evaded my search.

I have no desire to use the word Utopia, because it seems to me that people have such differing views of what Utopia resembles. However, two words do exist in other languages that, I believe, perfectly express the ideal of harmony between the two extremes of individualism and collectivism.

These two words both come from ancient times, in different cultures (neither of which is Western or Eastern per se), with sacred spiritual or religious roots, and yet, practical, down-to-earth values. Perhaps the reason that these words promote healthy, holistic views is that they have already overcome dualities. The two words which hold comprehensive and holistic visions for harmonizing human society are: "Shalom" and "Aloha."

At first, our familiarity with these terms may bring us to the conclusion that they simply mean "peace" and "hello," respectively. Such is far from the truth, however, although they do hold those meanings, and both can be used as greetings and farewells.

Both terms have a far greater vision for living life together, for we humans rarely live alone, and are indeed hard-pressed to do so successfully. We cannot start out life alone, and I cannot even conceive of a human who either has or who could live entirely alone for his or her whole life, unless they are one amazing yogi or yogini! Even people who like to live in the wilderness still need things like clothes, shoes, and utensils that have generally been made by other human beings. So, live together we seemingly must, at least to some degree.

What, then, do "Shalom" and "Aloha" mean? Let's start with Shalom.

As I learned in my divinity school days, the concept of Shalom is intended to include peace, justice, and wellbeing for not only all of humanity, but also for the earth and all her creatures. Of course, this understanding includes all the world as existing in "righteousness," or harmonious relationship with God.

The best concise description that I have ever read for Shalom is the following by Cornelius Plantinga as cited on Wikipedia:

> The webbing together of God, humans,
> and all creation in
> justice, fulfillment, and delight is what the
> Hebrew prophets call
> shalom.
> We call it peace
> but it means far more than
> mere peace of mind
> or a cease-fire between enemies.
> In the Bible, shalom
> means universal flourishing,
> wholeness and delight – a rich state
> of affairs in which natural needs are satisfied
> and natural gifts fruitfully employed,
> a state of affairs that inspires joyful wonder
> as its Creator and Savior opens doors and
> welcomes the creatures
> in whom he delights.
> Shalom, in other words,
> is the way things
> ought to be."[33]

We have here a set of values to guide us as a corrective to both individualism and collectivism, as well as two summary goals for our ways of relating:

- Justice
- Fulfillment
- Delight

---

[33] Cornelius Plantinga, *Not the Way It's Supposed to Be: A Breviary of Sin*, (Grand Rapids: Wm. B. Eerdmans), 1995. As cited by Wikipedia, accessed here: https://en.wikipedia.org/wiki/Shalom on September 23, 2016.

- Peace
- Universal flourishing
- Wholeness
- Joyful wonder
- Welcoming all creatures
- A sense of the way things ought to be, not just for ourselves, but for all

Put together, these values are meant both to embody and to lead to a "rich state of affairs" whose end goals are "natural needs are satisfied," and "natural gifts are fruitfully employed." Who couldn't be happy if their natural needs are satisfied and their natural gifts are fruitfully employed? Well, I guess some of us might feel unhappy if we have forgotten how to delight and wonder and be grateful for all that is. I'm sure that wonder can help lead us to truth, and perhaps delight and gratitude are the natural responses to the Truth we find.

Most importantly, I invite us to notice the wisdom embodied in the word Shalom, for if we are aiming for truth, surely any ultimate Truth that we find will entail such wisdom.

Like "Shalom," the word "Aloha" has similarly rich connotations well beyond the deceptively simple appearance and sound of the word. Friendly as it sounds, Aloha is a deep embodiment of the wisdom of the Huna spiritual tradition in Hawaii, which expresses natural relationship values based on the balance of nature and living as part of that harmonious balance. We greet one another with wisdom and harmony. We greet one another as part of the nature that surrounds us, and we learn from nature's wisdom how to live with one another.

Yes, one who is wise is a great Kahuna, but few of us Westerners seem able to maintain this kind of wisdom in our actions in this age of technology and extreme energy usage. Even if we try, we begin from a place that is already far out-of-balance relative to nature's perfectly balanced ecosystems, which beautifully sustain life. Perhaps "Aloha" is a perfect invitation to us to begin again at learning how to live in balance with nature as part of it, rather than as dominators of it.

At any rate, Aloha invites us to discover the natural wisdom within nature, trusting that it holds truths which will be evident if we respect her ways.

What does Aloha mean? Simply, "Aloha" means "hello," "goodbye," and "love," as well as a way of life. Children in Hawaii are taught this first meaning of Aloha:

>Aloha is being a part of all,
>and all being a part of me.
>When there is pain - it is my pain.
>When there is joy – it is also mine.
>I respect all that is as part of the Creator
>and part of me.
>I will not willfully harm anyone or anything.
>When food is needed
>I will take only my need
>and explain why it is being taken.
>The earth, the sky, the sea are mine to care for,
>to cherish and to protect.

This is Hawaiian - this is Aloha![34]

The ethics of Aloha may be expressed like this:

> "Come forward, be in unity and harmony
> with your real self,
> God, and mankind.
> Be honest, truthful, patient,
> kind to all life forms, and humble.
> God in us."[35]

The "prime directive" of Aloha has been stated as: "The joyful sharing of life energy in the present," and "to consciously manifest life joyously in the present."[36]

Please notice how both Aloha and Shalom include concepts of joy for all life. We may discover many truths which do not automatically make us feel joyful, yet ultimately, surely Truth and joy are just as inseparable as Truth and Wisdom. If the truth we find does not indeed bring us joy, is it any sort of ultimate truth?

Both Shalom and Aloha base their sense of wisdom for human life in the harmonies of nature. If we spend time observing nature, we will witness great beauty as well as great balance among species and energies of the earth. The sun, the rain, the snow all have their seasons, the wind and the clouds move as part of the

---

[34] "The Deeper Meaning of Aloha," by Curby Rule, accessed here: http://www.huna.org/html/deeper.html on September 23, 2016.
[35] Ibid, quoting kahuna David Bray. I feel great appreciation for the fact that "Aloha" echoes the meaning of "Namaste:" that we recognize the Divine in every human being.
[36] Ibid, Curby Rule.

flow of air, water, and particles through the atmosphere. The seas flow, the rivers flow, and even plants and animals grow, live, and die in a flow of life.

This may appear to be "just" my simplistic, nature-loving suburban view, yet I invite us to contemplate the many implications of these simple observations. I once was amazed to learn from an Amish man that you can tell when it is going to rain by the behavior of ants. Well, if we have intensely studied nature we can – but we city folks probably have no clue! The ants, apparently, have us all outwitted, for they somehow know beforehand that it is going to rain and are able to prepare for it without any technological assistance.

Natural systems tend to be both beautiful and truly functional and sustainable in a physical sense, as well as dynamic and flowing in an energetic sense. The harmonies of nature outlast the life of each individual, yet each individual receives from, contributes to, and becomes part of the flow. Nature thus models harmonious living in a web of life that is both individualistic and collective, and maybe even truly capable of maintaining a certain degree of Aloha and Shalom!

Would we not be wiser to model our own lives together after the wisdom and balance of nature? Doesn't nature in so many ways model truths for human life? If you think not, I would encourage you to spend a lot more time in nature, simply learning from her.

One example of modeling ourselves after nature's systems entails the concept of economies. We tend to view our economic theories as totally dependent on human behavior and an abstraction of resources called "capital," as though both humans and these resources are somehow separate from the earth, when in fact, the environment is both source, and final limit of all of our economic activity.

> **The environment is both source, and final limit of all of our economic activity.... Aloha and Shalom envision economies derived from the systemic harmony of nature that therefore also sustain nature.**

Nature's economies, or ecosystems, are sustainable for the most part. Why is it that we humans think that our economies can only be modeled on growth rather than sustainability? How can we think growth is our only option when economies depend on the sustainability of nature? Why don't we realize that the truth is that our economies would actually last longer if they were in fact modeled on nature's patterns of economic sustainability – as ecosystems, not just economies, but systemically and intrinsically sustainable parts of nature?

Then, not only would our economies depend on nature, but also the nature of our economies would be derived from nature.

If we derive our economic models from nature, then our economies would reflect the truth and wisdom of the natural world, and not just the extremisms of individualism, materialism, and fear-based human self-interest.

Shalom and Aloha both invite us to envision humans living as part of nature in economic sustainability and balance with one another and with nature. Aloha and Shalom *envision economies derived from the systemic harmony of nature that therefore also sustain nature.* For instance, in the Biblical year of Jubilee, all debts forgiven, so that those who are poor no longer have to struggle to repay. In this system of Shalom and Jubilee, land is also given a rest, just as domestic animals rest on the Sabbath. Ancient Judaism thus had a concept of allowing farm fields to lie fallow, giving the land an opportunity to return to its harmonic natural state.

Living in harmony with nature is an ancient, and sustainable concept to which humanity would do well to return.

We Western humans have (unscientifically) thought of ourselves as being at the top of the food chain in a model of domination, yet this is, I would suggest, part of patriarchy. Ever since patriarchal religions arose, warfare (not just the previous little skirmishes between tribes) and the cultures of domination also arose. Ever since the rise of patriarchy, our attitudes to nature have become win, dominate, exploit, and use it up for our purposes, even though our choices too often lead to such short-sighted goals that we are destroying the very nature on which we depend in the process.

If we cannot even figure out that we are part of nature, and that destroying nature does not bode well for ourselves precisely because we *are* part of nature, then how can we dare to think that we know much of anything that can be called "truth?"[37]

So, perhaps we have a final duality that is an entirely false dichotomy: humanity against nature. Why have we forgotten that we are part of nature, and that, as part of nature, it is not really going to work for us to keep being "against" it?

I do remember that, in eighth grade advanced English class in Chevy Chase, we had a highly intellectual male teacher who taught the available plots of fiction. I just remember being told that plots could take these forms: "man against man," "man against nature," and "boy meets girl." I think he may have also listed "man vs. self."

At that point, I realized that something was wrong with this picture. There was too much being "against" something and no sign of cooperation and other values I cherished. I kind of wondered why everything was about "man" and "boys," but I could not, in eighth grade in 1972, articulate androcentrism, sexism, and patriarchy. (Even spellcheck on Microsoft Word, as of 2017, does not know the word androcentrism!) It's about time we learn what patriarchy means for

---

[37] I know that some people seem unable to see that we have destroyed vast amounts of nature. Yet, as just one example, we have eliminated 50% of all species since 1970. **Yes, we have killed half of the species of life on earth in a mere 47 years.**
https://www.theguardian.com/environment/2014/sep/29/earth-lost-50-wildlife-in-40-years-wwf

humanity, before we continue to *be so against* ourselves and nature that we are *destroying* ourselves!

Some of the plots of the future need to include "women save humanity from themselves." Perhaps that needs to be our main plot of the stories we write together in the news each day.

Of course, I would prefer that together we cooperatively write the story, "women and men, led by the youth, save the world from patriarchy, greed, incivility, wealth disparities, weapons, war, and environmental destruction."

And of course, I would prefer that this story becomes non-fiction, for we need this story to become part of our collective truth.

In our quest for truth, our list of dualities which we must combine in order to gain some whole sense of truth now includes:

- feminine qualities as well as masculine qualities
- Western and Eastern worldviews,
- Northern and Southern worldviews,
- left brain and right brain
- rich and poor
- love and fear
- intellect and intuition
- civility and incivility
- materialism and spiritualism (meaning spirit as distinct from matter)
- individualism and collectivism

Without harmonizing all of these perspectives, our understanding of truth is likely to remain skewed, biased, and incomplete. Without realizing that there *is no* duality between people and nature, we may be doomed to destroy ourselves, finding out the truth only too late. I am, however, a hopeful person, and a person of faith. Hope and faith definitely shape my sense of what can qualify as truth!

Just as we need to overcome dualities by harmonizing them, so also we need to harmonize our individual and collective human voices for truth. Ultimately, from a spiritual perspective, it may be possible to affirm that there is "One Truth, Many Paths."[38] Could it not be that humans are designed to pursue many paths towards the same Truth?

I have explored Eastern traditions, Sufism, contemporary spiritual teachers, as well as the roots of Christianity and Judaism, and what I have found is that the greatest saints from all religions and throughout human history have come essentially to the same great spiritual discovery. The one great spiritual truth that the greatest saints of virtually all religions have found is that we are all one with God and one with one another, at the level of our soul.

Before Buddhists remind me that Buddha taught the concept of "no-self," please allow me to agree that he taught there is no "self" that arises from the world of form. However, the qualities Buddha sought to

---

[38] I recently learned that this is the understanding promoted by the Integral Yoga Center of Princeton, New Jersey.

cultivate in ourselves as individuals and among us in sangha (community) are sacred and universal qualities that lead to a sense of oneness. Buddha also taught meditation, which sooner or later tends to lead to a sense of oneness.

Indeed, this may be the other false duality that humanity needs to overcome. Like the false dichotomy of humankind and nature, there is another false dichotomy of humanity and divinity. Discovering our unity with God and with the divine in others and in nature has been the teaching of many of the wisest teachers of virtually all cultures. This gives us twelve dualities in all, although I would argue that the nature of humanity as one with nature and one with God arises only from a false sense of separation.

This false sense of separation arises primarily from left-brain consciousness. Dr. Jill Bolte-Taylor, a neuroscientist, has written a book and provided an excellent TEDTalk on this subject. Dr. Bolte-Taylor had a stroke, and as a neuroscientist, she was able to observe her own consciousness go in-and-out of left brain and right brain awareness as the stroke occurred on the left side of her brain. As she experienced right brain awareness, she discovered that there was no longer any separation between herself and the rest of the universe. In her right brain, she experienced no separation, and no judgment. Fortunately, her left brain functioned again enough to help her realize she needed help and, with great difficulty, finally managed to call for help.[39]

The great news is that meditation can lead all of us to this discovery of a state of oneness, or unity with being. Because meditation helps harmonize left brain and right brain awareness, meditation has actually led many of us to this same conclusion. Moreover, a regular practice of meditation can lead to replication of mystical visions similar to and lessons much the same as those the greatest saints of all religions have generally experienced and endeavored to share.[40]

For the truth is that, just like the physically replicable studies used in physical sciences, in the spiritual realm of human life through the millennia, it has been found that spiritual disciplines can also lead to replicable experiences. There is just as much an intuitively or mystically verifiable scale as there is a physically verifiable scale for the experiences of humankind on this earth.

Surely, the truth is that we will only be more human when we discover how to engage the mystical scales of

---

[39] Dr. Jill Bolte-Taylor's book is called *My Stroke of Insight,* as is also her TEDtalk, accessed here:
http://www.ted.com/talks/jill_bolte_taylor_s_powerful_stroke_of_insight on September 25, 2016.

[40] Please consider reading two sources reflecting saints of two religions: *The Feminine Mystic; Readings from Early Spiritual Writers,* by Lynne M. Deming, (Cleveland: The Pilgrim Press), 1997, which showcases writings of famous Christian women mystics; and *Autobiography of a Yogi,* by Paramahansa Yogananda, (Los Angeles: Self-Realization Fellowship), 1946, which shares the spiritual journey and teachings of Yogananda, who continually relates the connections between Self-Realization concepts in Hinduism and the teachings of Jesus Christ.

intuition just as much as the physical scales of measurement. This book seeks to do both. By engaging intuition and intellect, I believe our quest will lead us to a greater and broader truth that enables us not only to be more fully human, but also wiser, kinder, more compassionate, more understanding of one another across our differences, and ultimately, closer to a more Universal Truth. Or at least to understand ourselves and the universe more accurately than we did before!

If we ever find that Universal Truth and manage to live it together, I believe that "Lived Truth" might take the shape of a Utopia as described in a poem by Peter Maurin. In 1933, Peter Maurin co-founded the Catholic Worker Movement with Dorothy Day. His poem "A Case for Utopia" is a perfect expression of non-Western, non-materialistic, civil, love-based Aloha-Shalom:

> The world would be better off
> if people tried to become better.
> And people would become better
> if they stopped trying to become better off.
> For when everybody tries to become better off,
> nobody is better off.
> But when everybody tries to become better,
> everybody is better off.
> Everybody would be rich
> if nobody tried to become richer.
> And nobody would be poor
> if everybody tried to be the poorest.
> And everybody would be what [they] ought to be

> if everybody tried to be
> what [they] want the other fellow to be.[41]

This "Case for Utopia" presents a very idealized truth for our consideration. Just as we ourselves may be our only obstacles to achieving such a Utopia, we ourselves may also be our only obstacles to accessing truth. I do hope this book assists us in gaining further insight into how we can, individually and together, overcome our own obstacles to Truth.

---

[41] Although I believe that somewhere I have kept a copy of this poem since I was in college, I was able to find it on a blog by Canadian Richard Renshaw, accessed here: http://richardrenshaw.blogspot.com/2016/02/the-case-for-utopia.html on September 23, 2016. I changed the verb "tried" to "tries" in two places because that not only fits better grammatically, but also because I believe that was the way the original version read.

CHAPTER TWO

Spiritual Worldviews and The Politics of Knowing The "Truth"

"Science without religion is lame; religion without science is blind." [42]
– Albert Einstein

Many people may object to the idea of bringing spirituality or religion into a discussion of truth and illusion. I do understand that many of us tend to see religion as having obscured the truth for hundreds, and perhaps thousands of years, because of the history of the church's objections to scientific discoveries, as well as the anti-scientific Biblical stances held by many Americans still today. Yet this is precisely why we need to bring spirituality and religion into a discussion of how one person's lie can be another one's truth, because our spiritual worldviews largely determine what we are willing to consider as possibly being true.

In fact, I would like to challenge *all of us* on our assumptions about "reality" throughout this discussion of spiritual worldviews. Albert Einstein once wrote that a scientist naturally engages in epistemology[43] while investigating the natural world, *in order to question what we think we already know.* Only by questioning

---

[42] Accessed here on September 12, 2016:
http://www.higherperspectives.com/albert-einstein-quotes-1406166918.html
[43] Epistemology is the study of knowledge – what we can know and how we are able to "know" it.

what we believe we already know can we actually begin to discover if it is true or not.[44] For instance, despite long-held views that the earth was flat, people finally questioned this idea. Today, we know the earth is round.

Since epistemology is the study of how we human beings can know anything, I dedicate this section in particular to Einstein, because what I seek to do here is to invite all of us to question what we think we already "know."

First, I would like to share my very simple definition of "politics," which implicitly includes more traditional views involving governing people along with shrewd ploys to get more power, but which strives to speak the *essence* of the word "politics." In its essence, "politics" refers to how we human beings relate to one another in terms of power: who has the most power; whether we share power; whether we wield power over others unilaterally; whether we wield power for our own benefit or for the benefit of others; whether we hoard power, or whether we take turns wielding power.

The power dynamics between people depends on three central factors: our spiritual worldviews; whether we operate more from a consciousness of fear or a consciousness of love; and whether we balance both feminine and masculine qualities and strengths within ourselves. These three factors together explain much of

---

[44] Obituary for physicist and philosopher Ernst Mach (*Nachruf auf Ernst Mach*), *Physikalische Zeitschrift* 17 (1916), p. 101 as referenced here: https://en.wikiquote.org/wiki/Albert_Einstein

human behavior, when analyzed according to the chakra system of the body, as we will be doing later in this book. Understanding politics as a constellation of attitudes toward power in relationships will help us understand ourselves, others, and our sense of truth.

Secondly, and most significantly, I would like to distinguish between religion and spirituality. Religion, for the purposes conceived here, usually has exclusive claim on founding figures (in the last 5,000 years, these figures have usually been men), who are honored by the traditions, along with sacred books, rites and rituals, dogma or teachings that can be considered a prescription for "right" and "wrong," "true" and "untrue," often along with consequences for not adhering to the teachings and practicing the rites and rituals.[45] Religious leaders often make exclusive claims of knowing the "truth," based on their religion's historical views and teachings, especially over against the teachings of other religions.

My favorite way of describing spirituality is that it consists of the intangible essences of life and the universe.

Spirituality at its root simply refers to anything immaterial, that is, the essence of things. Spirituality can therefore have religious foundations, philosophical

---

[45] To my knowledge, only the Buddha seems to have resisted the tendency to see religious teachings as permanent. He taught that the Dhamma (dharma) changes. What I believe he meant by this is that, as we evolve spiritually, the truths that we are able to perceive evolve as our understanding evolves, allowing our consciousness to expand. For information on the life and teachings of the Buddha, I am indebted to Karen Armstrong for her book: *Buddha*, (New York: Penguin Group, 2001).

foundations, or humanistic foundations. For example, engaging in religious rituals can enhance one's experience of the life of Spirit, or one's spirituality. Virtues were a common spiritual topic of ancient Greek philosophers like Aristotle. Ethics as a field of human study expresses ethical and therefore spiritual ways of relating to other human beings without being based on religion, but more often on cultural values which reflect a humanistic spiritual concern for the wellbeing of all human life.

Understood in this way, spirituality is our experience of, understanding of, and relationship with all things spiritual – spiritual qualities within ourselves, spiritual aspects of the universe and others, and spiritual qualities conceived of as being beyond the physically-perceived universe.

Spiritual qualities consist of aspects of humanity and the universe such as:

- kindness,
- compassion,
- empathy,
- faith,
- belief,
- trust,
- love,
- inner strength and determination,
- "joie de vivre,"
- nurturing,
- creativity,
- insight,

- intuition,
- consciousness,
- strokes of genius,
- "gut feelings,"
- intellectual and aesthetic senses of beauty,
- strength beyond our expected physical strength, (or mind-over-matter),
- breath,
- self-discipline,
- mindfulness,
- awareness beyond the five senses,
- loyalty,
- faithfulness, and so on.

Such qualities reflect spiritual aspects of who we are and how we live life as human beings on this earth. Spirituality can be lived as a religion, and religion can be lived spiritually.

Religion is more about being taught by a book or a religious teacher; spirituality is more about inner knowing. Spirituality is more a way of being; religion is more a way of doing. Both can be experienced individually, and also communally. Both religion and spirituality, when placed together and lived out communally, can become a way of life.

Even if we consider ourselves scientific, we tend to deal with the immaterial. For instance, one could equally ask if mathematics is the language of the universe, or if mathematics is the language of God, or both.

Albert Einstein tied science, religion, and God together in this way:

> "I said before, the most beautiful
> and most profound religious
> emotion that we can experience
> is the sensation of the mystical.
> And this mysticality
> is the power of all true science.
> If there is any such concept as a God,
> it is a subtle spirit,
> not an image of a man
> that so many have fixed in their minds.
> In essence,
> my religion consists of a humble admiration
> for this illimitable superior spirit
> that reveals itself in the slight details
> that we are able to perceive
> with our frail and feeble minds."[46]

Scientific theories, in and of themselves, are immaterial just like ideas in general, even though such theories refer to the physical universe. Theories tend to have both spiritual and physical consequences, which is why double-blind experiments become important, so that theories do not influence the outcome of scientific studies.[47]

---

[46] As quoted in *The Private Albert Einstein,* (1992) by Peter A. Bucky and Allen G. Weakland, p. 86, accessed here on September 14, 2016: https://en.wikiquote.org/wiki/Albert_Einstein

[47] Some time ago, I realized that the nature of the universe is that of consciousness plus energy. This is an ancient teaching of Eastern thought, but it finally began to make sense to me through energy healing. Because the nature of everything is consciousness plus energy, double-blind experiments

In addition, if someone theorizes that there is no God, there is actually no way to control for that theory in a scientific study, unless one limits one's definition of God, which would have spiritual consequences and would limit the possibilities of "truth."

If, by contrast, one theorizes that God is everywhere and acting all the time, it does become seemingly impossible to control for "God" as a "variable," thus rendering the concept of God pretty well outside the purview of scientific theory, at least from a Western, left-brain perspective. Thus, Western science excludes the concept of God from its field of study, which is a spiritual consequence of this theoretical worldview.

With great appreciation for Western science, I highlight this to point out that, while it has spiritual consequences, Western science does not teach us about God one way or another per se, unless we, like Einstein, humbly revere the mysteries of the Universe with awe and wonder.

Please know that I highly value Western science. I love science, from nutrition to space exploration to the nature of quantum particles (what little I know of that!). One of my greatest joys of parenting is not only the successful educational and career status of both of my two adult children, but also that my son is studying for a Ph.D. in physics, and spent about a year-and-a-half, smashing particles together at almost the speed of light at the Large Hadron Collider at CERN, just outside of

---

become essential so that consciousness from the experimenters and their theory does not affect the outcome of their studies.

Geneva, Switzerland. I delight in humanity's discovery of new particles and the nature of quantum mechanics.

Also, I highly value spirituality and to some degree religion as well, depending on how it is understood and lived out. I have valued religion my whole life, but what opened me up to spiritual experiences was having been widowed at the age of 28. The rather horrifying experience of watching my late husband die of a cerebral aneurysm as it hemorrhaged opened a whole new level of spiritual experience and interest for me.

One generally does not find meaning and comfort in sheer science alone when faced with the death of a loved one. Again, I find the words of Albert Einstein, written for a friend grieving the death of his son, beautifully appropriate for spirituality in the face of life and death:

> "A human being is a part of the whole,
> called by us "Universe",
> a part limited in time and space.
> He experiences himself, his thoughts and feelings
> as something separated
> from the rest — a kind of optical delusion
> of his consciousness.
> The striving to free
> oneself from this delusion
> is the one issue of
> true religion.
> Not to nourish the delusion
> but to try to overcome it
> is the way to reach the attainable measure

of peace of mind."[48]

As shared in the introduction, my own worldview and understanding of truth has shifted from three-fourths scientific and one-fourth religious to half scientific and half spiritual. Indeed, since 2010, I have regularly experienced intuitive "knowing" and even mystical visions which have completely changed my own spiritual worldview.

These intuitive and mystical experiences lead me to perceive Einstein's statement above as absolutely true of the perfect essence of spirituality, and preferably of religion as well. I hope you noticed in the above quote by Einstein that he also considered false any potential dichotomy between humanity/God/universe.

From personal experience, then, I know that spiritual worldviews can change, and this is significant for expanding our ability to understand one another and view "truth" from a variety of perspectives. Please note that I am not asking you to do anything that I myself have not done: as a matter of fact, I highly recommend being open to changing your spiritual worldview!

---

[48] Letter of condolence written on February 12, 1950, by Albert Einstein to Robert S. Marcus, then Political Director of the World Jewish Congress, after his son died of polio. Accessed here on September 14, 2016: http://www.lettersofnote.com/2011/11/delusion.html I hope you notice that Einstein also sees as false any potential dichotomy between humanity and nature/God/universe.

In this book, we will look at two systems of explaining spiritual worldviews, in order to understand ourselves and others, as well as to maximize our potential to grow.

The best existing introduction to a variety of spiritual worldviews with which I am familiar is an overview taught by the Rev. Dr. Walter Wink, which I discovered in his video series entitled: *The System Belongs to God.*[49]

Spiritual Worldviews

Starting with Dr. Wink's terminology, I will paraphrase a few of his concepts and then expand his observations with my own comments. For any error in representing his ideas, I apologize; the outcome intended is to expand from his base and express new ideas as well, in order to help us more fully understand how our worldview impacts our ability and willingness to perceive "truth."

The Ancient Worldview

The first worldview in Dr. Wink's systematic overview is the "Ancient Worldview." In the Ancient Worldview, the earth and heaven are conceived of as being in relationship with one another, with a one-to-one correspondence between heaven and the earth. In other

---

[49] Apparently, Walter Wink's video series *The System Belongs to God* is now available on YouTube:
https://www.youtube.com/playlist?list=PLF0703044A8D5BBDF

words, what happens in heaven is seen as affecting what happens in the world, and vice-versa.

Typical of the Ancient Worldview is the saying, "As above, so below." This worldview can be highly spiritual in its intention. For example, the philosophy of "as above, so below" is reflected in the beautiful line of the Lord's Prayer (the "Our Father") which prays: "Thy will be done on earth as it is in heaven."

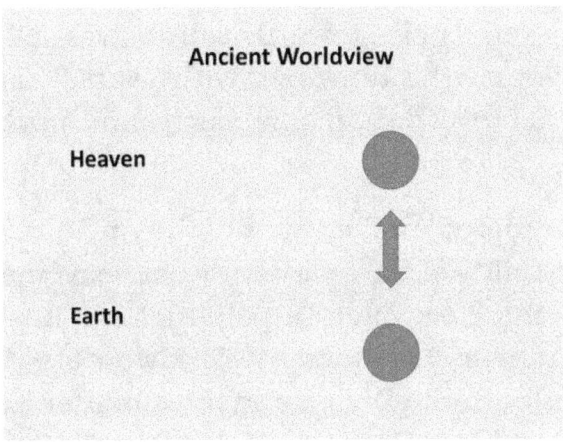

This worldview can also be more anthropomorphic in its understandings of the deity, as in the concepts of the Greek and Roman gods and goddesses, or concepts of God as being male, or "the man upstairs." Or God can be seen as walking about in a garden as in the story of the Garden of Eden in the book of Genesis.

In addition, this worldview can tend to be anthropocentric, meaning more focused on the human self, human life, and fulfilling human desires, as though we human beings do somehow form the center of the universe. One contemporary trend which exemplifies this "as above, so below" philosophy of the Ancient Worldview, along with an anthropocentric spirituality may in some ways be reflected in a spiritual emphasis on prosperity consciousness.

This worldview may therefore become limited by our own humanness and tendency towards self-interest, anthropomorphizing the Divine, as well as our anthropocentric views of the universe. And yet, by equally emphasizing heaven, this view does call us out of our own tendencies towards self-interest into a larger view of life and the universe, with sacred implications for our lives together on this earth, and prosperity for all.

One of the sacred implications of the Ancient Worldview is the possibility of harmony between heaven and earth. This view therefore offers a potential emphasis on love rather than fear. The Ancient Worldview also prioritizes connecting with the Divine and one another rather than focusing on separation and alienation. Because the Ancient Worldview emphasizes a harmonic balance in life, the focus is on the good, the positive, and the divine potential of life. This harmonic balance has been expressed quite beautifully through the abiding metaphor of the Garden of Eden.

The Spiritualistic Worldview

The next worldview we will consider is the "Spiritualistic Worldview." This view can be found in many religions, especially those which can be expressed, or perhaps misunderstood as expressing, a dualistic view of life and the universe.

On a positive note, the spiritualistic worldview highlights the holy, the sense of the sacred. Thus it emphasizes the importance of all that is sacred, holy, and good in life in general, as well as in our experiences of life individually and communally. Spiritual disciplines are often practiced fervently in this view, and can lead to heights of mystical union with the Divine. The Divine is idealized and worshiped for its (his/her) perfection, and emulated as our model for how to live and be as human beings.

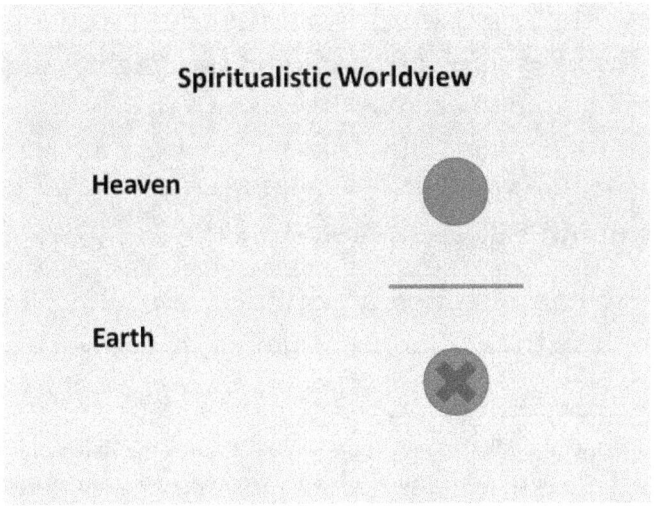

On a less positive note, in the spiritualistic worldview, human life is seen as fallen and sinful; therefore, fear can easily enter in along with guilt, shame, and blame. The story of Adam and Eve epitomizes this view, when understood quite literally, since it entails an acceptance of the duality of good and evil, and because blame for sin was placed primarily on Eve (secondarily on Adam), and therefore more-so on women in general. This blaming of women for sin creates a hierarchical duality in which men are seen as potentially more spiritual, and women less so. The evidence of this patriarchal bias resides in hierarchical, all-male "priesthoods" in Catholicism, Eastern Orthodoxy, many Protestant traditions, as well as the all-male Imams of Islam,[50] the priestly class in Hinduism, and also the traditionally male spiritual hierarchy in Buddhism.

In the spiritualistic worldview, what matters most is heaven, and generally, we humans are seen as having to believe the "right way" or act the "right way" or belong to the "right group" of people or the "right religion" in order to be able to escape this less-than-desirable world and get to heaven. In this view, there is something inherently wrong with or evil in this world, and so leaving it and getting to heaven is the number one goal.

This view has historically sounded appealing for those living in less than affluent societies, because then there

---

[50] My kind friend and Muslim neighbor, Saqiba, assures me that women are allowed to lead prayers with groups of other women, and that it is only the position of prostration before men that keeps women from being able to lead prayers with men, because of the supposedly inherent sexuality of the prostrated position. I appreciate learning that women can lead other women in prayer, but I still hear this as objectifying women as sex objects along with blaming women for the sexual desires of men during prayer, rather than men taking responsibility for their own desires and honoring women for their spiritual qualities during prayer and in life. Saqiba clarifies that women can serve on board positions in mosques and that scholars are the most highly revered in Islam, including female scholars.

is the promise of escape to heaven if we just live and/or believe the right way in this life, no matter how bad it is. Historically, this view has also been used in Christianity at least implicitly to justify classism, racism, slavery, and the like, because what counts is believing in an external savior whose goodness saves us all so that we can go to a "better place."

This view can also be appealing to those of us who tend to view the world on a dualistic level of "right and wrong," or who believe "my religion is right and takes me to heaven, but yours does not." Any tendency to view the world dualistically may find some resonance here.

In this Spiritualistic Worldview, one's own religion's sacred scriptures, whether the Bible or the Koran, the Sutras or the Vedas, becomes the only true and correct rule book and means of salvation from the fallen state of this world. Dualistically, the other religious texts are generally, though not always, seen as wrong and part of the "fallen" or "unsaved" nature of this world.

This view can therefore become very divisive in human relationships, and can limit the harmony and balance with which we live together on this earth. This view has predominated during the last 5,000 years of patriarchal religions, which has also been the period of human history in which the rise of warfare has increasingly spread around the globe.[51] It is easier to fight one

---

[51] While attending Vanderbilt University Divinity School, circa 1990, I heard a guest lecture by the Rev. Dr. Rita Nakashima Brock, who spoke of the simultaneous rise of the five "Axis" or "Axial" religions, patriarchy, and warfare. Before this time period, matriarchal religions were evident, based on

another if we don't care about the consequences for a fallen world and if we believe the other "guy" really is wrong!

The Spiritualistic Worldview also comes with an inherent tendency to bring bias in favor of one side of each duality, especially in the case of male and female. Generally, women have been blamed for "sinfulness," and have been seen as "less spiritual" because we have, of necessity, spent more time having and raising babies and generally less time, until very recently, being educated and having time to reflect on spiritual matters. Only women who have been renunciates in different religions have had the freedom to "specialize" in spirituality throughout most of our patriarchal history. And then largely male priesthoods have still generally discriminated against them.

Through this emphasis on dualism which has led to denigration of women, the world's religions have largely held humanity on this path of dualistic thinking, in which humanity is divided, fallen, and the earth itself has been seen as even more fallen. This, of course, has led to the possibility of exploiting not only women, but also the earth itself.

In this context, how could a woman theologian or spiritual teacher possibly think, know, or express "truth" that could be heard, let alone accepted by predominantly male priesthoods?

---

archaeological records. Rev. Dr. Brock is the Co-Founder of the Soul Repair Center at Brite Divinity School, Fort Worth, Texas.

The feminine voice has long been suppressed, but finally has begun to emerge on a global scale. Empowering women to have an equal voice in the discussion of what is true exists as one of the primary pillars essential to feminism, which is simply the belief that women are human beings equal with men as human beings. The spiritual version of the feminist belief is simply that women are equally spiritual and equally valuable souls, reflecting the Divine equally as much as men.

> **The experiences of pregnancy, childbirth, and breast-feeding richly teach wisdom about the connectedness of humanity in ways that male bodies simply cannot experience nor teach. Being a mother...one's whole being, from pregnancy onwards, begins to exist, at times, completely for the wellbeing of another human being.**

How can we possibly discover truths of what it means to be human if we do not hear women's voices? I remember a conversation I once had with my son while he was a student at St. John's College in Annapolis, Maryland, the "Great Books School," and a superbly excellent school in my opinion. He was reading and writing about the nature of being human, but none of the readings were written by any women, nor about women's experiences of being human.

The experiences of pregnancy, childbirth, and breastfeeding richly teach wisdom about the connectedness of humanity in ways that male bodies simply cannot experience nor teach. For instance, on Mother's Day this year, I realized and shared with my adult son that what I cherish the most about being a mother is how one's whole being, from pregnancy onwards, begins to exist, at times, completely for the wellbeing of another human being. My son's response was "it feels good to be on the receiving end of that."

Moreover, humanity needs to hear the voices of women when it comes to experiences of sexuality, intercourse, and the sacredness and holiness that are potential in acts of making love. In particular, there is a metaphorical sacredness for the bodily experience of a woman during heterosexual intercourse: she invites the other human being to enter into her own being.

What does it mean for life, human connection, and our ways of relating to one another if we truly honor this act of connecting by inviting another human being to enter into our own being, both literally and metaphorically speaking? Does this not invite true intimacy, trust, and sacredness for every human interaction?[52]

The essential word here is "invitation." The sacredness of deep, intimate connection between and among human beings is by invitation only, never by force. The culture of rape in many places around the world is clearly the denial of the sacred feminine, which is

---

[52] I am aware of writing this from a feminine, heterosexual point of view. I welcome other sexual orientations and gender points of view as to the sacredness of our bodies connecting in loving, non-objectifying ways.

largely a result of patriarchy, but also of the combination of patriarchal dominance both culturally and through the Spiritualistic Worldview. The combination tends to be dismissive, destructive, and denying of the rights, the values, the voices, and the empowerment of women.

How can we possibly understand the truth of human potential if we do not include the experiences of women in our studies of truth? How can we possibly know the "Truth" if we do not know what women's bodies and lives teach us about it? How can we possibly understand one another if we don't even hear what women's experiences are? What possible value can be placed on these human expressions of love and care as foundations for individual and collective wellbeing if we devalue pregnancy, childcare and breastfeeding, because these activities "don't earn any income?"

We have come to the point in much of American culture at which even women devalue our own bodies and what our bodies are capable of even when it comes to giving birth and breastfeeding.[53] And yet, breastfeeding might be one of the most sacred acts of humankind! If you have not read John Steinbeck's *East of Eden*, there is a

---

[53] I write this with particular emphasis on breastfeeding, because in 2014, I worked with two dentists, Dr. Michael Gelb and Dr. Howard Hindin, researching and writing the book *GASP: Airway Health, the Hidden Path to Wellness*, on the importance of breastfeeding for facial morphology and the resulting structures of the mouth, including the bite, for the overall physical and mental health of people of all ages. This importance of breastfeeding has been found in relation to significant epigenetic changes of the mouth, face and sinuses which have resulted from generations of little-to-no breastfeeding since the Industrial Revolution, which changes have led to both cognitive and physiological health issues, potentially at epidemic levels.

poignant story in the book which makes this point: during the Great Depression and migration of starving people west, one woman who was still breastfeeding her child was tasked with nursing an elderly man who was so starved he was incapable of eating. The sacredness of that act of self-giving is evident among the reactions of the characters in the story.

How will we access truth, when so many of the world's religions teach that the Divine is exclusively or at least preferentially masculine, especially from this Spiritualistic Worldview? These teachings are hierarchically imposed with no room for questioning the "revelations of truth" in each religion. From the spiritualistic worldview, then, how can we open our minds even to be able to hear one another speak our own "truths," let alone a sense of universal "Truth?"

Even in this world view, though, there is hope for hearing one another. The ability to hear other's "truth's" comes from being able to remain calm and non-anxious, which can only occur if we remain in the energy of love rather than fear. We will discuss this more later, but for now, let us affirm that even those of us who tend to have spiritualistic worldviews can shift from a deterministic dualism which emphasizes fear and separation to one which indeed emphasizes connection and compassion through viewing the deity as primarily loving and merciful.

May this discussion be the voice of wisdom calling us all to shift to a less literal and more metaphorical spirituality which speaks of love, empathy, human equality, justice, and compassion as important precisely for connecting us and bridging the divides among human beings.

The Materialistic Worldview

The third spiritual worldview we will consider is the "Materialistic Worldview." In this worldview, only the earth comes into focus, and heaven is seen as either irrelevant or truly unimportant. In this view, what really matters is getting all that we can out of life, because "you only go around once," and "the one who dies with the most toys wins."

The Materialistic Worldview leads us to focus on health and wealth, pleasure and material wellbeing. Or "abundance," as many spiritual people like to refer to this bountiful banquet of material wellbeing which appears to be available for a fair proportion of the roughly 9 billion people on the planet. I would like to note, however, that billions of people on the earth are not yet receiving this abundance, in part because of our exploitative global economies.

In the Materialistic Worldview, we "look out for number one," we compete for a perceived limited supply of goods, and we emphasize what we can get out of life rather than what we can give back. Heaven either doesn't exist, or it isn't watching, or it doesn't care.

We buy more shoes, TV's, better houses, save more money, stock up on everything we might want or need, "build a nest egg," attend the best universities, get the best jobs, raise the smartest children, and so on. We try to live forever or at least as long as we can because we

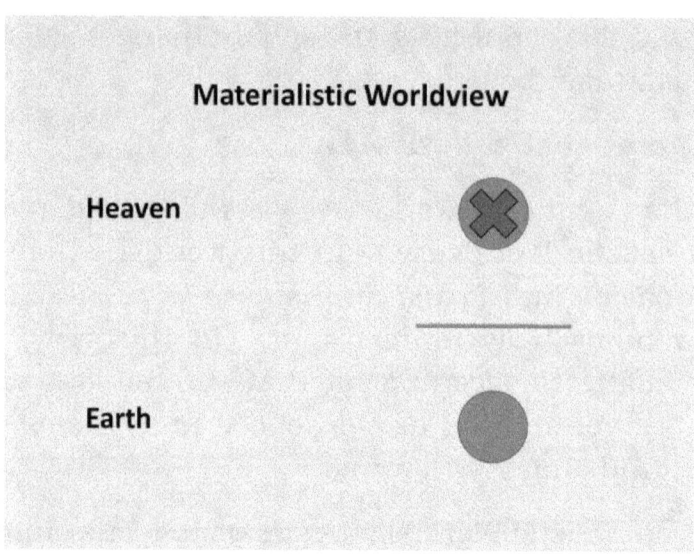

don't trust that there is anything worth living for beyond this lifetime. The only thing we do trust, in this view, is the world that we can see, touch, feel, think, create, earn, own, hear, taste, wear, smell, win, and hold onto.

If we come from a place of fear rather than love, we may also seek to dominate and exploit the rest of the world in order to "get our fair share," which behavior is defensible in this view because we "earned it." The result is again an overemphasis on fear and separation (not to mention an inability to understand that most of the rest of the world also works very hard).

It may actually be easier to go into fear and to feel chronic anxiety from this worldview, because if our sense of security lies in the material or tangible world, our feelings of safety will go up-and-down with the appearance of material and tangible wellbeing and relative safety that we experience.

For most of us, material and tangible wellbeing tends to go up-and-down in a variety of ways, especially if we include relationships and the people in our lives as part of the tangible aspects of life. Depending on externalities rather than internalities with this worldview can lead us into great anxiety, which can also lead us to make some rather hurtful or desperate decisions, because our "truth" is so easily threatened by what is external to us.

Instead, if we come from a place of love, we may desire to share all this great worldly goodness with everyone, celebrating life and the abundance of nature all around us. If we come from this place of love, humanistic ethics may give rise to social democracies where the wellbeing of all citizens is seen as a top value, rather than exclusively the wellbeing we can "earn" for ourselves.[54]

The truths that we are able to "hear" in the Materialistic Worldview are truths that support our physical and material wellbeing. If any other view, claim, or statement is viewed as a potential threat to our sense of material wellbeing, then we may reject it automatically as untrue, because it threatens the values which form our core sense of security, which is primarily about survival and thriving physically on this earth.

Notice, though, please, that one can either come from the Materialistic Worldview in an individualistic perspective, or a collective socialist perspective. If fear

---

[54] Countries like Norway, Sweden, and Denmark seem to have accomplished this approach of balancing economic freedom with more-or-less universal economic wellbeing exceptionally well through the Nordic model of social democracy.

and sense of isolation (please hear America's patriarchal culture of "rugged individualism")[55] drive the Materialistic Worldview values in us, then we generally strive for our own wellbeing, even at the expense of the wellbeing of others. Many of the one-percenters of the world may reflect this approach, although I do not know since I do not know any of them personally.

Or, if we come from a more gender-balanced and truly democratic perspective as well as a materialistic worldview, then the social democracies we create are likely to be more comprehensive in providing for the wellbeing of all citizens as well as the environment, as can be seen in countries like Denmark, Norway, and Sweden.

The Theological Worldview

The fourth spiritual worldview may seem to have an unexpected name relative to its description, but please bear with me. The next worldview is the "Theological Worldview," and in this understanding of the universe, earth is actually seen as above heaven, and there is no relation between the two of them. Scientific understandings of the universe and of life prevail.

In this view, theologians, priests, rabbis, Imams, and shamanic or other spiritual teachers can teach all they

---

[55] This would be an example where the lessons learned from a woman's bodily experiences can create a different set of values, leading to nurturing and caring for others equally as much as for one's self.

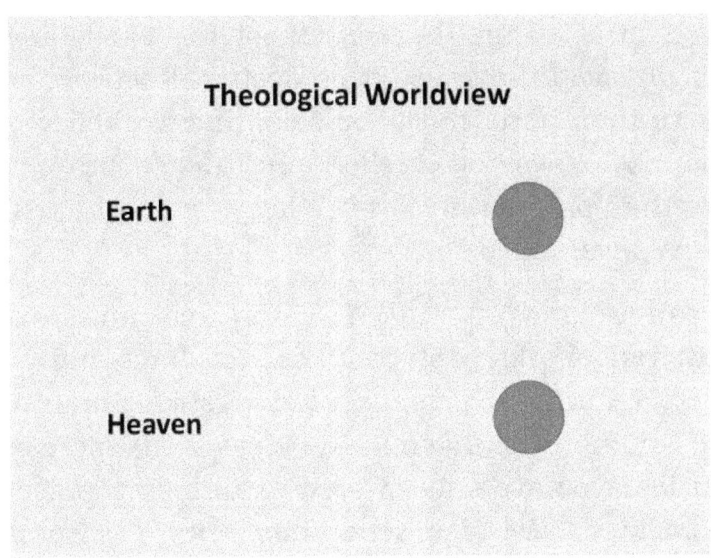

want to and study heaven all they want to, but most of their teachings are seen as irrelevant to how life and the universe operate. Theologians are free to discuss concepts such as "how many angels can dance on the head of a pin," but most theology is considered just as unimportant as that very discussion.

In this view, scientists are primarily the ones who discover and understand "truth." This view has dominated in the West for about five hundred years, ever since the rise of the scientific worldview. The scientific worldview might be considered another name for this spiritual worldview, except with that name, it might leave the theologians entirely out of the discussion of truth!

Herein lies the problem relative to knowing truth: the scientific worldview predominantly blocks any consideration of the presence of Spirit, God, or divinity in any form within the context of the earth and the larger physical universe. This occurs, I believe, largely because the approach of the scientific worldview relies almost exclusively on intellect and the left brain alone, rather than on the right brain's larger metaphorical and intuitive awareness.[56]

How can we arrive at truth if we only use one side of our brain, and employ only one way of "knowing?" For millennia, humans have recorded mystical and intuitive senses of knowing. Even in the West in the more recent centuries, we have still referred to and often relied on a "gut feeling." We also sense moments of inspiration, whether with the creation of music and poetry, or the ability to understand and apply mathematical equations to the physics of the universe. Einstein himself lauded imagination, which relies on both left and right brain work,[57] "as more important than knowledge." Einstein also credited intuition for many of his scientific ideas: "I believe in intuition and inspiration. ... At times I feel certain I am right while not knowing the reason."[58]

---

[56] I am aware that this analysis of the left-brain/right-brain split is simplistic and no longer supported by some research. Nonetheless, I believe the points convey some basic truths that can lead us to valuing all parts of our brain, and all ways of knowing.

[57] *Psychology Today* online, Christopher Bergland, *The Athlete's Way*, "The Right Brain is Not the Only Source of Creativity," September 17, 2013. https://www.psychologytoday.com/blog/the-athletes-way/201309/the-right-brain-is-not-the-only-source-creativity

[58] Cosmic Religion: With Other Opinions and Aphorisms (1931) by Albert Einstein, p. 97; also in Transformation : Arts, Communication, Environment (1950) by Harry Holtzman, p. 138. As found on this site: https://en.wikiquote.org/wiki/Albert_Einstein Accessed September 18, 2016.

Einstein also wrote: "Unthinking respect for authority is the greatest enemy of the truth."[59] One of the potential problems with any of these spiritual worldviews arises when we do not question the authorities who train us to have these worldviews. How can we possibly know if our worldview creates an accurate portrayal of what really exists if we do not even question our own worldviews and if we do not learn about other worldviews?

I applaud scientific inquiry. I am, in a way, asking us to consider spiritual worldviews from a standpoint of systematic inquiry as to their causes and effects. However, the "Theological Worldview" has left theologians largely positing (and believing in) a God who is absent from this universe: the Deistic view that God is like a clock-maker who made the clock, wound it up, and then left it to run on its own power. If this were so, how could we possibly know God? Would we merely know God by what God created and the effects of what God created? How could we possibly experience God directly?

It would essentially be impossible, in the Theological Worldview, to experience God directly. This idea of "truth" creates major dilemmas. First and foremost is the dilemma that, if we believe, as many of us do, that God is the ultimate Truth, then the Theological Worldview says that we have no way of directly discovering that ultimate Truth.

---

[59] In a letter to Jost Winteler, quoted in *The Private Lives of Albert Einstein,* by Roger Highfield and Paul Carter, 1993. Referenced here:
https://en.wikiquote.org/wiki/Albert_Einstein

Another dilemma arises because many spiritual people from different religions, around the world, as well as throughout history believe that they *have* actually experienced God. If people do experience God, what kind of explanatory value does this scientific and theological worldview have? Very little, it turns out, for those of us who have mystical experiences of any kind.

Writing about Deism and its influences on some of the Founding Fathers of the United States of America, Professor Darren Staloff of City College of New York clarifies: "Deists insisted that religious truth should be subject to the authority of human reason rather than divine revelation."[60]

I would like to suggest that the dichotomy between reason and revelation is a false dichotomy, based in part on Newtonian physics and a theological worldview that leaves no room for the great variety of human experiences of revelations, miracles, visions, and the like, which experiences have globally persisted throughout human history, even today. [61]

If a worldview is limited in its ability to explain what is happening to people in a way that takes into account their experiences of truth as well, it obviously has limits in its ability to perceive and to explain a more comprehensive "Truth."

---

[60] Staloff, Darren. "Deism and the Founding of the United States." Divining America, TeacherServe©. National Humanities Center. September 6, 2016. <http://nationalhumanitiescenter.org/tserve/eighteen/ekeyinfo/deism.htm>
[61] For some miracle stories that I have actually experienced, please see my book, *Mornings with the Masters: Mystical Journeys in a Postmodern World*, chapters two and thirteen.

The presumed dichotomy of reason and revelation is much the same as the presumed duality of intellect and intuition, and so reason and revelation represent just another aspect of that duality which we need to harmonize and thus to overcome. When considering the yin and yang of reason and revelation, maybe we need a little bit of yin in our yang, and a little bit of yang in our yin!

The Integral Worldview

In the Integral Worldview, earth and heaven are no longer separate spheres, but rather swirl in relationship together, intertwined like a spiral galaxy flowing with stars. In this view, spiritual and material expressions of "reality" flow together and affect one another. This view is incarnational, viewing God as everywhere present. (In classical Christian theology, this is the view of God's omnipresence.) Many religions view the presence of Spirit this way, from Native American traditions to ancient Tantra to some versions of Hinduism to some versions of Christianity.[62]

In the Integral Worldview, there is no need to escape the world, but there is every reason to shape the world and

---

[62] In my experience as a minister, quite a few Christians are more Deist in their way of viewing God as rather separate from the Universe, or at least believing in an "Enlightened" view of the universe as following natural laws rather than allowing miracles and revelations. Many of the Founding Fathers of America, including Benjamin Franklin and Thomas Jefferson, were influenced by Deist beliefs, whether one could label them outright Deists or not, as was much of Christianity in the "Age of Reason."

Spiral Copyright:
<aref='https://www.123rf.com/profile_sakkmesterke'>sakk mesterke / 123RF Stock Photo</a>

human life through the life of Spirit, the presence of the sacred, the Holy, or call it what you will.

Both reason and revelation are valued highly in this view, and without both, humans are seen as living out of balance, which balance is often deeply rooted in spiritual understandings of nature and the harmony of nature evident through both science and spirituality.

The Integral Worldview therefore typically and ideally values both feminine and masculine in harmony and balance together, along with valuing not only God, humans, and angelic beings, but also animals, plants, and the forces of nature.

In the Integral Worldview, love finally and fully replaces fear, and so the very best elements of each worldview in turn are included. As in the Ancient Worldview of as above, so below, in the Integral Worldview, there is also a trust that humanity is supported in being able to live life in balance and harmony. As in the Spiritualistic Worldview, there is a trust that there is "more" to this life than meets the eye, and that we can raise our vibration through love to attain all the best that the life of Spirit has to offer, even here, as well as beyond this earth-plane.

There is also trust that support will be provided for the physical and material wellbeing of humanity, especially as we intend to share that wellbeing rather than hoarding it for ourselves. There is trust that the ways of nature and the laws of the universe make sense and provide for a greater harmony as well as greater potential for the wellbeing of humanity. There is trust in both intellect and intuition.

This latter trust opens the door to an infinite potential of learning and knowing "truth" and Truth.

The essential element of the Integral Worldview may be trust. For through faith and trusting in the ultimate goodness of heaven and earth, the Integral Worldview finally harmonizes the dualities. Perhaps trust is our missing element for fully realizing love rather than fear, and so enabling us to overcome all the other dualities of human thinking.

Maybe love and trust shape the small dots on either side of yin and yang, emphasizing harmony and the potential for wholeness!

The Integral Worldview invites us beyond duality, then, into a world where wholeness and universal flourishing are not only possible, but also become real. Aloha and Shalom find their home in the Integral Worldview. Because the Integral Worldview empowers us to overcome all dualities, I would suggest that this worldview, out of all of Rev. Dr. Wink's models, offers us the fullest potential for discovering "truth."

CHAPTER THREE

Intellect, Intuition, and Illusion

Whether you can observe a thing or not depends on the theory which you use. It is the theory which decides what can be observed. [63]
– Albert Einstein

The humorous and ironic truth we need to acknowledge first is that what intuition perceives to be true, intellect often considers to be illusion; and yet, what intellect considers to be true, intuition often considers to be illusion.

For instance, an intuitively-guided mind may experience a vision, a psychic message, or otherwise just "know" something without any perceived external source of information. Or, a yogi, mystic, or spiritual healer may experience miracles occurring through their healing intentions.[64] Intellect would generally consider all these experiences to be illusions.

---

[63] "Einstein was objecting to the placing of observables at the heart of the new quantum mechanics, during Heisenberg's 1926 lecture at Berlin;" related by Heisenberg, quoted in *Unification of Fundamental Forces* (1990) by Abdus Salam. Accessed here https://en.wikiquote.org/wiki/Albert_Einstein on September 19, 2016.

[64] I met my first mystic, a gentleman from India being studied by Duke University for his psychic abilities, when I was 13 years old, in 1972. I actually witnessed him curing a woman's headache with his hands. I am also a big fan of *Autobiography of a Yogi*, and even though I initially did not believe the miracles recounted in the book to be true, I now trust that all the miracles were true. Many religious traditions speak of saints performing miracles. I have

On the other hand, great saints and yogis of all time have often reached a state of consciousness in which they view the physical world as a world of illusion. In Eastern thought, this view of the world as illusion is called Maya, which has been identified philosophically and written about for many thousands of years.

Indeed, the material world, from the highest intuitive consciousness, can be seen to be illusion, and only the highest forms of consciousness are real. This is similar to claiming that only ideas are real, but it is not the same concept. These highest forms of consciousness exist beyond the consciousness of this world of form, including our everyday thoughts and ideas.

Our commonplace thoughts relate to the world of form, or the physical universe. Only the observer mind and highest intuitive awareness, which can occur without words, per se, exist as real. This higher consciousness aspect of reality, expressed as the really real, could also be called ontological reality – or actual being-ness, or Source.

I invite us to seize this opportunity to consider the fact that continuing to view intellect and intuition as opposites and as competitors for truth may actually serve humanity much less effectively than viewing them as harmoniously intertwined in our quest for truth, harmony, and balance for life on a global scale.

---

even experienced numerous "miracles" through the healing work I do. (To read about some of these miracles, please see my book, *Mornings with the Masters: Mystical Journeys in a Postmodern World.*)

The choice is ours: a cooperative view, or a competitive view. Wisdom suggests that we cooperate with one another while competing only with ourselves by continually seeking a greater understanding of truth. Ignorance tempts us to keep competing with others for the voice of our own truth, at the expense of hearing the voices of others. A competitive paradigm blocks an openness to true inquiry, and how can we discover truth without inquiry?

The great Spiritual Masters have tended to ask questions on their quests for truth, as well as when helping others in their quests for truth. Buddha not only asked questions, but also experimented with different spiritual practices, until he found the Middle Way. The great philosophers have tended to ask questions in their quest for truth as well. Great scientists like Einstein have also tended to ask questions in order to discover truth.

Perhaps the greatest example of the value of this questioning approach is the Socratic method, which famously led people away from ignorance and into truth. As a great philosopher, Socrates focused on virtue, even asserting that "virtue is knowledge." This focus on virtue suggests that Socratic philosophy offers a corrective to the intellect's quest for truth, by including a love of wisdom and virtue as inseparable from a love of truth.

As one scholar points out, Socrates' contribution to a discussion on the relationship between wisdom, virtue, and truth might be expressed thus: "Virtue is not knowledge in any ordinary sense, but true virtue is nothing other than wisdom."[65] The three might be considered inseparable, and if we wish to distinguish truth from illusion, I would suggest that this is indeed the case. Truth, virtue, and wisdom are thus inseparable.

What good is truth if it does not reduce suffering[66] and increase compassion and justice in the world? If a truth does not do these things, is it the "whole truth?"

> **What good is truth if it does not reduce suffering and increase compassion and justice in the world? If a truth does not do these things, is it the "whole truth?"**

Wisdom asks questions to open the mind to new discoveries, thereby expanding the reach of knowledge. Extending our knowledge base out in all directions empowers us to grow closer to a more comprehensive and universally explanatory truth. When seeking truth through questions, we may seek knowledge that can explain everything – a unified field theory of truth!

By contrast, ignorance takes refuge in what it already knows, stockpiling the bricks and mortar of its own

---

[65] My expression of the meaning of this statement, which can be found in Lorraine Smith Pangle's *Virtue is Knowledge: The Moral Foundations of Socratic Political Philosophy*, (Chicago: The University of Chicago Press), May 2014. The above quote was accessed here:
http://press.uchicago.edu/ucp/books/book/chicago/V/bo18008895.html
September 7, 2016.

[66] **The Buddha's whole motivation for seeking Truth was to reduce human suffering.**

small ideas, merely layering the same or similar ideas one on top of the other in order to build a wall of defense to keep out any potentially threatening new ideas, people, or events. And ignorance simply labels any new or threatening idea "wrong" without first engaging in inquiry.

Like Einstein, we need to question what we think we already know, or we might simply remain ignorant.

Wisdom calls for a continued humility (yes, here's a virtue!) in order to expand our own knowledge to be able to embrace truths which set us free, not just individually, but also as human beings. Truths which set us free from suffering, war, violence, and hatred, are surely truths worth pursuing. Such truths embody true wisdom.

> **Wisdom and truth are inseparable. The only way to attain Truth is through being wise, and the only way to become wise is to become increasingly aware of what is True.**

Wisdom and truth are inseparable. The only way to attain Truth is through being wise, and the only way to become wise is to become increasingly aware of what is True.

One simply cannot attain both wisdom and truth without asking questions, and pondering the potential implications of ideas that could answer those questions.

Let's practice: I invite you to consider that, if wisdom and truth are inseparable, what are the implications of this statement? Can wisdom discover not only what is true but also what is illusion? Can truth make illusion become evident as well? Why would we claim that wisdom and truth are inseparable? What if the only truths we could discover led to injustice and greater suffering; would they really be truths, or just part of the illusion of this world?

What are the implications for humanity if one can only find truth through wisdom, and if one can only attain wisdom through seeking truth?

Why is wisdom pertinent here? The only way we can attain both wisdom and truth is by combining intellect and intuition.

> **The only way we can attain both wisdom and truth is by combining intellect and intuition.**
>
> **Science cannot, by itself, completely discover all Truth.**

Science cannot, by itself, completely discover all Truth. Science, as currently understood in the West, simply cannot answer questions such as: "What is the meaning of life?" or "Does God exist?" or "What is the purpose of your individual life or my individual life?" "Are angels real?" "Are miracles possible?" "What happens when we die?" "Is reincarnation possible?"

What kind of life would we have, and what kind of ironically limited beings would we be, if we could have the ability to ask such questions, but not also have access to answers to these questions?

Theoretically, from the very highest spiritual perspective, intuition could indeed lead to all knowledge and Truth, and indeed the greatest spiritual masters seem to have operated at this level.[67]

However, most of us do not yet operate at that level of intuition. Interestingly, Socrates believed that divine revelation led to some access to knowledge of the truth. He also believed that the soul can be led to "remember" what it already knew before it incarnated into this lifetime.[68] Using today's terminology, I hope Socrates would agree that both intellect and intuition are necessary to access wisdom, and in turn, to perceive truth.

Intellect alone won't get us to the answers, and intuition without intellect can be morally dishonest, because it is capable of denying the very facts presenting themselves to us as though truth cannot exist in every layer of the "being-ness" of the universe.[69]

And yet, if truth is anywhere, isn't truth everywhere?

---

[67] For one book which gives numerous examples of spiritual masters whose intuition seemed capable of accessing all Truth, please see Yogananda's *Autobiography of a Yogi*.

[68] See for example, the explanation of anamnesis given here: https://en.wikipedia.org/wiki/Anamnesis_(philosophy)

[69] For example, please remember the clergy colleague who believed God created stars with the light already shining all the way to the earth at the time of their creation.

One spiritual text wisely asks: "can truth have exceptions?" The implication, from a spiritual perspective, is "no;" not if one is contrasting truth with illusion, as in the context of this question.[70] Isn't life worthy of pursuing the kind of truths that have no exceptions? Won't we truly need both our intellect and our intuition to lead us on such a quest? Won't we have to start from scratch and ask a few questions, or many questions, to get us there?

> **Won't we really have to question everything we think we already know in order to arrive at some kind of permanent truth that has no exceptions?**

Won't we really have to question everything we think we already know in order to arrive at some kind of permanent truth that has no exceptions?

In the West, we have for so long emphasized the science of the intellect in a way that has almost entirely excluded intuition. In parts of Asia, however, intuitive sciences have flourished for hundreds, and probably even thousands of years. In many practical instances in Asia, both intellect and intuition have been combined to bring harmony to both human health, and human life. Traditional Chinese medicine would be just one example of this, as would also Ayurvedic medicine, in both of which careful scientific observations are

---

[70] *A Course in Miracles,* Foundation for Inner Peace, (New York: Viking Penguin), Second Edition, 1996, p. 281.

balanced with intuitive understandings of health and life.

By contrast, ever since the "Age of Reason," we Westerners have opposed intellect and intuition, as if one can be trusted, and the other cannot. And yet, intuition has somehow survived this onslaught against its inner wisdom. In the West, we still speak of having a "gut feeling," of "sensing the possibilities," of having an optimistic view, and so on. We also have descriptions of intuitive experiences such as "feeling the excitement in the air," and "the tension in the room was so thick you could cut it with a knife."

These latter two statements get at a topic that much of the West thinks of as "hocus pocus," "fluff," "airy-fairy," or "woo-woo." And yet it's real.

That topic is the topic of subtle energy. In Chinese medicine, the body is understood as an energy system, with the energy, or chi, flowing up and down the body along meridians. In acupuncture, certain energy points are recognized as relating to certain bodily functions, so that sticking needles in these points can enhance the bodily parts or functions by unblocking the flow of chi, or subtle energy. This flow of chi is also what is enhanced through practices such as Tai Chi and Qi Gong.

Subtle energy can also be called spiritual energy or life force. In yoga practices, this spiritual energy is referred to as prana. Prana and yoga entail a whole spiritual science of studying how the prana affects us physically, emotionally, mentally, and spiritually. In yoga, this life force is understood to flow throughout the body as a system of energy through energy centers called chakras.

If you are thinking this is all "hooey" or "baloney," please pause and ask yourself if you *actually know* what you think you know, or if you merely think you know, but have not yet asked enough questions to know for certain sure.

> **If you are thinking this is all "hooey" or "baloney," please pause and ask yourself if you *actually know* what you think you know, or if you merely think you know, but have not yet asked enough questions to know for certain sure.**

For instance, have you ever been to a ball game or stadium, or auditorium full of people where you could "feel the excitement in the air?" Many people have; which is why we commonly use that phrase.

That excitement energy is a form of subtle energy, and we human beings are all intuitively programmed to pick it up. Notably, no one had to stop and explain to you, "Do you feel that energy in the air? That's excitement you're feeling, and it comes from all these people being gathered into one place and feeling excited until there's so much excitement energy in the air that you can actually feel it!"

No; no one had to explain this to any of us who have felt this, because we are intuitively programmed to be able to sense subtle energies.

As another example, have you ever been in a room full of people, perhaps at a meeting, where "the tension in the air was so thick that you could cut it with a knife?" Many of us have actually felt that subtle energy of tension around a group of people. And again, no one had to explain to us, "excuse me, but this is not excitement energy. This is tension, so be really careful what you say right now." No explanation was needed, because we are all intuitively designed to be able to detect subtle energy and to be able to discern excitement from tension in the air around us.

> **Have you ever been in a room full of people, perhaps at a meeting, where "the tension in the air was so thick that you could cut it with a knife?" Many of us have actually felt that subtle energy of tension around a group of people.**

Have you ever been near someone who was really angry, and you could literally feel the anger coming off of them? Again, no one had to say, "Watch out, that's waves of anger that you are feeling; you need to be extremely careful right now."

Have you ever felt the energy of love as someone has hugged you or held you? I certainly hope that everyone has, and that no one has needed an explanation that what they were feeling was love.

Our "gut feelings" usually tell us exactly what kind of energy is around us at any given time when we are with other people.

Having a gut feeling is the same as knowing something intuitively.

Having a hunch is also an expression of an intuitive, or inner knowing.

So, even in the West, we have not been able entirely to shut down or lock away intuitive knowing, and that is a very good thing, because it is impossible to be wise without engaging both intellect and intuition. And it is impossible to know the truth, without also being wise. Human beings, then, require both intellect and intuition in order to attain the kind of wisdom that seeks, and finds, truths in many forms.

In our quest for truth, then, it will be necessary that we:

- Question what we think we know
- Seek to be wise as well as to know the truth
- Pay attention to our gut feelings and hunches
- Study intellectual ways of knowing
- Study intuitive ways of knowing
- Accept that we will have different senses of truth and illusion, and that we will most likely get closer to the truth if we listen to one another and ask genuine questions than if we shut one another down by telling each other that the other one is wrong.

Lastly, there is a science of the intellect, but there is also a science of intuition, or a science of the soul; that is, a spiritual science. Just as Chinese medicine studies the subtle energy system of the body scientifically, yoga studies the life force and its flow in the body through the chakra system to understand how human beings are one with, and can return to a full state of oneness with, the Divine.

I learned this when studying Raja Yoga meditation, and when reading *Autobiography of a Yogi*. Yoga is the spiritual science of union with God. Yoga as a science has been studied through intuition and experiential practice over many thousands of years. Purely and simply defined: yoga is a set of practices, especially including meditation, designed to lead a person into a state of union with the Divine. "Yoga" means union, as in union with God. Yoga is an intuitive science.

Intuition is another way of knowing. Science essentially means knowing, although clearly it is also a system of study which enables us to discover truth and to know things as they are in themselves. What I would like to invite us to embrace is a sense that intuitive knowing can be just as scientific as intellectual knowing. Both intellectual science and intuitive science study nature; the aspects of nature they study simply differ in terms of how they can be experienced and measured.

For those of us who have cherished the saying "women's intuition," knowing that it speaks of a deep, inner wisdom that women seem *perhaps* to be able to access more easily, at times, than men, the idea of intuition being a science can be very affirming.

However, the science of subtle energy goes way beyond women's intuition, or gut feelings or hunches, whether they are experienced by women or men. What we are going to explore next, then, is this science of subtle energy, and how it enables each of us to be so human, and yet, at times, perhaps even divine.

After all, what human concepts of truth would be complete without both concepts of humanity and concepts of divinity?

If you are an agnostic or atheist, I understand that you may well be cringing right now. Yes, humanity has created some really bad ideas of who God is: angry, judgmental, punishing. I trust that, if you are an atheist or agnostic, then you have done an excellent job of rejecting some really bad ideas about God. Thank you.

I invite us to consider concepts of divinity in a new light. First, let us consider that perhaps life itself is sacred. If life is sacred, does that not imply that there is indeed something divine about the sheer fact of someone or something being alive? I would suggest that the sheer fact that anything can be alive, is an essence of divinity – that is, the ability to be alive is a divine quality.

In other words, the essence of life is divine.

> **After all, what human concepts of truth would be complete without both concepts of humanity and concepts of divinity?**
>
> **I trust that, if you are an atheist or agnostic, then you have done an excellent job of rejecting some really bad ideas about God. Thank you.**

Secondly, let us ask, "If life itself is divine, then what is essential for life?" I would suggest that anything that creates, nurtures, supports, protects, and sustains life has at least some divine characteristics. Anything that is essential for life is, in some way, divine.

Now, we may disagree on all of this, but when we bring it back to our own personal and communal lives, we generally consider some things essential. So, if you are an atheist or agnostic I invite you to consider what is essential to you in life, and to consider whether or not that which you consider essential may in some way be sacred, or worthy of being cherished.

Your input could be helpful to us as we consider what is truth together.

For instance, I ask all of us to consider: what do you value or cherish? Do you cherish kindness and compassion or peace? Or do you value unconditional love and gratitude? Do you cherish friendship and family commitments? Do you value harmony and freedom? Are these virtues not something that we could at least call sacred, perhaps even divine?

Human nature has, for many thousands of years, conceived of something or someone as divine. Even Buddha, who apparently did not teach about God per se, strove to encourage qualities within each human being which might be revered as divine qualities such as compassion, or virtues, to use the Socratic term.

Whatever your views, I invite us to seek truths which we can cherish as sacred and meaningful, not only for ourselves, but for all of humanity, indeed for all life on this planet. For surely truth is something we cherish. We humans even tend to cherish our own illusions of truth.[71]

Why not seek truths that we can cherish together? Wouldn't that be wise? Wouldn't that also be virtuous?

Speaking of virtues, there is one more element of human knowing that we need to include in our understanding of truth and illusion. The ancient Israelites believed that the heart was the seat not only of emotions, but also of human intelligence.[72]

Recently, scientific studies have begun to be conducted which demonstrate that the heart actually does contribute information to the brain on many levels, not only hormonally, but also for decision-making. Perhaps this is the missing piece for including virtue in our paradigmatic quest for truth!

The Heartmath Institute offers extensive insight into the involvement of the human heart in human ways of knowing and doing.

For instance, they cite the fact that, in 1983, a new hormone was discovered that is produced by the heart

---

[71] I write this having recently experienced a vigorous debate, often lacking in wisdom, humility, and civility, about whether or not God and free will exist, that over 140 people participated in on LinkedIn. I sense wisdom when I hear questions or at least openness, along with expressions of civility. Incivility may sound clever, but it rarely, if ever, conveys wisdom.

[72] I cannot give you a reference on this; however, I distinctly remember learning this in a course at Vanderbilt Divinity School, most likely in the Hebrew Bible class I took with Dr. Renita Weems. If she was not the source of this information, I do apologize! Dr. Weems was a great professor. At the time, I remember thinking how unscientific and "wrong" this ancient view was. Clearly, my views have changed.

itself. Nicknamed "the balance hormone," ANF is one of the many ways that the heart has been found to communicate with the brain, causing not only physiological changes, but also possibly even influencing behavior. The heart also produces oxytocin, the "love or social bonding hormone," which has been found in relationships involving trust, friendship, and enduring bonding.[73]

Trust is another virtue paramount for creating healthy human communities and I would argue that trust is also essential for accessing truth. A lack of trust stems from fear, and, as pointed out earlier, fear can block our openness to perceiving truth. So, finding truth necessitates multiple virtues: wisdom, love, trust, honesty and humility, as we have discovered so far.

> **Finding truth necessitates multiple virtues: wisdom, love, trust, honesty and humility.**

Perhaps the wisdom of the heart contributes to such values, along with other values such as empathy and compassion. Moreover, perhaps such values, or virtues are necessarily intertwined with truth, which, after all, is a virtue, right? If virtue is defined as "moral excellence; goodness; righteousness,"[74] then surely truth is embedded in the very nature of virtue itself. Socrates

---

[73] Research findings cited by the Heartmath Institute, accessed on September 8, 2016 here: https://www.heartmath.org/research/science-of-the-heart/heart-brain-communication/

[74] As defined here: http://www.dictionary.com/browse/virtue?s=t Accessed on April 11, 2017.

considered knowledge to be the basis of all virtue, and only what is eternally true to be true knowledge.[75] So, let us consider truth, in the spirit of Socrates, to be the very foundation of all virtue.

The distinction I would draw from Socrates, is that knowledge must be infused with love rather than fear, in order to be true knowledge; that is wisdom. This is where the heart enables us to grow in our ability to access truth, for the heart chakra brings in the power of love to discern truth from fiction.

Other researchers have found that the heart influences bodily communications and psychophysiological reactions in numerous ways. McCraty, et al, in an article entitled "The Coherent Heart" theorize, based on extensive research, that "the heart encodes and distributes energetic information holographically," and thus operates as a "global organizing mechanism to coordinate and synchronize psychophysiological processes in the body as a whole." They further cite research that lends itself to understanding that both the heart and brain receive intuitive information on an ongoing basis.[76]

If the heart as well as the right and left brain are actually involved in our information-seeking processes, then our quest for truth surely does necessitate

---

[75] I am again indebted to Lorraine Smith Pangle's article "Virtue Is Knowledge" accessed on April 11, 2017, here:
http://press.uchicago.edu/ucp/books/book/chicago/V/bo18008895.html

[76] McCraty, et al, "The Coherent Heart," *Integral Review*, December 2009, Vol. 5, No. 2, pp. 57-58, accessed on September 8, 2016, here:
http://www.integral-review.org/issues/vol_5_no_2_mccraty_et_al_the_coherent_heart.pdf

intellect, intuition, and virtue, in order to be complete. If right brain, left brain, and heart are inseparable in communication processes within human beings, then it stands to reason that wisdom and virtue, along with intuition, are inseparable from our intellectual intelligence as we quest for truth.

CHAPTER FOUR

Cultivating Wisdom: The Inner Path to Truth

*"We all need something good, beautiful, and true
To believe in.
Mindfulness is the light that shows us the way.
Mindfulness gives rise to insight, awakening, and love.*[77]
– Thich Nhat Hanh

When we think of truth as something exterior to ourselves, we still never know for certain that it is true. All that we ever really know is what we experience in our heads. Even our sense perceptions from our extremities either travel to our brain, or to our spine, or to our spine and then onwards to our brain. So, all we know is the signals we receive from nerve endings, and what happens in our spinal cord and brain.

Therefore, everything we think we know is, ultimately, uncertain, other than through replicability and the subsequent interior verification of the outward experiences. What exists as "true" consists of the interior verifications. Even if these are collective experiences of replicability and collective interior verifications, we still only have interior verification on an individual basis for anything we might consider to be true.

---

[77] Thich Nhat Hanh, *Living Buddha, Living Christ*, (New York: Riverhead Books), 1995, pp. 120-121.

In our minds, we represent what is outside us with ideas, images, memories, concepts, feelings, and so on. All we ever really know is what is inside our own heads. (This is true until our consciousness expands through the crown chakra, but we'll have to wait to explore this concept in a later chapter.)

> **All we ever really know is what is inside our own heads.**

I make this claim having briefly studied phenomenology, and therein discovering, if I understood correctly, that indeed, all we ever have is an interior experience of outward events, things, and persons, which interior experience merely represents those exterior phenomena.[78]

This basic existential truth that we may experience phenomena as happening outside us although we really

---

[78] This is indeed my own view of phenomenology. I confess I did not study phenomenology with great enthusiasm at the time while I was a young widow and single mother studying at Vanderbilt Divinity School, unfortunately, although now it interests me far more! Gabriella Farina (2014) has pointed out: "Phenomenology should not be considered as a unitary movement; rather, different authors share a common family resemblance but also with many significant differences. Accordingly, "**A unique and final definition of phenomenology is dangerous and perhaps even paradoxical as it lacks a thematic focus. In fact, it is not a doctrine, nor a philosophical school, but rather a style of thought, a method, an open and ever-renewed experience having different results, and this may disorient anyone wishing to define the meaning of phenomenology**." Some reflections on the phenomenological method. Dialogues in Philosophy, Mental and Neuro Sciences, 7(2):50-62.http://www.crossingdialogues.com/Ms-A14-07.htm Quote accessed here on October 5, 2016:
https://en.wikipedia.org/wiki/Phenomenology_(philosophy)

only "know" the truth of that experience through our own interior mirroring of that experience, is probably the single biggest obstacle to knowing truth in any mutually and communally verifiable way.

This is, for instance, why human beings even manage to argue over data, even when studies have been replicated and employ sound methodology. If an exterior truth just doesn't fit our interior sense of "reality" or our inner "truth," then we reject it, resist it, and often argue against it. Very often, we consciously or unconsciously deny that we have anything inside us that might be blocking our perception of truth.

> **Only through cultivating inner wisdom can we clear out our interior obstacles to knowing what is true.**

As long as we depend on what is outside us for our barometers of "truth," we will tend to resist or reject external information or experiences vehemently or stubbornly when they do not match our inner "truth." Until we learn to cultivate inner wisdom, we will continue to argue with the "reality" outside us, without being aware of our own internal barometers for truth.

Only through cultivating inner wisdom can we clear out our interior obstacles to knowing what is true. It might turn out that our interior truth is the correct or most useful information, theory, idea, approach, intuitive knowing and so on, but until we access that inner knowing without human ignorance and human bias, we cannot be sure that it is true.

How do we cultivate inner wisdom? From my own experience, it can take years and a lot of practice with mindfulness, meditation, and learning about the ways that we may block truth by our own current state of being. Our own current state of being and consequent access to "truth" is determined by our current knowledge, worldview, experience, emotional needs, desires, intentions, ability to access intuitive truths, ability to reason intellectually, openness to harmonizing dualities, and so on.

Basically, cultivating inner wisdom occurs when we can cultivate inner awareness, and develop our ability to remain open to outer awareness without judgment, attachment (desire), projections, or assumptions. So often, we are unaware of our projections and assumptions, perceiving what is inside us as originating outside ourselves when the reverse is actually true. Thus, increasing our internal self-awareness is central to being able to perceive truth.

Ignorance can be a big factor in influencing our sense of what is true. Ignorance limits our ability to consider all potentially available information in order to see a synthetic whole, or universal truth. One of the reasons that education is so empowering is that, without it, we remain stuck in a considerable degree of ignorance, and therefore, also stuck in an equal measure of illusion. We might feel happy living in illusion, like a "happy drunk," but our lives will most likely become less effective in contributing to a greater good as well as a more universal truth.

With ignorance, humanity tends to become less humane. Long ago, I read Paulo Freire's *Pedagogy of the Oppressed,* and the one key concept I remember is that education is humanizing. Anything that helps us be more human empowers us to be our very best selves, individually and together. By contrast, ignorance is dehumanizing, because the more ignorant we are, the less we understand ourselves, others, and the world around us. Ignorance cannot lead us to truth.

I would also like to observe, that, in the concept of "humanizing" our life together, it is imperative that we balance both masculine values and feminine values, for without both, we can hardly claim to be humanizing. One or the other without both is simply feminizing or masculinizing, but not humanizing.

> **Ignorance is dehumanizing, because the more ignorant we are, the less we understand ourselves, others, and the world around us. Ignorance cannot lead us to truth.**

This is an example of truth that has too often been overlooked due to patriarchal domination of religions and cultures around the world. Part of patriarchy includes fearing the feminization of men. Yet, for all of us to be fully human, we need to balance the feminine and masculine qualities within ourselves. Otherwise, we all just live out of balance to some degree. This is an obvious truth, but one that we have not really emphasized in our culture.

Once we learn a truth, we can learn to deal with it, but without knowing what is true, we are left groping around in the darkness of illusion. This is a primary reason that honesty in relationships is so essential to maintaining harmony, love, and peace. Dishonesty designed to protect someone merely leaves them living in illusion. For instance, a man who refuses to inform his wife of a potentially dangerous situation near their home so that she doesn't get upset, may simply be protecting himself from dealing with her emotions rather than actually informing her so that she can figure out how to protect herself.

Ignorance and dishonesty, or the withholding of information, metaphorically leave us in the dark in our search for truth. Missing information also leaves us in the dark. Truth and open flows of information are foundational for effective democracy as well, for without truth and an informed public, we cannot make decisions that serve the greatest good for the greatest number of the citizens in a democracy.

As a simple example in terms of individuals, if we are building something or learning a craft and if we need access to both written instructions *and* visual diagrams, but we *only* have visual diagrams, we may not be able to figure out how to create or construct the whole item.

The same is true for building complete and effective information-based systems, whether those information systems are political, economic, or spiritual. The more information we have for designing those systems, the more complete or universally effective those systems become. Obviously, we are going to have to overcome ignorance if we are going to build human systems that lead to truths that bring us health, harmony, and peace on a larger scale.

Ultimately, Truth explains the complete system of the entire universe in all aspects of its being. While Einstein launched us on a quest for a Unified Field Theory, most of us appear to have far to go to understand the universe as a whole, multi-dimensional and integrated system.

Beginning with cultivating inner wisdom is the only sensible way to approach such an unwieldy prospect of finding truths that explain essentially everything in the universe, systematically at that. Since cultivating inner wisdom is a process, and because some of us may already be cultivating our inner awareness, let us now either begin cultivating, or continue enhancing our inner awareness.

The first step is to look inside for where we feel wounded, fearful, or emotionally vulnerable. Inner emotional wounding causes us to become overprotective of ourselves in many situations, and to lash out against anything or anyone who "makes" us feel unsafe. No one can actually make us feel unsafe, although others can indeed act in a threatening manner. What makes us feel unsafe are our own subconscious memories of having been hurt. These past painful memories often exacerbate any future experiences of emotional pain. Due to the past emotional pain, we tend to develop both a fear of being hurt and an emotional attachment to avoiding feeling or being hurt.

Until we gain enough self-awareness to perceive our own fears and what feels threatening to us, we cannot be fully open to perceiving truth.

For instance, if someone tells us that they literally gave away their last dollar to a homeless person so that the homeless person could eat, we might not believe that person. If we feel very threatened by the idea of running out of money, we may not be able to believe that someone else could live that way. And yet, it may be true. Some people live with a whole lot less fear about having money or depending on money. Often, people who are able to be generous to the point of giving away much or all of their money fully trust and rely on a higher power to provide for them.

> **Until we gain enough self-awareness to perceive our own fears and what feels threatening to us, we cannot be fully open to perceiving truth.**

When I returned to Kinshasa, the capital city of the Democratic Republic of Congo in 2005 for the first time as an adult, I felt honored to be able to preach at a church service. The Regional Minister translated my sermon into Lingala[79] while I preached. When the offering was collected, people gave and sang joyfully, and the offering was carried down the aisle to the front

---

[79] Lingala is the trade language spoken among ethnic groups in most of the Democratic Republic of the Congo. Many Congolese speak at least three languages, and often more, including their ethnic group language, Lingala, and French, sometimes along with German or English and other African languages.

of the church by people who were singing, dancing, and playing percussion instruments. Giving was a joyous and celebratory occasion.

The Regional Minister, who was sitting next to me, commented, "Some of these people are giving to the offering even when they do not know where their next meal is coming from." Who in the United States would have expected this? Do you find this hard to believe? I think many of us do, and yet, having lived in the DR Congo, I trust that it is true.

Fear has frequently blocked not only a lot of kindness and generosity from occurring in the world, but fear has also blocked our openness to new truths.

As another example, if we are scientists developing a new scientific theory, and after spending years in research, we come to the conclusion that this theory explains just about everything we need to be able to explain in the data, then we might feel very threatened if someone questions our conclusions. We might resent their questioning and resist considering whether they raised a legitimate point. We might decide that they don't really know the data as well as we do, as our defense. However, they might have done other research and so they may know something that we don't know. This would be an example of both fear and ignorance blocking our search for truth.

How often has this happened in science that one person's new information threatened someone's old understanding of the "facts?" Historically, this resistance has repeated time and time again, as historically "new" ideas, from the earth revolving around the sun, to evolution, to Einstein's theory of relativity have all been initially resisted. Even today, scientists and physicians often resist new information about what is "healthy" for us when that information conflicts with existing paradigms.

Familiarity and comfort with what we already think we know often represents fear of moving out of a comfort zone of information, again, potentially leaving us in a cloud of ignorance.

> **How often has this happened in science that one person's new information threatened someone's old understanding of the "facts?"**

So, let us cultivate inner awareness to know our own vulnerabilities and our own fear-based potential blocks to truths, whether those "truths" are facts, theories, intuitions, or our own or someone else's experience.

Next, let us look at denial. If we have fears, we often also tend to go into denial. There are many things the human mind is capable of denying. One of the strongest may be the effort to avoid guilt. We often fear either the feeling of guilt or we fear being punished for being "guilty," or both. Again, we will generally not feel overwhelmed by guilt, unless guilt has been conditioned into us early in life by family, friends, teachers, or religious leaders.

As an example, we might feel guilty about having a bad habit, and therefore suppress our own awareness of how much we honestly engage in that bad habit. If we are going to be able to change or eliminate the habit though, we need to become more aware of it, not less. In order to get out of denial and become more self-aware, we actually need to stop feeling guilty.

Guilt, feelings of guilt, and denial together frequently limit our self-awareness. Please understand that I am not advocating denial of responsibility, for we need to accept responsibility for our thoughts, beliefs, intentions, and actions in our quest for truth. Feeling guilty in a lingering sense, however, does not assist us in accepting responsibility effectively.

One step in increasing self-awareness, then, often entails healing our sense of guilt and shame, as well as our old emotional hurts and emotional traumas. Emotional healing may be necessary in order to increase our self-awareness. As we become more self-accepting, we can become more self-aware. Self-acceptance is central to increasing self-awareness, and vice-versa; self-awareness is essential for increasing self-acceptance.[80]

If we are unable to accept ourselves, we are unable to accept a fundamental aspect of truth, so self-acceptance may be the fundamental starting point for our quest for truth. Every human being has positive as

---

[80] This is one kind of work we life coaches often do with people. Healing emotional pain, shame, blame, and guilt while moving to greater self-acceptance and self-awareness is crucial for enhancing one's life as well as one's search for truth.

well as negative qualities, and if we reject the positive qualities by focusing on the negative ones, we are not fully accepting the truth of who we are. If we cannot accept ourselves, we are in denial about ourselves, and when we are in denial, we cannot access the full truth.

Again, if we are in denial or simply unaware of our positive or negative qualities, we remain unaware of the truth of our own selves. So, self-awareness and self-acceptance together form the foundation of the inner wisdom we need in order to recognize and access truth. As the ancient sayings have long advised us: "Know Thyself," and "To thine own self be true."

In our quest for inner wisdom, let us look next at blame and shame. Why? Well, not only are blame and shame two very toxic energies or emotional states, but also the thinking that goes behind them is judgment, which reflects a dualistic mindset, which in turn tends to limit access to truth, as we have earlier discussed. In addition, judgment typically entails both assumptions and condemnation, with or without adequate facts.

For example, let's say a couple is arguing over whose responsibility it is to take care of certain household chores, as some of the important chores did not get done the night before. One person in the couple blames the other one, saying, "you never help out enough; you just think you're too important to have to do the dirty work."

Now, if this couple were seeing me for coaching, I would approach this problematic comment several ways, but in our quest for truth, we need to point out a few problems here. First, the person is sharing an opinion, "you never help out enough," which is not necessarily a fact, although that is his or her experience of the situation. Without stating a fact, though, the information gets murky due to basing this comment on an opinion rather than a clear statement of feelings, expectations, or facts.

Second, the person made an assumption about the other person's motive. Assumptions are not facts; they obscure the truth. Third, the assumption is stated in a blaming fashion, which brings in potential emotional resistance to truth on the part of their partner. Fourth, the assumption is actually an attribution of motive, or projection of what is inside the person speaking, and blaming our own issues on the other person.

> **Not only are blame and shame two very toxic energies or emotional states, but also the thinking that goes behind them is judgment, which reflects a dualistic mindset, which in turn tends to limit access to truth.**

Now, we don't know why the second person does or does not do "enough" chores. Accusing them of "thinking they are too important," just tells us that the person doing the accusing experiences their partner that way, whether or not the partner actually is that way. The truth expressed here is an experience, not an actual motive necessarily on the part of the partner.

When a person has been talked to in such a blaming fashion with a projection of really negative motivation onto them, we might feel too defensive and go into denial because now we don't feel safe sharing our own emotional pain. Such defensiveness can lead to denial rather than helping the person feel safe enough to share their feelings in order to access and speak their true motives.

We would gently and lovingly have to ask the second partner, "Why don't you do more chores?" in order to find out their actual motivation. If we ask from a place of genuine empathy, they are more likely to be able to get in touch with their own feelings and true intentions.

When we blame, shame, and project negative motivations onto others, we generally inflict emotional pain onto them, possibly causing them to deny any negativity rather than feeling loved enough to face their own inner truth.

Love heals our emotional wounds and can empower us to face our inner truths, "good," "bad," hurtful, or precious and vulnerable. From a loving, non-judgmental place, we will avoid using labels such as "good" and "bad."

We also shut ourselves down when we judge and label ourselves as bad and shame ourselves into thinking we are somehow unworthy. Instead, we need to give ourselves empathy and understanding, in order to accept our reasons for doing what we do, and to care about our feelings.

Everyone needs empathy and understanding along with love in order to feel emotionally safe enough to access our own inner truths. Without this supportive safety, and genuine concern for our wellbeing, we cannot open up the wounds to access how we hurt emotionally and why. For instance, if we feel sad, and care about the fact that we feel sad, then we can decide to accept responsibility for our feelings and make choices that help us feel less sad.

Only by becoming more aware of our own inner thoughts and feelings can we understand our own motivations and our own truths. This also helps us understand what might be blocking us from perceiving truths that would feel too emotionally painful. To access truth more accurately, we need to bring ourselves more love and compassion to heal our own emotional needs.

So, accessing inner truths requires both empathy and understanding, along with loving enough to care about another person's wellbeing as well as our own. Cultivating inner wisdom entails love, empathy, and understanding, as well as compassionate caring. In fact, these qualities are inseparable from inner wisdom. Without inner wisdom, we cannot fully access truth.

Once we create an emotionally-safe space inside ourselves, we can access truth both inside ourselves,

> **Once we create an emotionally-safe space inside ourselves, we can access truth both inside ourselves, and outside ourselves more openly and readily.**

and outside ourselves more openly and readily. Inner wisdom calls us to do just that. We create this emotionally-safe space inside ourselves through practicing empathy and compassion with ourselves.

Once we are able to feel emotionally safe, we will be able to practice empathy and compassion with others. This ability to empathize and to care for others is essential in our quest for truth, because without empathy and compassion, we will be unable to understand others, let alone hear what truth sounds like to them.

If we are unable to hear the truth that others hear, we will be unable to consider what elements of truth, such as important values, are expressed in what they hold dear. If they see "value-added" somewhere we don't, we need to honor that this is something important to them. When we feel emotionally safe inside, hearing other people's values and understandings of truths becomes easier.

When we are able to feel emotionally safe inside ourselves, we will also stop blaming and shaming ourselves. When we can stop blaming and shaming ourselves, we will be more prepared to stop blaming and shaming others. When we stop blaming and shaming others, we will be able to listen to their actual motives, rather than projecting our own emotional needs and judgments onto them.

As we offer empathy and compassion to others, we create an emotionally-safe space for them as well. Creating emotional safety in relationships, including in groups at school, work, government, church,

> **Creating emotional safety in relationships, including in groups at school, work, government, church, synagogue, mosque, and temple, is essential to being able to open our minds to perceiving more universal truths, rather than more limited, self-serving truths. However, to create emotional safety in relationships, we must honor ourselves and every human being as an equally valuable person on this earth, simply because we breathe, think, feel, cherish, and exist.**

synagogue, mosque, and temple, is essential to being able to open our minds to perceiving more universal truths, rather than more limited, self-serving truths.[81]

However, to create emotional safety in relationships, we must honor ourselves and every human being as an

---

[81] As I listen to many of my clients, I realize it will be so helpful in work environments if I can manage to teach this to the "bosses" of the world!

equally valuable person on this earth, simply because we breathe, think, feel, cherish, and exist. As each person breathes, thinks, feels, cherishes, and exists, we form our potential for giving, teaching, creating, working, and sharing.

An important truth, however, is that, for many of us, we will only be able to fulfill our potential if we are valued simply for being, because feeling valued just for being ourselves makes us feel safe. As we feel safe, we grow and develop our full potential to be who we really are.

Being human is enough to be cherished and to be worthy of a safe emotional space in which we can share our truths. This means that we do not get to demean each other for being on welfare, or for being part of the 1%, for working or for not working. Just *being* creates a value added to society. Of course, we need to work to accomplish what is needed in life and for life, but our primary value comes from who we are, not what we do. This concept may become clearer by the time we read the last chapter of the book.

If we have ever stopped and spoken with homeless people on the street, we may have discovered the depths of their thoughts, as well as their struggles, as well as the heights of their hopes in life. If we listen with empathy and compassion, we may at least learn how difficult another human being's life is, or how limited their wealth has been in terms of emotional support and education or motivation to be who they can be. By learning how difficult their life must have been, we can learn truths of what still needs to be improved in our society – not so much in them, but in society which has failed them in some way.

I know many of us want to blame people as individuals for not being successful, but the truth is that we are all part of a system of human behavior interconnected through groups at the level of home, school, community, socioeconomic neighborhoods, other groups such as religious ones, government, and also society in general.

If we are unable to learn "even" from homeless people on the street, we are not yet there to where we can practice empathy and compassion sufficiently to help humanity know the truth. If we would like to learn a universal truth, we must listen to all of humanity.

From the point of view of nature, we are all contributing to life just by being alive. By being alive, we are part of Life. From a spiritual standpoint, we all live and breathe by Divine Spirit. Either way we look at it, life in each of us is sacred, that is, worthy of being cherished, therefore each of us contributes to life simply by sharing our own experience of living and our perspectives on life.

We are all part of this greater existence called Life. We are all part of nature, and part of the universe. We are all part of what may be called Spirit. When we can accept ourselves in this light of seeing ourselves as all part of something greater than ourselves, we can begin to see each of us as necessary, as sacred, and as having a greater potential than we might be expressing in the present moment.

In this view, there are no "bad guys." What we formerly may have referred to as "bad people" are only people who have not yet understood the sacredness and equality of everyone, and have not yet learned to honor that sacredness and equality in all people, including themselves or ourselves.

When we can honor everyone as part of this greater good called Life, or nature, or the universe, or Divine Spirit, then we can finally overcome the most basic root of all dualities: the idea that I am separate from all else, and that everyone else thus becomes "other" than myself. Here "other" means a radical split, a complete separation of self from other. This split between "self" and "other" is the root of all duality.

This may well be why Buddha emphasized the concept of the "no-self." By letting go of the sense of a separate self, we can create harmony and lessen suffering together. We will return to these ideas in later chapters.

By becoming aware of our tendency as human beings to categorize other people and other views as radically "other," rather than as part of the same whole of which we ourselves are part, we will be able to begin to harmonize all the dualities. Connecting rather than opposing creates unity, where opposing has created separation. Separation maintains dualities.

When I use the word radical, I mean "drastically." I don't mean to imply that people who might be conservatives don't do this segregation of "self" and "other;" in fact, from my observations, it seems to me that many people hold conservative religious, social, and economic views precisely because of a belief in this false duality, that we are radically separate and different from one another. What is so often trying to be "conserved" is the similarity of being like oneself, and protecting oneself from those who are "different," rather than allowing differences among people and rather than perceiving these differences as "safe" and positive.

One of the basic dualities that we can overcome through cultivating inner wisdom is the duality between what we want, and what is. Often, life presents us with situations, people, and events that appear to be something other than what we really want in life. Whether we experience a real disaster like a hurricane or a fire destroying our home, or smaller challenges like another driver cutting us off on the highway, or a co-worker getting the promotion that we wanted, life gives us situations which we may find ourselves resenting or lamenting.

> **One of the basic dualities that we can overcome through cultivating inner wisdom is the duality between what we want, and what is.**

When we resist what life is offering us, though, we are actually resisting Life. Yet, from a spiritual standpoint, Life is always giving us what we need for our spiritual growth and evolution. As human beings, we are capable of overcoming so much as individuals. We are also capable of overcoming so much more together. When we choose to accept what is, we will be able to overcome our circumstances by changing ourselves. By changing ourselves, we can change our lives, and by changing ourselves and our lives, we can change the world.

Accepting what life offers us does not mean allowing a child to run into the street and get hit by a car, nor does it mean staying in an abusive relationship nor remaining "stuck" in addiction. Accepting what life offers means being aware of what is, and choosing to accept it in the sense that our responsibility becomes changing ourselves and how we respond to what is, rather than resisting or denying what is. If we want to save someone's life when they are caught in a fire, first we must acknowledge there is a fire, then we can act to save their life and put out the fire!

Accepting our responsibility to change ourselves empowers us to accomplish what Life really needs from us. Maybe we are the ones who are meant to get that community block grant to transform our neighborhoods[82] or maybe we are the ones who are meant to bring reconciliation between co-workers and thereby create harmony in the workplace.

If a "problem" occurs, I am sure many of us understand that every crisis or problem really creates an opportunity. Yes, a problem offers us an opportunity. What is the opportunity? From the standpoint of inner wisdom, every problem that appears outside us is an opportunity to change ourselves, beginning with our thinking. When we can change ourselves, we just might become the change we wish to see in the world. If all of

---

[82] As I write, the president has proposed a budget which I believe entails eliminating community block grants, yet these grants are often a means of self-transformation for whole communities.

us would do that, life for everyone would get so much better.

Accepting life as it is in each moment opens us up to being aware of truth on a larger scale. Being aware of truth beyond our own limited desires enables us to see what is needed in Life, not just by ourselves, but by others as well.

In order to get really good at accepting life and seeing a greater possible truth, that is, a greater possible good, we need to be able to practice non-attachment. What is non-attachment? Non-attachment is the ability to be aware of our own desires in each and every situation, relationship, or interaction, and to be able to let go of our desired outcome if that outcome interferes with peace, harmony, or love for all involved, or if it interferes with the greater good of humanity.

> **Non-attachment places both a larger truth and a larger good before our own desires. Non-attachment also helps us open our hearts and minds to hear the truths that others speak.**

Non-attachment places both a larger truth and a larger good before our own desires.[83] Cultivating inner

---

[83] I just received the intuitive realization that this is what Jesus meant when he said, "You cannot serve God and wealth." (Cf. Matthew 6:24, NRSV) Paraphrased for today, what Christ meant was: we cannot prioritize this illusory world of form and prioritize God at the same time. What matters is Divine Spirit, in and through all things, and so we need to accept what is, and become part of the Divine flow of pure potential for transforming what is in order to serve a greater good for all humanity, not just ourselves. When we do

wisdom requires non-attachment, so that we can remain at peace and accept what is facing us in each present moment. Non-attachment also helps us open our hearts and minds to hear the truths that others speak.

In order to hear the truths that all of humanity can contribute to the greater truths of life, then, we have to:

- Become self-aware
- Accept ourselves
- Heal our own inner emotional wounds
- Stop the guilt syndrome by no longer shaming and blaming ourselves and others
- Listen to our own deep thoughts, values, fears, and feelings with empathy and compassion
- Listen to the thoughts, values, fears, and feelings of others with empathy and compassion
- Create a safe space for ourselves emotionally
- Create a safe space for others emotionally by making no assumptions, no judgments, and no projections
- Overcome the split between "self" and "other" by understanding that we are all part of the universe, therefore we all contribute to a universal truth which encompasses all of us
- Develop non-attachment and practice acceptance
- Honor ourselves and every human being as an equally valuable person on this earth, simply because we breathe, think, feel, and exist. In

---

that, we can trust that we will also receive what we need, although it may come from an unexpected source.

honoring ourselves and others just for existing, we honor Life, of which we are all part.

If we can do all these things, we will be on our way to cultivating inner wisdom. One sign that we have found inner wisdom is that we will tend to feel a greater sense of peace and contentment in life. Feeling peaceful and contented conveys an inner wisdom that is open to discovering greater and greater truths.

Now, there are some tools that we can use to help us develop and live by this inner wisdom. Some of these tools are also helpful for enabling us to hear the truths that others speak. Most if not all of these tools contribute to greater self-awareness, often helping us get out of our own patterns of subconscious denial.

Our first tool is mindfulness practice. Mindfulness practice is about opening and expanding our awareness of what is. As we focus on the present moment, we become more aware of what is present in the moment, and we become more present in the moment.

Mindfulness practices vary, but when I lead people in a mindfulness practice, I have us start by focusing on our breath, and then spend time noticing how our bodies feel, allowing our bodies to relax as we focus on and fully experience each part. Next, I have people focus on our breathing again, and then begin noticing our emotional feelings, in the moment, and then noticing what emotional feelings come up. Next, I have people notice our thoughts, and allow ourselves just to observe our thoughts, not becoming attached to those thoughts, but just letting them go.

There are a few other bits that I add in here-and-there, depending on the group and their spiritual orientation, but basically, we just start by focusing on the breath and increasing inner awareness.

Too often, in our culture, beginning in our schools and often in our families, we are told implicitly or explicitly to shut down our emotions and to keep our feelings to ourselves in public places. We end up learning to tune out our physical and emotional feelings, rather than increasing our self-awareness. Mindfulness helps us return to a fuller sense of self-awareness.

How many of us older generation individuals had parents influenced by Victorian era (Patriarchal and classist) values of keeping our mouths shut, and chins up without giving expression to our inner feelings? Or how many of us have been influenced by patriarchal values from other systems such as churches or the military, where expressing feelings is not allowed and people are expected to suffer in silence? When we bottle up our feelings like that, we can lose our own sense of self, awareness of our inner truths, and awareness of our own needs.

One of the fallacies of the patriarchal approach is the idea that we become weak and vulnerable if we express our needs and feelings, and therefore, we must remain strong by rarely or never expressing needs and feelings. The problem with that belief is that it tends to make us lose our own self-awareness. The truth is that when we lose awareness of what is going on inside ourselves, that lack of awareness makes us weak.

We may or may not need to speak our emotions, feelings, desires, and needs out loud, at least as adults, but we do need to become experienced and adept at being aware internally of our own feelings and desires.

> **One of the fallacies of the patriarchal approach is the idea that we become weak and vulnerable if we express our needs and feelings, and therefore, we must remain strong by rarely or never expressing needs and feelings. The problem with that belief is that it tends to make us lose our own self-awareness. The truth is that when we lose awareness of what is going on inside ourselves, that lack of awareness makes us weak.**
>
> **When we become consciously aware of our feelings, we become *stronger*, because then we can accept responsibility for speaking or acting to provide for our own emotional needs.... Once we know our own needs and accept responsibility for them, we can be open to hearing the needs and truths of others, if we open our awareness from a place of love rather than fear.**

When we become consciously aware of our feelings, we become *stronger,* because then we can accept responsibility for speaking or acting to provide for our own emotional needs. Knowing our own feelings also strengthens us by preparing us to remain considerate of what other people need. Once we know our own needs and accept responsibility for them, we can be open to hearing the needs and truths of others, if we open our awareness from a place of love rather than fear.

Without self-awareness, we also cannot identify our own biases that lead to blocking a variety of aspects of truth, whether rational, objective truths, or intuitive truths. Our own fears and biases may block us from accepting scientific evidence, as exemplified by climate change denial. From a spiritual perspective, our emotional pains and attachments often systemically lower the vibrations of our subtle energy, which can interfere with higher intuitive awareness. This statement will become clearer later in the book.

Our second tool for increasing inner awareness and wisdom consists of communication techniques for expressing our own feelings and needs in a way that they can be safely heard and understood by others. I add "safely" heard because if we express ourselves well, we will be tuning into our own sense of self, our feelings, and our needs and *taking responsibility for ourselves,* which enables the other person or persons to feel safe tuning into their sense of self, feelings, and needs.

The best method that I know for communicating safely with others is the technique referred to as "I" statements. "I" statements are contrasted to "you" statements, which can be hurtful, blaming, shaming, accusatory, projecting, assuming, and so on, leaving the other person feeling threatened, attacked, and emotionally unsafe. Such lack of emotional safety tends to block our quest for truth, because people tend to shut down, go into denial, and hide their inner selves when "you" statements are being used.

An example of an emotionally toxic "you" statement is: "You never try to be there for me when I need you; you're always just off in your own world putting yourself first and you don't even care about me!" Now, that is a loaded "you" statement, virtually guaranteed to block any dialogue leading to clarity and truth.

There are two forms of "I" statements which I believe can be effective for helping us communicate in ways that lead us closer to discerning truth. The first form focuses on expressing our own feelings, and taking responsibility for them, rather than blaming the other person. It is expressed as an observation of relationship dynamics, but neither a definition of them, nor a judgment of them.

An "I" statement expressing feelings follows this format: "I feel _____ when you _____, and I need you to _____.

One example of an "I" statement is: "I feel so hurt when you come home late without calling me, and I need you to communicate with me, telling me when you won't be coming home on time and why."

When we can get in touch with our inner self, our inner truth, our feelings, and our desires, and *own* them, then we can speak with others from a place of detachment, allowing the other person space to be aware of their own inner truth. One way of developing our detachment is first to be aware of our feelings, and then to remind ourselves to "Go with what you know, not with what you feel." Our feelings are one source of information, but we also know things about the other person, ourselves, the relationship, the situation, and we can draw on what we know to choose a more constructive response than our feelings might allow.

For instance, a second form of "I" statements draws on our own inner awareness to help clarify relationship issues. We start these "I" statements with what we know about ourselves in the relationship: "When you say 'that,' I hear 'this.' Then I feel 'this.' I would prefer that you talk to me 'this' way." Please notice how we take responsibility not only for what we hear, but also for how we feel. This personal responsibility is super important in creating healthy relationships.

Our third tool for creating greater awareness within ourselves as well as among people consists of listening techniques. Empathic listening techniques enable us to empower others to express themselves with full awareness of their own sense of self, their feelings, and what they need.

The format of this listening technique follows like this: "What I hear you saying is _____. Is that right? Is there more?" Obviously, each person takes turns talking and listening.

When both partners use this technique, or when all parties in a group use this technique, greater clarity occurs and everyone can begin to "get on the same page," understanding each other better, and questing for truth on whatever the topic may be much more effectively.

When groups are seeking to reach greater understanding together, it can help if everyone engages in some de-stressing and mindfulness exercises before beginning. Whether the group is a family, a group of co-workers, or a classroom full of children, engaging in mindfulness practices together can clear the negative emotional energy and distracting thoughts and feelings, so that everyone can engage in a quest for greater truth and understanding together.[84]

When I work with groups, as often as possible, I invite everyone to sit in a circle. I then explain that we are sitting in a circle for three reasons, and I ask them to guess what those three reasons are. Children are able to come up with some interesting and often delightful answers!

In some people's traditions, circles are considered sacred. What is sacred about sitting in a circle, in my view, are these three things: 1) everyone is included and no one is left out of the circle; 2) everyone is equal in a circle, and no one is seen as better or more important than anyone else; and 3) when we sit in a circle, we can hold the space in the center for all that is sacred, such as love, compassion, personal responsibility, empathy, strength, respect, listening, honoring, cherishing, Spirit/Source/God/Allah, peace, patience, and so on.

---

[84] I have developed some programs that assist with this process: a "Stress Reduction Workshop" available for corporations and other work groups, a program for 3rd to 12th graders called "Mastermind Stars: Master Yourself & Your Life," and a "Family Yoga Day." I also offer in-home family therapy to help families as a group engage in these techniques.

By honoring ourselves, and honoring others, we can cultivate inner wisdom together. Creating greater self-awareness together enables us to access the deep, inner wisdom within each of us. Cultivating greater self-awareness and wisdom within each of us as well as among us in ever-wider circles will accelerate our human quest for truth in all areas of our lives.

CHAPTER FIVE

Your Intuitive Self: The Chakra System of the Body

> *"Everything in the universe is within you.
> Ask all from yourself."* [85]
> — *Jalaluddin Rumi*

If the idea of having an intuitive self sounds unbelievable to you, I understand your reluctance to engage in exploring this idea as a serious mode of inquiry into truth. After all, rationality used to be the only mode of inquiry I trusted as well. Please remember that we cannot get at a holistic and comprehensive sense of truth unless we engage both intellect and intuition. So, please enjoy the ride, and see if it brings you some interesting insights along the way.

In our search for truth, the body needs to be recognized as a source of awareness, not only perceptually, but also intuitively. If we block any sort of awareness of physical or energetic activities, then we partially block truth. So then, our understanding of intuitive awareness will begin with the body's own system of intuitive awareness of both ourselves and the world around us. This body-based intuitive system[86] also

---

[85] https://www.goodreads.com/author/quotes/875661.Jalaluddin_Rumi Accessed November 2016.
[86] Technically, here, when I refer to the "body," I am actually referring to the energy system of the body, rather than the physical aspect of the body. We will get to this, I just did not want to start out with too much confusion.

helps us get out of denial and rise to new heights of self-awareness, which in turn clarifies our quest for truth by alleviating blocks and biases.

The chakra system of the body is an ancient system for understanding the flow of subtle energy in the body. Much like the energy meridians of Traditional Chinese Medicine and acupuncture, the chakras represent flows of life force energy in the body. This life force is literally what keeps us alive.

The life force can also be understood as spiritual energy – the energy of our soul, as well as the energy from the Source of life force. Whether you call that source nature, or God, or whatever is not the most important issue here. You may consider it the energy of nature, much like the energy that we recognize as making us feel good when we go outside and get some "fresh air." Life force is what makes fresh air feel so great, along with possibly greater oxygen levels present outside than inside our buildings.

We often feel especially good in the fresh air and extra life force energy on a mountain top. We may also feel great in fresh air especially when it is combined with the life force present in the ocean – many of us find ourselves feeling renewed and revitalized by both the air and water at the beach. Life force energy is more noticeable in spring and summer when the plants are putting out a lot of life force energy around us. That is why many of us enjoy climbing mountains or hiking in a forest; the life force energy all around makes us feel more alive and healthy.

The life force energy is also why we don't like stuffy rooms; it is not just the lack of oxygen that we intuitively sense in stuffy rooms, but also the lack of life force energy. That is why we tend to feel better if we spend time outside or bring plants indoors. Sunshine also provides a subtle energy that feeds us energetically, impacting our sense of wellbeing in addition to the air as we spend time outside.

Our bodies also receive and contain this life force energy. We can study the life force within us through the chakra system of the body. The chakras are centers of vitality that affect the health and wellbeing of the whole person. For instance, each chakra has a gland associated with it, and each chakra feeds different organs of the body the life force energy they need. Because the life force or subtle energy feeds all of life, every cell of the body depends on this for wellbeing.

The word "chakras" means "wheels of light." The chakras may also be called energy vortices. There are seven chakras in the body, or seven main energy centers which feed the body, with much smaller chakras along the arms, legs, and so forth. The chakras are the swirls of energy that radiate the energy outward to all the surrounding cells.

We do have one Western symbol that reflects this ancient knowledge, although our full awareness of what this symbol means seems to have gotten mostly lost long ago in the West. This Western symbol representing the chakra system is the Caduceus.

The Caduceus, or Staff of Hermes

Copyright: <ahref='http://www.123rf.com/profile_zoljo'>zoljo / 123RF Stock Photo</a>

Although not yet recognized as such by the medical establishment, the symbol of traditional medicine in the West is, despite a lack of record-keeping to the effect, based on the chakra system. As such, the caduceus serves as a reminder of the little-known presence of such esoteric wisdom crossing over between East and West long ago, or perhaps arising in the Middle East with ancient figures such as Hermes Trismegistus, images of whom can be seen holding a Caduceus.[87] While this is not the meaning that Western intellectual analyses of the origins of the Caduceus give it, nonetheless, the one-to-one resonance of the chakra system and the Caduceus is clear. [88]

The two snakes represent the kundalini, or spiritual energy, rising up the etheric spine (the center line in figure 1 below). Starting at the base, where the two snake tails emerge, we can see that there are seven points of convergence for the snakes, including where they meet at their heads, symbolizing the seven chakras as energy centers. The ancient traditions of yoga have terms for the "serpents": "nadis" or channels of energy, which rise around the central energy channel, which is called "sushumna."[89]

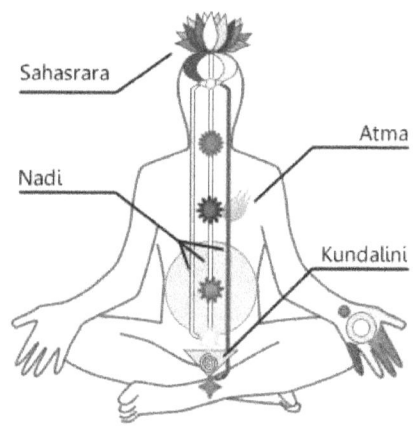

Figure 1 The Kundalini system simply represented, without the coiling of the Nadis which spiral energetically upward like snakes. Source: https://commons.wikimedia.org/wiki/File:DiagrammaChakraKundalini.jpg

---

[87] See for instance: http://www.worldglobetrotters.com/Links/Caduceus/caduceus.htm Accessed September 28, 2016.
[88] Caduceus image: Copyright: <a href='http://www.123rf.com/profile_zoljo'>zoljo / 123RF Stock Photo</a>
[89] For one explanation of this system, cf. this site: http://www.tantra-kundalini.com/nadis.htm Accessed September 29, 2016.

One nadi is considered masculine and the other feminine, as they carry their respective masculine and feminine energies up the spine. The kundalini energy rising up the spine through the chakras to the crown is the path of not only physical and mental health, but also of spiritual liberation through which one reaches a state of union with God.

The central sushumna channel carries the pure intentions of attaining oneness with God, as well as the energies of faith and devotion. This energy enables us to increase both our trust and our purity as it rises up the spine, so that ultimately, we will trust the Divine implicitly, as expressed through ourselves, in others, in the world around us, and beyond the universe as well.

As we trust the Divine more and more, we increasingly grow in faith and devotion. This growth generally occurs gradually as the kundalini energy rises, helping us develop through the chakra system. Occasionally, we may experience "leaps" which raise our consciousness significantly. Ultimately, the raising of the kundalini energy entails the resurrection of the Divine Consciousness within each human being, leading to our Ascension and oneness with God.

The wings of the Caduceus make sense as symbols of spiritual freedom, as we break free from earthly life and connect with the Divine. The wings here represent the Atman, the transcendent Self, or eternal soul, as it breaks free from attachment to the material world and unites with Cosmic Consciousness, or Eternal Spirit.[90]

The wings of the Caduceus also make sense as symbolic of angels[91] or angelic messages from God as one attains higher intuitive consciousness when the upper chakras are energized. Fully energized by the kundalini, the crown chakra opens up to Oneness and Cosmic Consciousness which feels like bliss, and thus one's state of being becomes heavenly, that is, one attains Nirvana.

The main point about the Caduceus as a symbol of health and medicine is that, the healthier our spiritual selves are, the healthier our bodies tend to be. The chakra system both represents and empowers our spiritual health and wellbeing.

Thus, the Caduceus symbolically represents our spiritual wellbeing and our resulting subtle energy as the root of our health and wellbeing on all levels. Now, that is an ancient secret worthy of Hermes and the Hermetic teachings! It also makes sense energetically, because body-mind-spirit connections are all energetic, so our wellness in one affects our wellness in the others via our subtle energy system, or chakras.

As I searched online for information about kundalini, I discovered many references to people, especially in the

---

[90] For a clear explanation of this concept of the Atman, you may consider: http://www.hridaya-yoga.com/hridaya-yoga-articles/hridaya-philosophy/atman/

[91] For the best understanding of angels that I have ever found, please see Matthew Fox and Rupert Sheldrake's *The Physics of Angels*: *Exploring the Realm Where Science and Spirit Meet*, (San Francisco: HarperCollins), 1996.

West, having problematic experiences with kundalini rising. Both physical and psychological problems have often been reported. I believe this is due to a number of factors. First and foremost, there are few teachers in the West who are qualified to guide others into this higher state of awareness. Second, there is a lot less common knowledge about how to integrate spiritual practices with a spiritual lifestyle in order to engender greater physical and psychological health while developing one's spiritual health.

Spiritual teachers are needed in the West who can assist others in developing the kind of self-awareness, intentions, and lifestyle practices that enable the kundalini rising to become an experience that leads to pure bliss. Bliss is definitely worth finding!

One remnant of awareness of the chakra system can still be found in Christianity. This Christian remnant of awareness of chakras can be seen in the golden halo surrounding the head of Christ, the heads of the Holy Family, as well as the heads of various saints through history. The halo of golden light encircles the crown chakra of truly holy people, radiating out the divine holiness within them.

The golden glow of the halo is actually the bright light of the spiritual energy which emanates from those who have fully opened and energized their crown chakras through sanctification, enlightenment, Self-Realization, and God-Realization. (We will discuss these more at the end of the book). The halo reflects the Divine light of union with God.

The halo, when it exists, is part of a person's aura, as the energy that may be intuitively "visible" above a person's crown chakra. The chakra system also relates to our aura – the "bubble" of energy around us. Although some people do not "believe in" auras, many of us do feel it when someone else is "in our space."

When we feel uncomfortable with someone standing "too close" to us, this usually happens because their subtle energy does not match ours, and we sense their energy in our aura. Conversely, if we feel good standing close to someone, it means we like how their energy feels, especially if they are loving us!

Many people have heard of and do understand the reality of auras, or can even see them. Our auras reflect the subtle energies of our body; not just the chakra energy, but also the energies of our thoughts, emotions, intentions, and beliefs. Our auras also extend our intuitive awareness out around our bodies. The clearest example of this is when we feel someone else in our personal bubble, but we can also sense near-by objects such as walls, if we learn to pay attention.

There may be a relationship between auras and what scientists are now researching as "bio-photons" emitted by living beings, including plants and animals (inclusive of humans). These bio-photons occur in the low end of the visible light spectrum, which may explain why some of us can "see" auras and/or the life force of living beings. Bio-photons are also referred to as ultra-weak photon emissions (UPE) from living systems. These bio-photons function as part of a larger electromagnetic field.[92]

Communication through fields of energy is just beginning to be researched and understood through Western scientific approaches.[93] For instance, researchers are now discovering that brain waves can transmit information via electromagnetic fields. This also implies that information transmitted by electromagnetic fields can be received and perceived by the brain.

An aura is basically a field of energy. Energy and information are stored there, received there, perceived there, and transmitted there. Auras hold incredible amounts of information in them. I have had direct experience of this numerous times, first through a class

---

[92] "UPE also supports the understanding of life sustaining processes as basically driven by electromagnetic fields." "Spontaneous Ultraweak Photon Emission from Biological Systems and the Endogenous Light Field," Forsch Komplementärmed Klass Naturheilkd 2005;12:84-89 (DOI:10.1159/000083960). Accessed here:
http://www.karger.com/Article/Abstract/83960 on September 29, 2016. See also: "An Introduction to Human Bio-Photon Emission," Forsch Komplementarmed Klass Naturheilkd. 2005 Apr;12(2):77-83, accessed on September 29, 2016 through the US National Library of Medicine of the National Institutes of Health here:
https://www.ncbi.nlm.nih.gov/pubmed/15947465
See also: http://articles.mercola.com/sites/articles/archive/2009/08/15/your-body-literally-glows-with-light.aspx Accessed on April 11, 2017.
[93] See for instance: "Scientists discover that our brain waves can be sent by electrical fields," *Science Alert*, Peter Dockrill, Januray 15, 2016, accessed here: http://www.sciencealert.com/scientists-discover-new-method-of-brain-wave-transmission-electrical-fields on September 29, 2016. See also: "Magnetic field provides a new way to communicate wirelessly," Liezel Labios, Jacobs School of Engineering, University of California at San Diego, August 31, 2015, accessed here: http://jacobsschool.ucsd.edu/news/news_releases/release.sfe?id=1807 on September 29, 2016.

on "Aura Reading," despite the fact that I wasn't sure I believed in such things at the time.

Since then, I have experienced information stored in people's auras in everyday life, including two times where people's auras actually contained warnings for me or someone else. Virtually every time I do energy healing, I sense knowledge intuitively through people's auras, and the energy of their chakras.

> **From a spiritual perspective, then, subtle energy and consciousness interweave themselves, or dance together, to shape physical "reality."**

For thousands of years, Eastern spiritual scientists have understood the subtle energy equivalent of Einstein's famous equation: $E = MC^2$. The conceptual equivalent, though not the mathematical equivalent of the relationship of mass and energy in terms of *subtle* energy, is that the C stands for consciousness or information and messaging, rather than for the constant speed of light. From a spiritual perspective, then, subtle energy and consciousness interweave themselves, or dance together, to shape physical "reality."

It is the interplay of consciousness and subtle energy that creates the physical level of "reality," from the perspective of spiritual science. For many thousands of years in India, this interplay of consciousness and energy have been represented by Shiva and Shakti, the masculine and feminine principles of divinity, representing energized consciousness (Shiva) and conscious energy (Shakti).[94]

Our conscious and subconscious states of thinking, feeling, intending, and believing all emanate subtle energies which create the larger field of energy around us. All of these subtle energies put together with the subtle energy of our physical state of wellbeing and our level of spiritual development, create our auras. Our auras thus compare to an energy field, which helps us to be intuitively aware of information that is not directly available to our rational minds.

As I have mentioned before, we have "gut feelings" and "flashes of insight" that may be signs of our intuitive awareness. This sort of intuitive awareness arises from or through the individual chakras themselves, not just through the aura. While the aura may work as an *antenna for subtle energy* messages, the chakras are the receivers/perceivers of the actual meaning of the messages as they interact with our own internal sense of "truth."

We have seven major chakras in our physical bodies. There are other spiritual chakras above our heads, which connect with larger energy fields of consciousness than our own. We also have smaller chakras, like whirls of energy, along our arms, legs, and

---

[94] I found it interesting to witness that there is a dancing Shiva sculpture at CERN, the Large Hadron Collider outside of Geneva, Switzerland. I visited in late November 2015, while my son was getting to do his Ph.D. research there.

throughout our body. Each tooth functions like a mini-chakra.

Our first chakra is at the base of the spine. Our second chakra is directly below the naval. Our third chakra is right above the naval, and our fourth chakra is at our heart center. Our fifth chakra is at our throats, while the sixth chakra is right between and slightly above our eyebrows, and our seventh chakra is at the top of our heads. Please see the diagram below, showing the location of the chakras, and the symbols for each one.

Let's start with each chakra in turn, and notice what kinds of intuitive signals we may receive from each one. The first chakra is the root chakra, and unlike most Americans, I am going to assert that the root chakra, which is linked with the gonads (testes and ovaries), is the seat of our sexual energy.[95]

At the level of the root chakra, our intuitive awareness often includes a sense of sexual attraction with someone, as their sexual energy may get released from their root chakra if they feel aroused in our presence.

---

[95] This assertion is based on my training from the spiritual center where I studied in England, and also on my own experience both with working with clients through energy healing, as well as intuitive self-awareness. If I am in error on this, I take full responsibility; however, I stand by this assertion despite having read or heard many Americans assert that the sacral chakra is the seat of sexual energies. This assertion makes no rational sense to me, since the gonads (sex glands) are related to the root chakra, and the spleen and pancreas are related to the sacral chakra.

Image: The Seven Main Chakras of the Human Body[96]

Or, our sexual energy may be released as we feel aroused in their presence. Either way, we intuitively feel sexually attracted to another person, without

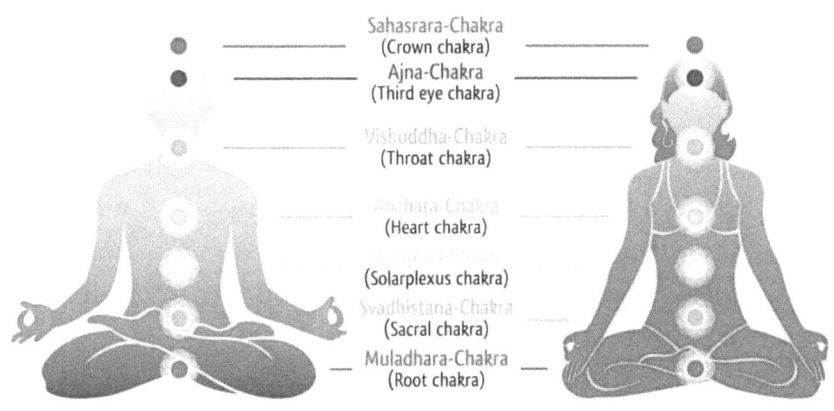

consciously realizing that our root chakra is making the connection for us. For those of us who have become more adept in chakra awareness and the ability to influence the energy in each chakra, this experience of sexual attraction and feelings in our root chakra may be more obvious, and we may develop the ability to prevent it from occurring, as well.

---

[96] Copyright: <a href='http://www.123rf.com/profile_sahua'>sahua / 123RF Stock Photo</a>

The sexual energy released from two people's root chakras can actually connect both people, and – voila! – sexual attraction occurs, sparks fly, and chemistry has happened! That subtle energy field created when two people connect energetically through passion of body and soul is usually what we mean by chemistry. Many of us, and perhaps most of us, intuitively sense such chemistry, in ourselves and others.

Moving up to the second chakra, the sacral chakra, we arrive at the beginning of the gut feeling area. In this energy vortex, we sense whether or not something feels right to us. If something feels right, it will feel fair, and it will feel as though we can remain in balance instead of being thrown off-center. If something feels wrong in the sacral chakra, it feels unfair, and we feel powerless as though someone yanked the rug out from under our feet. In this chakra, we have a sort of intuitive signal for justice and fairness, fair play and foul play.

The third chakra, the solar plexus, helps us express our emotional and creative self – creative and personal self-expression. This is the chakra of independence, rebellion, and "doing things my own way." It is also the chakra that relates to feeling fear. In the solar plexus chakra, we feel that "butterflies in the stomach" feeling, which we can enjoy as a feeling of excitement, as though we are on a thrill ride and loving it. For some of us, we may dislike that "butterflies in the stomach" feeling if we experience it as a touch of fear.

The solar plexus chakra relates energetically with the adrenal glands so it interacts with our fight-flight-freeze-fold response. So, if we feel fear, we feel it in our solar plexus, and that chakra tells us either we feel safe, or we feel unsafe.

The solar plexus energizes romantic attachment and "falling in love," in tandem with the heart chakra. As this romantic love is energized more by the solar plexus than the heart chakra, it reflects the emotional, dependency-type of connection between two people, where they may feel or believe that the other person completes them in some strongly-felt emotional way.

The solar plexus is where we can feel emotional tugs-of-war with people energetically. The solar plexus is also where we can feel people co-dependently latched onto us, draining us of our energy. This is the chakra that tells us if other people are "good" for us emotionally and energetically, or if they are a threat or an energy vampire (yes, there is such a thing!).

If you have ever felt drained after talking with someone or after just being around them for a while, chances are that they were draining your subtle energy, and your solar plexus felt pretty drained. Remember, if you will, that the solar plexus is tied with the adrenals, which can lead us to feeling fatigued if we have over-extended ourselves in some way, including feeling energetically depleted by others.

We can also feel emotional resonance with other people here: the excitement of the crowd, or the sheer fun of creativity "dancing to the music." This chakra can energetically encourage us, when we feel safe, to "let our hair down" "relax" "chill out." When we do those things, it is because our solar plexus chakra is saying "it's okay – go ahead, everything's peachy."

The solar plexus chakra is also the seat of the "belly laugh," or feeling so comfortable being ourselves, super relaxed and having a good time, that we can just completely let go and enjoy the humor of the moment. Even fun energy is something we intuitively feel. In the solar plexus chakra, we can feel the fun!

The heart chakra is our next chakra up – the fourth chakra. Obviously, the heart chakra is where we feel love when we do, whether we are feeling loved by someone else or feeling love towards someone else. The heart chakra gives us this signal, then, of "that loving feeling" which we generally enjoy and feel good about.

> **The phrase "open our hearts" comes from the experience of energetically opening our heart chakras to give love, receive love, and feel the love!**

If we don't "get that feeling" of love, then we tend to be more cautious in our relationships with people, so this is a very important intuitive signal to us.

One thing that can confuse us intuitively in the heart chakra is whether or not the love we experience is conditional or unconditional. We may struggle a bit in figuring that out until we have more experience with recognizing the intuitive signals from our heart in tandem with the intuitive signals from our other chakras. I would suggest though, that the phrase "open our hearts" comes from the experience of energetically opening our heart chakras to give love, receive love, and feel the love!

Our fifth chakra is the throat chakra. When I do energy healing on people, I tend to feel three very strong signals from this chakra. First, I feel that person's "sense of self" energetically speaking. The throat chakra gives us our sense of voice, our sense of power to speak up and be heard for who we are. How strong this is in someone is something I actually tend to feel in the flow of their energy there. I also feel whether or not the flow of energy, and therefore their sense of self, has been "knocked sideways" by something or someone in their life. Third, I am able to feel if the person drives themselves by high, narrow expectations and a lot of "should's" and "ought-to's" in life. I call this the "chin-up syndrome," because this pattern of thinking leaves them feeling they have to deny themselves so they cannot easily be true to themselves.

The throat chakra signals us when we feel something is "right" or "wrong," "true" or "untrue" and we tend to speak up with our sense of what is right, accurate, or true. When we speak untruths, our throat chakra reacts energetically, which can lead to a hoarse throat or other symptoms. If we feel shut down by emotions or someone or something more powerful than us, we may feel "choked up." I would suggest that the throat chakra and the sacral chakra are basically linked with both our sense of personal power and our sense of right-and-wrong, just-and-unjust, fair-and-unfair.[97]

The throat chakra is where we can energetically get into tugs-of-war over "who's right and who's wrong" in verbal arguments. Because our sense of self is tied-in energetically here, such arguments can feel very important until we learn to feel good about ourselves enough to separate ourselves from attachment to the outcome of such arguments.

At a more advanced level, spiritually and energetically speaking, the throat chakra is also the seat of clairaudience, or hearing truths intuitively. If we are truly pure in our intentions, dedicated to serving the highest good, and not dependent on drugs or alcohol, then we can hear the voice of God, as it were. Or at least, we can hear intermediaries such as angels, or other higher beings who speak on God's behalf.

If we are relatively spiritually advanced, and if we generally hold good motives of service, then we may hear helpful psychic messages through the throat chakra. Psychic abilities start here, although one can receive higher intuitive messages through energizing the brow chakra and crown chakra for spiritual truths.[98]

---

[97] I realize that I digress from common teachings on the seat of personal sense of power here. Part of my experience is also based on practicing Falun Dafa exercises, or Falun Gong, and experiencing a greater sense of physical and personal power in the sacral chakra as a result.

[98] I distinguish between psychic messages and intuitive messages like this: psychic messages can come from the earth plane or other dimensions of consciousness without necessarily being directed by God, angels of light, or

However, if we have raised the kundalini energy through drug use and have thereby blown open our chakras, we may have left ourselves energetically open and vulnerable to outside influences. Through drug use, we may have activated the throat chakra before being ready emotionally or spiritually, and so we may hear voices that are unkind, disembodied, or even malevolent. This is the root of much of schizophrenia: lack of emotional, mental, and spiritual development before opening the throat chakra energetically. If this has happened to us, we may feel very confused about motivations, and extremely confused in our sense of self, with or without going into full-blown schizophrenia.

Continuing to raise the kundalini energy, or spiritual life force energy, or the energy of enlightenment, up to the brow chakra, we arrive at the Third Eye, which is energetically found directly above and between the eyebrows. In the brow chakra, we begin to have mentally and visually-based intuitive knowing. These can be intellectual, related to our life purpose, or purely spiritual.

The brow chakra is the seat of being visionary, regardless of the field, especially if our visionary ideas have a positive impact on the world. So, when people who are not overtly spiritual yet who have a highly-evolved chakra system work in secular settings, we may be the visionary movers and shakers who draw people

---

other Higher Beings of light; whereas intuition is the divine guidance we receive, either through energy fields of consciousness on this earth plane, or more directly through higher spiritual planes of consciousness, or through Higher Beings such as angels, Archangels, and Ascended Masters. If one is highly intuitive, one can talk with God.

into our visions of how to make the world better, whether it is through technology or through developing a non-profit organization, or whatever our vision creates.

At a more advanced level spiritually-speaking, the brow chakra is the seat of clairvoyance, or of seeing visions. Perhaps we experience lucid dreams or receive our answers to life's questions through our dreams. Perhaps we see visions and have mystical experiences while meditating. Perhaps we have intellectual insights through intuitive nudging, as Einstein often seems to have done.

Again, purity of motivation makes a difference in what we will experience here. The purer our motivations of serving a greater good for humanity and for divinity, the more insight we are likely to receive or perceive through the Third Eye. Our level of emotional and spiritual development overall affects whether or not the Third Eye is open and "seeing." Again, preparation through practicing spiritual disciplines, studying, and being emotionally and mentally prepared are all essential to having positive experiences here.

The crown jewel of our intuitive self is the crown chakra, located on the top of the head. When we raise the kundalini energy to the crown chakra, we can experience direct perception of God, and direct divine knowing. The full flowering of the crown chakra leads to Oneness with the Divine. In the Hindu tradition, this is called Self-Realization, which is followed by God-

Realization. In a state of God-Realization, a person's consciousness is One with the Consciousness of God.

At the level of the crown chakra, life changes significantly. Perception of what is real shifts almost completely. Truth and knowledge can just pour into us as though we are an empty vessel awaiting Divine Truth to fill us up. Asking a question of the Divine, we can receive direct answers.

> **The crown jewel of our intuitive self is the crown chakra, located on the top of the head. When we raise the kundalini energy to the crown chakra, we can experience direct perception of God, and direct divine knowing.**

Life changes when we remain in this state of consciousness; life flows as though we are part of Pure Divine Potential flowing into the universe. Obstacles are mysteriously removed, miracles can occur, providence shines on us, and we understand our purpose in life to be blessing others. As long as we align ourselves with Divine Will and the intention of blessing others, we will be intuitively guided without having to think about what to do.

Ultimately, our minds become One with the Mind of God.

Our intuitive potential is therefore unlimited. The way we develop our intuitive abilities is through spiritual disciplines: meditation being the primary discipline along with prayer; but also through fasting, non-attachment to the material world, simple living, service to others for a greater good, humility, generosity, compassionate action, and so on.

How much truth would you like to access? Of course, it helps to have some rational and intellectual base of information and understanding, especially to ground ourselves and to help us connect with and serve others. Ultimately, though, we can access all knowledge directly through the enlightened awareness of our higher chakras. We are the only ones who limit ourselves in this quest for Truth.

CHAPTER SIX

Seven Spiritual Worldviews:

Why We Think So Differently From Each Other

"There are no facts, only interpretations." [99]
– Friedrich Nietzsche

Please remember that, like many Americans, I spent most of my life steeped in Western ways of thought, replete with rationality and intellect as primary values. Because I was also steeped in traditional Christian teachings, I saw no need for exploring Eastern ways of understanding religion or human nature.

However, once I started to wonder about things that I could not explain, such as why we all see the world so differently at times, then I needed something else to help me understand the world better. What I have needed, and what I believe we all need, is a way of understanding not only why we think so differently, but also how we can understand, value, and get along with each other.

For me, this depth of understanding did not begin to occur until I discovered ancient teachings from long-trod Eastern spiritual paths. Indeed, these teachings were developed many thousands of years ago, and have been explored, experienced, and passed on for

---

[99] https://www.goodreads.com/author/quotes/1938.Friedrich_Nietzsche Accessed November 28, 2016

thousands of years. Western scholarship does not always recognize just how ancient these teachings are, but these Eastern systems of knowledge reach back thousands of years, having been developed long before the current known writings.

Those who have more recently synthesized Eastern and Western understandings of spirituality have performed a great service for all of humanity. What we can learn from them can enable humanity to be able to create greater harmony for all life on earth.

Indeed, many of our greatest spiritual teachers of the 20th and 21st Centuries have already found this harmony that arises from synthesizing Eastern and Western thought and spirituality. Among these teachers, I would include first and foremost Paramhansa Yogananda, followed by Ram Dass, Eckhart Tolle, Deepak Chopra, Caroline Myss, and even the Beatles (the words in some of their songs teach deep spiritual concepts). Of course, there are many others.

I first encountered an understanding of psychology and spirituality from an Eastern perspective while studying a form of meditation called Raja Yoga in 1996. The meditation class was taught by a teacher from the Self-Realization Meditation Healing Centre in Somerset, England (SRMHC). I was reading Yogananda's *Autobiography of a Yogi* at the time, so the course and the book tied concepts together to make this new understanding much clearer to me.

The fifteen-hour Raja Yoga meditation course taught me not only how to meditate, but also about the chakra system of the body. With particular relevance to our quest for truth, the course taught a little bit about how the chakra system relates to our emotional and spiritual development as human beings, from birth through full spiritual maturity.

For four years, I engaged in further studies at the SRMHC in England, which helped develop my understanding of the chakras in relation to human development, health issues, psychological issues, and spiritual issues. I am deeply grateful for the training that I received from this spiritual center. The Centre is led by a woman guru, Mata Yogananda. Staying at the Centre and receiving training there leaves one experiencing God in ways I never had before, certainly not even in church. Ultimately, though, our paths separated, and I eventually felt led to offer meditation classes and other spiritual training for people.

Before I began developing training classes for others, I discovered Rosalynn Bruyere's book, *Wheels of Light,*[100] in which I first encountered the concept of each chakra having a different worldview. Some of what she wrote inspired me many years ago, but I have moved forward from what she wrote, in part relating it to teachings from the SRMHC, but also expanding intuitively from there. I am indebted to Bruyere for introducing me to this concept of worldviews related to each chakra.

---

[100] Rosalynn Bruyere, *Wheels of Light: Chakras, Auras, and the Healing Energy of the Body*, (New York: Fireside), 1994.

In 2010, I read Caroline Myss's excellent and groundbreaking book, *Anatomy of the Spirit*,[101] and again learned perspectives on life held by human beings according to our level of chakra development. I am indebted to and truly grateful to Myss for this book, because it helped me stay sane and remain centered when I first started having mystical experiences and naturally wondered if I were going crazy! Her book made it evident to me that this feeling of losing one's mind is a common experience as one becomes a mystic.

While Caroline Myss's paradigm is beautiful, it does not completely align with what I was taught by the SRMHC in England, nor with my own experience working intuitively with my clients during energy healing. Therefore, while I acknowledge, appreciate, and highly recommend *Anatomy of the Spirit*, the paradigm of spiritual worldviews I share here both relates to and moves beyond Myss's paradigm as well.

The reason I mention this is both to honor Bruyere and Myss, but also to explain that the system of chakra worldviews offered here disagrees with what many Americans will expect to read relative to each chakra. Part of the reason for the differences I teach about the chakras is that I focus on the glands associated with each chakra, as well as the energies as I experience them intuitively while healing people. Many Americans may experience a distinct conflict of ideas, but what is presented here is a cohesive system, with great

---

[101] Caroline Myss, *Anatomy of the Spirit: The Seven Stages of Power and Healing*, (New York: Three Rivers Press), 1996.

explanatory value, particularly with regard to our quest for truth.

We will consider each chakra and its worldview in turn. What is important to understand is that, the chakra system of the body represents our spiritual evolution as we raise the kundalini energy up the spine. At birth, we energize the root chakra, and as we grow and develop

> **At birth, we energize the root chakra, and as we grow and develop through our lifetime, we gradually energize each chakra in turn.**
>
> **Chakras thus reflect our level of spiritual development, as well as our emotional and mental development.**
>
> **It can take many thousands of lifetimes to energize all of the chakras fully to attain a transcendently enlightened state of being.**

through our lifetime, we gradually energize each chakra in turn. It can take many thousands of lifetimes to energize all of the chakras fully to attain a transcendently enlightened state of being.

Chakras thus reflect our level of spiritual development, as well as our emotional and mental development. In order for chakras to develop and grow, we must learn the spiritual lessons associated with each one, and also develop the related emotional and cognitive abilities. Chakra development is an interactive process involving life events, such as healthy, supportive relationships that lead to emotional developments and spiritual progress, or experiencing traumas that lead to emotional and spiritual setbacks. As life events affect our physical wellbeing, spiritual learning, spiritual evolution, and faith development, life either helps us develop our chakras, or allows us to shut down our chakras through developmental stunting. As we develop and grow by accepting life and learning through its challenges, each chakra is energized by the subtle life force or divine energy.

Let's look at an example. If we are energizing the heart chakra, we may suddenly become aware of all the times when we have failed to love people unconditionally, and we may begin to desire to learn to love people unconditionally, no matter how much they have hurt us or how much they continue to hurt us.

Before we begin spiritually energizing the heart chakra, we tend to love only people who love us and only when they don't hurt us, and we may see no reason to love anyone else. After fully energizing the heart chakra, it becomes easier to love people unconditionally virtually all the time. (For some of us, myself included, it may take longer to "get there" in this process!)

Spiritual evolution, from this Eastern perspective, is a life-long (and indeed multiple lifetime) process that progresses through the chakra system of the body by fully energizing, healing, and unblocking the flow of energy of each chakra in turn, beginning at the base of the spine, and traveling up to the top of the head.

Ideally, our spiritual, emotional, and mental development evolve at the same rate, so that we progress in a balanced way on our spiritual path. Often, however, life gives us multiple lessons on multiple levels, slowing our progress with challenges and traumas for which we may not feel prepared. We may forge ahead anyway, or we may need to circle back around to some of our earlier lessons to heal and make progress once more.

The concept of spiritual development is not new in the West, though it may be far older in the East. In 1981, theologian James Fowler developed a model of stages of faith which paralleled Jean Piaget's stages of cognitive development. I am grateful to Fowler for first tying together these two concepts, which truly are tied together through our evolution through the chakra system. Fowler's model even recognizes enlightenment as entailing awareness of universality, and he notes that one reaches such enlightenment at final stages of faith development.[102]

As I reflect on how Fowler's stages of faith made sense to me long ago as a psychology major, at that time, I was only able to recognize advanced souls like Christ as being at the final stages. Now, after years of meditation and experiences of healing and energizing chakras, both my own and those of others, I recognize the validity of universality as a mystical form of enlightenment and as a metaphysical truth. I also now recognize the potential

---

[102] https://en.wikipedia.org/wiki/James_W._Fowler and also https://www.integrallife.com/node/40372 accessed November 19, 2016. See also James Fowler's book: *Stages of Faith,* published in 1981.

for enlightenment by all of humanity, sooner or later, through the chakra system of the body.

As Fowler recognized so long ago, our sense of truth changes through our questioning of faith as well as our explorations of faith. At younger ages, when we allow others to teach us truth, and unquestioningly believe the "truths" we are taught, then we often miss out on the universal aspects if we are taught very literal and concrete religious understandings based on religious texts.

> **Our worldview is deeply shaped by which chakra we mostly resonate with at any given time. Each chakra offers a sense of truth that makes sense to us when we are at this stage of development. This is why we see truth so differently from each other.**

Many adults remain at this stage, and even if we do question some things, our emotional security is often so tied to the teachings, the religious institutions, our current understanding of the religion's founding figures, and the religious texts (Bible, Koran, etc.), that we cannot conceive of truth being any different than the way we have been taught.

Since our emotional, cognitive, and spiritual development is different at each stage of chakra development, our worldview is deeply shaped by which chakra we mostly resonate with at any given time. Each chakra offers a sense of truth that makes sense to us when we are at this stage of development. This is why we see truth so differently from each other.

For instance, someone who is energizing their solar plexus chakra tends to be creative and expressive, and may have a passionate sense of what is real and true to them, but also passionately believes it is important for others to have their own sense of truth. In the solar plexus chakra, much of truth is relative, and our relation to it is determined by our life experiences. To someone with a solar plexus chakra worldview, everyone speaks their own truth.

By contrast, for someone who is primarily energizing a sacral chakra worldview, truth tends to be seen as very concrete and literal, whether based on a particular (and generally the only acceptable) religious worldview, or based on a materialistic worldview. To people energizing the sacral chakra, dualism is real, and there is right and wrong as well as true and false.

> **For each human being, and indeed for each chakra, an energetic interplay occurs between consciousness, worldview, and reality, such that our consciousness of what is real is determined to a large degree by what our chakra worldview is willing and able to perceive as "real."**

For each human being, and indeed for each chakra, an energetic interplay occurs between consciousness, worldview, and reality, such that our consciousness of what is real is determined to a large degree by what our chakra worldview is willing and able to perceive as "real." For instance, each chakra can be energized primarily with love or with fear. The consciousness arising from fear-based chakra worldviews tends to be easily threatened and defensive of its "rightness." Loving chakra worldviews tend to be more open and understanding of multiple perspectives on truth, life, and so on.

Each chakra can also express primarily feminine or masculine energies, which express and develop through feminine or masculine consciousness. This does not mean that men will necessarily progress or evolve differently than women, although they may. The expression of sacred feminine and masculine energies means that each and every one of us has, or needs to have, both feminine and masculine characteristics, or strengths. As one example, we all need to be emotionally strong and independent at times, and we all need to be gentle and nurturing at times. The more we develop both sets of energies, the fuller the development of each chakra will be.

For instance, in the heart chakra, the feminine energy heals, nurtures, and connects, while the masculine energy protects, strengthens, and remains strong even when solitary. This does not mean that men energizing their heart chakras only behave certain ways, nor does it mean that women only behave certain ways. We all have feminine and masculine characteristics, and we all need to energize our heart to do all the above, or our heart chakra development will not be complete.

The feminine and masculine energies travel through the two nadis, or energy channels, that spiral up around the central channel, the sushumna, or the etheric spine, that carries the main force of kundalini energy up the chakra system.

The masculine energies carry the intention of exercising power over oneself; that is, self-discipline, strength, perseverance, and so on. Because the masculine energy or power is all about self-rule, personal autonomy, a sense of sovereignty, and sovereign rights are all vitally important from the masculine perspective.

This energy of exercising power over oneself can also extend in a positive manner to exercising power over others in order to protect or guide them, as in the case of raising children, or as in the case of being a leader, teacher, or warrior. The dysfunctional expression of the masculine energy is exercising power over others without their permission, taking away the autonomy of others, or to inflict harm while serving one's own self-interest.

In political and economic terms, capitalism expresses both functional and dysfunctional masculine energies, with very little feminine energy input. Capitalism grants personal economic autonomy to the owners of capital, but subjects those persons who do not own capital (or who own significantly less) to the sovereignty of those who do.

The feminine energies carry the intention of sharing power with oneself and others; in other words, giving oneself the energy to create, nurture, fulfill, grow, develop, connect and relate with others, and so on. This is why feminine nature is into relationships and artistic expression – the shared energy connects, expands, and expresses the powers of love, passion, and beauty within.

Cooperative systems, social democracies, and egalitarian systems all reflect feminine energies, with more or less functionality depending on the balance of individual autonomy derived from the masculine energies. If our legal systems had been designed with the input of feminine energies, they would include more avenues for reform, rather than punishment, restitution rather than retribution, and mediation rather than adversarial settlements.

Since America is still dominated by patriarchal values, arising primarily through conservative Christianity, but also through patriarchal economic, legal, educational, and political systems, this excess of masculine energy is why so many Americans feel terrified of any economic system other than capitalism. To let go of capitalism seems threatening to the "pure" autonomy sought after by the male system in the absence of female energetic input. Only by balancing female and male energies can we create healthy economies along with healthy political and legal systems.

The male and female energies relate to each chakra in turn, and both are necessary for full emotional and spiritual development through the chakra system.

One caveat needs to be made about chakra development. Tragedies in life as well as excessive alcohol or drug use may blow open our chakras before we are developmentally ready. This can create problems, because we may be left energetically open and therefore emotionally and spiritually vulnerable.

Blowing open our chakras through drugs, alcohol, or tragic shocks can lead to a spiritual crisis and the proverbial dark night of the soul.

Excessive drug use, if it blows open the upper chakras, can lead to psychic vulnerability, which in turn can lead to conditions such as schizophrenia. In other words, shock, trauma, excessive alcohol, and drug use can all limit or even block our ability to perceive, access, and understand truth.

In our quest for truth, we need to explore and understand how the chakra system of the body affects our ability to perceive the truth. The worldviews that we will share here reflect the seven chakra stages of spiritual development, along with our cognitive and emotional development, as they all relate to our understanding of truth.

The chakras as a system of energy develop most fully and expansively through the energy of love. The chakras also develop the most harmoniously and therefore maturely through a balance of sacred feminine and sacred masculine energies. These energies in turn shape our very consciousness, expanding it and harmonizing it with the consciousness of others and with life itself. Through shaping our conscious awareness, the energies of our chakras shape our understanding of truth.

By contrast, if we live in fear, we will tend to limit our chakra worldviews to a less-emotionally and spiritually developed state. Fear will limit our ability to fulfill the chakra worldview's function of creating a healthier way of understanding and opening up to truth. We may remain stuck in lower chakra worldviews if we live with a lot of fear. Fear does not always show itself externally as fear; it may often be seen as blustering bravado or overpowering, dominating, bullying, and attacking, or just protectionism. Fear keeps us stuck from our full chakra development.

> **These observations about our emotional and spiritual development serve the purpose of helping us understand and connect with each other, *without judging one another.***

One important note, here: please understand that all these observations about our emotional and spiritual development serve the purpose of helping us understand and connect with each other, *without judging one another.* The point here is not to shame, blame, or think of anyone else as "bad" in some way.

The reason I keep using "we" and "us" language is that, according to this paradigm of spiritual development, we have all lived at each of these stages, so no one is "better" than anyone else. Indeed, throughout one life time, we may have many moments when we return to various "lower" chakra worldviews, especially if we feel afraid, unloved, or threatened.

What helps us to remain non-judgmental is that, as we grow along the chakra system, we gradually understand our essential oneness, rather than our separateness. Each chakra contributes positive aspects to our worldview, such as valuing family, or emphasizing our freedom to have our own views. No one is to be shamed for coming from a place of fear rather than love. Chances are, if we feel fear and interject that fear into our worldviews, it is most likely because we have been raised with a lack of unconditional love, as well as a lack of emotional maturity leading to greater empathy and understanding.

The finger-pointing of blame only goes backwards, and ends with ourselves as our starting points. What we need to accept for ourselves is not blame but our own responsibility for our personal spiritual development, including our willingness and ability to understand and respect others. The highest spiritual view is not about blame, but about empathy, understanding, love and forgiveness. We can only reach this highest spiritual level if we accept complete responsibility for our own spiritual progress.

Each and every one of us must progress through these chakra stages, and each and every one of us either contributes more love into the world to help us all "get there" at the top of our crown chakra, or we are contributing a lack of love through fear and judgment. Yes, judgment stems from fear.

When we let go into love, neither fear nor judgment have any role in our way of being and living anymore. On the spiritual path, it is our responsibility to help ourselves and one another advance with love, empathy, and compassion.

We reach different levels of truth in stages. Each "stage" or chakra worldview is energized by a different energy, or different level of consciousness. Ultimately, what we discover is that truth resides within the most universal, loving, peaceful, and harmonious consciousness.

CHAPTER SEVEN:

The Root Chakra: Worldview, Values, and "Truths"

> *"The individual has always had to struggle
> to keep from being overwhelmed by the tribe.
> If you try it, you will be lonely often,
> and sometimes frightened.
> But no price is too high to pay for the
> privilege of owning yourself."* [103]
> – Friedrich Nietzsche

The root chakra worldview is tribal, as Caroline Myss points out in *Anatomy of the Spirit*.[104] We are born into families, cultures, nations, and often into religious communities as well. Generally, we identify with our familial and local groups early on in life. Those of us who have opportunities to expand our worldview beyond our local community and family, as well as the spiritual capacity to do so, will explore beyond these views. Many of us, however, remain in the root chakra worldview for our whole life.

We can recognize ourselves as living from a root chakra worldview if we find ourselves:

- believing in the importance of family,
- putting family first,
- being all about involvement in our school,

---

[103] As quoted here:
https://www.goodreads.com/author/quotes/1938.Friedrich_Nietzsche
Accessed on November 21, 2016.
[104] Caroline Myss, *Anatomy of the Spirit,* p. 103 and following.

- being active in our church, synagogue, temple, or mosque,
- rooting for our favorite (usually local) athletic teams,
- cheering for our alma mater,
- being loyal to friends,
- being loyal to the business or organization for which we work,
- being patriotic and even nationalistic, and so on.

We can see that emotionally and developmentally, a root chakra worldview identifies with a group of people similar to us, creating a stable emotional base around a sense of home, belonging, and group identity. As our emotional and spiritual foundation, then, the root chakra represents our belonging and formation of identity through identifying with family, city, tribe, nation etc. The root chakra provides group cohesion and stability at a family, tribal, institutional, and sometimes even a national level.

The root chakra provides us with a sense of purpose defined as both being part of a family, and also protecting and taking care of our family. While all this loyalty to family can be very positive, it can also limit our understanding of truth to the degree that we resist the life experiences, knowledge, and worldviews of people who are different than us.

As far as emotional development goes, in the root chakra, the values are generally about me, my, and mine, along with us and ours. Our family, our team, our school, our hometown, our nation, our political party, our business, etc., are what are important to us. Therefore, also, we identify with people "like us," rather than being open to identifying with a variety of unknown people or groups perceived as very different from "us."

Anything that is perceived as not good for me, my, mine, and ours may well be perceived as not good in principle, and if it is seen as not good in principle, it will also probably be seen as false. Anyone who is perceived as not being part of my group and as "not good" for me, my, and ours, will likely also be perceived as a threat. A person not from "my group" will more easily be seen as someone who does not speak the truth.

A root chakra worldview can also become, in emotionally dysfunctional cases, exclusively about "me, my, mine," like an eternal two-year-old, or a perennial narcissist. Certain politicians and political views tend to sound like root chakra views, as people and politicians seek to protect "us," whoever that group of people like "us" happens to be, whether white males, people in business, farmers, the 1%, etc. This happens when we never advance enough emotionally to be able to empathize with people who are not "like us."

> **A root chakra worldview can also become, in emotionally dysfunctional cases, exclusively about "me, my, mine," like an eternal two-year-old, or a perennial narcissist.**

A root chakra worldview can even become extremely overprotective in very negative ways through violence, verbal abuse, threats, name-calling, and ultimately war against those people who are "not like us," if a root chakra worldview also combines with a spiritual lack of development leaving a person in a perpetual state of fear. When humans lived almost exclusively in tribes with spears and swords as primary weapons, this may have frequently led to skirmishes, but rarely to outright domination of one group by another.

Our advances in weaponry have happened faster than our emotional and spiritual advances have evolved up the chakra system of development, leaving many human beings fighting wars and choosing terrorist attacks from a root chakra perspective. War and terrorist attacks are justified from a root chakra basis: my group, nation, or religion must be protected at all costs, because it is the right thing to do. There is no higher order of thinking emotionally or spiritually from the underdeveloped root chakra worldview.

Fear takes the "me, my, mine," of family, ethnic group, religious group, or nation, and turns those who are not part of "my group" into enemies, whether the threat is real or not. If we go into fear from the root chakra perspective, we tend to draw lines of distinction between "me, my, mine, and us," vs. "them." We then protect ourselves at the expense of others. From fear and a root chakra perspective, we protect our families, our business, and our nation at the expense of others.

This kind of duality is also typical of patriarchy, where the drive to dominate others and leave certain males on top is the only way that some people (particularly men, along with women who find safety within well-defined roles in patriarchy) can manage to feel safe.

We have seen this root chakra behavior with its emotionally-limited focus of "me, my, mine" combine with fear-based patriarchy raise its worldview onto the national stage in American politics time-and-time again in 2016.

Patriarchy may be simply one form of expression of root chakra values, where the male principle of the chakra is expressed without also expressing the female principle. Specifically, the male principle of the root chakra is to procreate, to exercise dominion[105] (not domination), and to protect.

The female principle of the root chakra is to embody, to connect with, and to nurture. Honoring both the feminine and the masculine energies of the root chakra is necessary for full emotional and spiritual development of the root chakra and its worldview. By balancing the female and male energies of the root chakra, we create an emotionally and spiritually healthy root chakra worldview.

---

[105] By dominion, I refer to ancient ruling concepts such as expressed in the Suzerainty Treaty, wherein the one ruling was responsible for the wellbeing of (usually) his, or her, subjects. Dominion is the ruling over self for self-benefit as well as the ruling over others and land for everyone's benefit together, like a tribal chieftain, who rules in a circle rather than in a linear hierarchy. This is a distinction from the concept of domination, which is not the masculine energy of the root chakra as expressed with loving life force energy. Dominion is the sacred masculine energy; domination is not. Domination is an energy that arises from fear combined with masculine root chakra energy.

The healthy spiritual version of the root chakra is the concept that we are all one family, and that we all take care of each other. Therefore, truth is perceived as all that takes care of life and that gives life. Creating, protecting, strengthening, connecting with, and nurturing life are consciously or subconsciously seen as the foundations for truth.

What is perceived as true from the root chakra perspective then, is anything that creates, nurtures, sustains, connects, and protects life for us. Anything that is divisive and destructive of life for us is seen as threatening, and therefore likely to be untrue. This healthy understanding of truth from a root chakra perspective can only occur when the root chakra is energized by love rather than fear.

> **The healthy spiritual version of the root chakra is the concept that we are all one family, and that we all take care of each other.**

What is pertinent here in our discussion of truth, then, are four major concepts. First, from an underdeveloped root chakra perspective, if a person is not perceived as being "one of us," they are seen as less likely to know the truth or speak the truth, and what they say may be seen as dishonest if it does not help "us."

Second, if someone with a root chakra worldview has only the masculine or feminine principles energized, a duality will exist in their emotional and spiritual perceptions, so that truth will become limited to the more masculine or more feminine views of what is right, good, and true. Without the feminine nurturing energy, the masculine root chakra of dominion turns into the energy of domination, and so dominating others and the environment is seen as good, and therefore the basis for what is valuable and true.

Third, a duality can occur if the focus of root chakra energies becomes predominantly material rather than spiritual or a balance of both. This happens through a process of objectification, or failing to recognize the unity of humanity and divinity, as well as the unity of humanity and divinity with nature. If we recognize the divine as present in others, we cherish and nurture our relationships. If we recognize the divine in nature, we cherish and nurture the environment.

If we see ourselves, others, and nature as devoid of divinity, we tend to focus merely on material well-being for ourselves and our group. Thus, focusing on material wellbeing rather than on the wellbeing of our relationships can arise as a duality in the root chakra. This duality really expresses the duality of materialism over spirituality.

One example of this view of truth that arises from Western materialistic culture in America is that getting a job and providing for one's family is seen as "reality," or the only way to live one's life. Money, jobs, saving for retirement, and acquiring material wellbeing become the all-important values. Truth becomes a matter of material wellbeing; other aspects of life may be irrelevant and other perspectives on life may be seen as invalid. From a materialistic root chakra perspective, what is true is that which supports jobs, earning money, and providing for oneself and one's family.

From a materialistic root chakra worldview, going on a spiritual quest or living a spiritual lifestyle may be seen as out-of-touch with reality, and therefore missing the main truths of life. Spiritual practices may be seen as having no value, discovering no truths, etc.

When we are focused on material wellbeing without valuing relationships as part of our spiritual wellbeing, and if our circle of who is included in "us" is small and nationalistic, then trusting that immigrants are not going to take our jobs is seen as naïve, because the belief is that immigrants will take our jobs. From this nationalistic view the assumption that "they" do "take our jobs" is seen as truth.

However, when one draws the circle of "us" not only globally, but also universally, inclusive of a benevolent Creator, not only is fear decreased and love increased, but also a very basic energy of trust is developed. Trust may be an essential root chakra energy.

Trust is the energy that allows us to let go of a strictly materialistic root chakra worldview, which is so often limited in its ability to perceive truth other than in a literal and concrete sense. When we develop trust in ourselves, one another, and the universe, then living a spiritual lifestyle, serving the needs of others, and trusting God to provide for us represents a truer way to live.[106]

When one lives a life of pure and total trust in the universe, one can continually give away one's money and possessions, and trust that the Universe will continue to give back. This idea of providing for and sustaining life is equally a root chakra truth, except the truth becomes that we focus more on providing for the needs of others rather than for ourselves. Of course, if everyone did this, we *would* all be provided for!

> **When we develop trust in ourselves, one another, and the universe, then living a spiritual lifestyle, serving the needs of others, and trusting God to provide for us represents a truer way to live.**

There is a story that has circulated in churches, often told during children's sermons. In this story, a man died and went to heaven, but when he got to the pearly gates, he asked St. Peter, who reportedly guards heaven's pearly gates, if he could go see what hell was

---

[106] The truth of God providing and therefore the need to live a life trusting that God will do so is espoused repeatedly in *Autobiography of a Yogi*. In 2013, I started getting the intuitive guidance to stop trying to get a job, despite the fact that I live in the enormously expensive Washington, DC area. In 2015, a God-Realized Indian saint, J.P. "Dada" Vaswani, of the Vaswani Mission in Pune, India, (whom I met in New Jersey on May 31), told me to stop thinking that I needed to earn a living. He added that the laborer deserves to be paid (a Biblical quote), and later added that I needed to "live the truth." That is the ultimate challenge – first we have to know the truth before we can live it!

like before entering heaven. So, St. Peter led the man down to hell.

There, in hell, the man saw a tragic sight: people were sitting around a table laden with a feast of food that smelled so heavenly that it was torture, because they could not eat it. Everyone had wooden spoons with long handles tied to their arms, so that they could not bend their elbows to get the food into their mouths. And so, they suffered having to smell the food, but never getting to eat it.

Then, St. Peter led the man back up to heaven, and they entered the pearly gates. There, in heaven, the man again saw a group of people sitting around a table laid with a heavenly smelling feast, and again they had long-handled wooden spoons tied to their arms so that they could not bend their elbows.

However, in heaven, everyone was smiling, laughing, and eating happily, for instead of merely trying to feed themselves, they were feeding each other. Because they focused on feeding each other, everyone ate, feasting on the heavenly food.

The root chakra can either lead us to the sense of "truth" that there is only enough for me and my people, or it can lead us to the truth that if we all share and focus on making sure that everyone receives some, there will indeed be enough for all.

Fourth, the energy of fear rather than love limits the root chakra worldview and consequently a person's ability to expand their understanding of truth. For instance, if we have a root chakra view which leads us to see someone else as not "one of us," and if we are truly fear-based, we are less likely to allow the "different" person to become "one of us."

When a person combines a root chakra view with the energy of fear, we usually perceive people who are different than us as untrustworthy. In other words, a root chakra worldview plus fear equals the projection of difference, danger, dishonesty, and destruction onto others. This act of fear-based projection destroys the truth.

> **When we come from a fear-based root chakra worldview of "me, my, mine," and only feel safe with politicians who appear to protect "me, my, mine," then we vote for them, failing to discern whether they speak the truth or not, because the message we hear is that they will protect "us."**

We have seen that dynamic in the 2016 presidential election.

This worldview appeals to those of us who have never had to be exposed to other worldviews or to large numbers of people who are different than us. Vitally, though, it is such exposure to people with different cultures and different world views that can pull us out of our ethnocentric and local-centric worldviews. When we come from a fear-based root chakra worldview of "me, my, mine," and only feel safe with politicians who appear to protect "me, my, mine," then we vote for them, failing to discern whether they speak the truth or not, because the message we hear is that they will protect "us."

The root chakra values safety, and without further emotional and spiritual development to energize the root chakra with love more than fear, that valuation of safety first can rise to extreme levels. When that happens, we may want to "build that wall," find our sense of safety by being able to protect ourselves with guns and weapons, and "throw Muslims out of the country."

On the other hand, once we learn to energize the root chakra with love rather than fear, we can at least identify with and respect people with different worldviews as well as honoring families of other cultures. If we feel loved, we may more readily accept people who are different from us into our local communities, and even into our families through bi-racial marriage, or by marriage to someone of another religion.

That ability to feel loved and safe is an important aspect of being able to grow up and beyond a limited root chakra worldview. Feeling loved and safe can enable us to expand our circle of family, local community, or even nation to include people who are different from "us." When we feel loved and safe in our families, nations, and other groups, we can develop an expansive root chakra view in which we begin to desire that everyone will feel safe and loved and included in the family circle, whether they are like us or not.

Feeling loved and safe can therefore help us open ourselves to perceiving truth beyond the truths taught by our own group, family, tribe, nation, or religion. Feeling threatened makes us shut down intellectually, so that new ideas do not have a chance to create cognitive dissonance, or cause us to feel confused to the point of not being able to make sense of what we're hearing or experiencing. When we feel threatened, we merely reject the ideas that threaten us as if they are untrue.

People often don't feel safe when we feel confused and unable to understand what's happening. Because of this, we may avoid new situations, unfamiliar people, traveling to new places, or whatever might challenge our current understanding of reality, so that we will keep feeling safe. Root chakra people who live from fear more than love may not travel a lot, and may not have an interest in "expanding our horizons," because that could threaten what feels safe and "normal" to us.

When those of us who are still developing our root chakra do travel, it may be more from the perspective of going forth to conquer and accomplish our goals, without a particular interest in absorbing new information and without any great interest in understanding the differences of others and the world around us.

Speaking of "normal," the root chakra worldview also considers the familiarity of the people, culture, and religion to which we are accustomed to be "normal." Any views, ideas, or practices that are distinctively different from those of our own group are usually viewed as suspect, because they may be threats to the way our "tribe" is supposed to live and get along.

If we only feel emotionally comfortable with what is "normal" for our group, then our truths will be similarly limited. Truth that is outside the norm of current cultural belief and thought will automatically be suspect. Therefore, receptiveness to new ideas may be minimal.

If we feel loved and safe, we will more fully energize and harmonize our root chakras. Feeling loved and safe will also help us to develop emotionally and spiritually so that we energize all the higher chakras as well. By feeling loved and safe and energizing our upper chakras, we can energize an expansive root chakra worldview.

If all our chakras are expansively energized and we have reached emotional and spiritual maturity, our root chakras will be developed enough so that we will see all of humanity, indeed, all of life as part of our "family" – as part of our own circle of care and concern. From an expansive root chakra view, no one will be left out. At the very least, we will have to develop and energize all the lower chakras and the heart chakra as well to view others as part of one big family.

I once knew a very loving woman in a church I served, who was not especially intellectual or interested in ideas, but she was generously warm and loving and easily included others into her circle of care. While her orientation in life seemed very local and family-oriented, her chakras would have been well-developed through the heart chakra, so that she chose to see virtually everyone as someone whom she could welcome into the circle of family and love. I honor her memory with gratitude for the generosity of her love.

The more we develop emotionally and spiritually through the worldviews of the other chakras, the more expansive our root chakra worldview will become. Since the journey up the chakras along the spine continues sequentially, we will next consider the worldview, values, and "truths" of the sacral chakra.

Before we move on, however, we will first ask the question: "how are sin and evil perceived in the root chakra?" From the root chakra worldview, sin and evil have to do with denying life; destroying life; undermining, being disloyal to, or betraying the tribe, the family or the nation; as well as speaking and acting against us, me, my, or mine.

If sin and evil reflect destruction and betrayal, who is God in the root chakra worldview? At a most basic level, God is the One who provides for us and protects us. From the root chakra worldview, God is seen as Father, as Mother, or as Mother/Father.

From a root chakra perspective, God can also be seen as the Earth Mother and/or the Great Spirit, often represented by the sky or the sun. The fully-developed root chakra view becomes balanced in its understanding of divinity when it perceives both the masculine and feminine aspects of the divine. This development occurs with our spiritual evolution as well as the energizing of both feminine and masculine energies in the root chakra.

Let's look at a prominent spiritual teaching, one which we will consider from the perspective of all the chakras and their spiritual worldviews. This teaching arises from Judaism, but the larger spiritual truth to which it speaks has echoes in most religions, in one form or another, for it raises the issue of Oneness.

The teaching I would like us to consider, first from the point of view of the root chakra, is: "Hear, O Israel, the Lord our God; the Lord is One."[107] From the root chakra perspective, this teaching is often heard as: "God is everywhere we go and all the time with us, for God is OUR God." Often, in ancient Judaism, God as expressed in Biblical terms seems to have been a rather tribal God, though omnipresent and existing as the only God. For any religion, those who see the world through root chakra eyes, God is more of "our God" and very tribal. By extension, our God is not "your God."

However, the truth of this teaching, "The Lord is one" has also been expressed in Judaism and Christianity as the omnipresence of God. I realize that, at this point, some scholars and theologians may think I have misunderstood this verse; I ask that you bear with me, for I am sharing an intuitive perspective that this verse represents ancient knowledge of truths not always fully understood as being expressed in this verse.

---

[107] From Deuteronomy 6:4. The capitalization of "One" is my choice, and not drawn from the text.

There are a variety of ways, depending on one's religious traditions or lack thereof, that the root chakra perspective may hear and understand this truth:

- God is OUR God and we are God's chosen people (communal truth)
- God is everywhere present and everything is sacred (Tantra and panentheism)
- Spirit imbues everything with life – Animism
- Everything is god – pantheism
- The energy of magic is everywhere – earth-based paganism[108]

For the root chakra worldview, the community is the source of our experience of truth, and the community is the test of our understanding of truth. Whether the community agrees with our understanding of truth or not, our ability to bring greater harmony into a community is a test of our accessing the truth of divine oneness. For those of us living from a fully-developed root chakra worldview, the truth of God's oneness is experienced within both the human community and the earth-based community of life.

For the root chakra: Truth Is Shared, and Truth Is Communal.

---

[108] This website defines a very balanced and harmonious root chakra understanding of magic:
http://www.thewhitegoddess.co.uk/an_introduction_to_paganism/what_is_magick.asp Accessed on December 9, 2016.

CHAPTER EIGHT

Sacral chakra: Worldview, Values, and "Truths"

All things are subject to interpretation; whichever interpretation prevails at a given time is a function of power and not truth.[109]

– Friedrich Nietzsche

The sacral chakra is located just below the belly button, and is associated with the spleen as well as the pancreas. The spleen purifies the blood and supports the immune system, so the energies of the sacral chakra include purification and strength as protection. The spleen also organizes the immune system by destroying old red blood cells and storing new white blood cells and antigens. Thus, organization is also one of the functions energized by the sacral chakra.

As the pancreas aids in digestion, giving us energy for life, the sacral chakra is also the seat of personal power in a physical sense. Similarly, as the pancreas helps maintain healthy blood sugar levels, the sacral chakra also energizes self-discipline, balance, and harmony. The sacral chakra therefore develops our sense of personal power to rule over ourselves, as well as developing our personal power in relation to others.[110]

---

[109] https://www.brainyquote.com/quotes/quotes/f/friedrichn109379.html
[110] For those who are accustomed to thinking of the solar plexus chakra as the "seat of personal power," I agree, but with a caveat: the personal power in the solar plexus chakra is about setting oneself free to become one's individual self,

In terms of human development, the sacral chakra reflects the young child who begins to develop a sense of preferences, focuses on concrete, sensory reality, develops a love of routine, and counts on routine for a sense of stability and safety in life. This is also the baby or child who becomes fussy and out-of-sorts when his or her routine is not followed.

The sacral chakra also reflects the school-aged child who begins to learn to get along while playing with other children by following the rules, by sensing what is fair for everyone, and by obeying the rules set by powerful adults. This sense of harmony through equality, connection, and fairness reflects the feminine energy of the sacral chakra, as we learn how to connect with others harmoniously and peacefully, respecting each other's equality, rights, and relative authority.

> **This sense of harmony through equality, connection, and fairness reflects the feminine energy of the sacral chakra. The masculine energy of the sacral chakra is self-discipline, rules, focus, and being organized.**

---

as well as about personal creativity and emotional expression. Please see the next chapter. ॐ

The essence of the feminine energy of the sacral chakra is reflected in the Golden Rule: Treat others the way you would like to be treated.[111]

The masculine energy of the sacral chakra is self-discipline, rules, focus, and being organized. If one is lacking the masculine energy, it can lead to disorganization or fear of stepping out of one's comfort zone. For true inner strength for living life to our fullest potential both individually and collectively, we need both the masculine and feminine energies of the root chakra.

The sacral chakra also reflects the adult who easily develops and strongly maintains a routine with a lot of self-discipline and focus. This is, clearly, the adult who is well-organized. Yet, this may sometimes become the adult who gets stuck in a rut of routine, who cannot break free in order to adapt to new situations, new relationships, or new demands in life.

The sacral chakra thus gives us the energy of self-discipline, focus, organization, equality, connection, rules, and fairness. Sacral chakra energy leads to appreciating the orderliness of nature, as well as preferring organization in human life, individually, culturally, and institutionally. People who are strong in sacral chakra energies can make good managers, who generally follow the rules, although they may do so with excessive legalism and a lack of flexibility.

---

[111] The Golden Rule was a command of Jesus Christ, which I have paraphrased for today here. See Matthew 7:12 in the Bible.

The sacral chakra teaches us that our life purpose is to work, to take care of our responsibilities, to manage our relationships according to rules and social expectations, to "do our duty," and to manage our physical and financial assets. Life is very practical and concrete for the sacral chakra, so our purpose is very practical and concrete as well.

For the sacral chakra, fear-based needs for security and safety focus less on the group we're a part of, and more on our own power, or that of others, to control the situations and material world around us. Like the root chakra, the feeling of safety and security is important, but the focus begins to move from group identity to our own inner power to control ourselves, the things around us, and sometimes others as well. The sacral chakra emphasizes the tribe less, and the ability to wield power a whole lot more.

An overbalance of fear instead of love can lead to the legalism and inflexibility with regard to rules and expectations. For a fear-based sacral chakra worldview, the need to control is how one manages to deal with fear and a lack of trust in life. That high need for control can arise through a need for black-and-white decision-making, strict adherence to rules, laws, and procedures, or through efforts to manipulate and control other people through whatever means one can accomplish and maintain control.

A fear-based solar plexus chakra worldview can lead to an excessively authoritarian parenting style, teaching style, leadership style, or way of governing. Dictatorial approaches to governing fit in here. The fear-based

> **This purification of our intentions energizes us to act from a sense of principles such as fairness, cooperation, justice, following the rules, respecting the law, and being truthful for the sake of accuracy and accountability.**

emphasis in all these styles of exercising power results in a high need for control in each setting.

When the sacral chakra is more fully energized, that is, more fully developed emotionally and spiritually through the power of love, the sacral chakra also invites us to purify our motivations as we interact with the world around us. This purification of our intentions energizes us to act from a sense of principles such as fairness, cooperation, justice, following the rules, respecting the law, and being truthful for the sake of accuracy and accountability.

Having a sense of duty and being motivated by a sense of duty also arises from sacral chakra energy, but if this sense of duty is not based on higher principles, the sacral chakra is not yet fully developed. Duty relates to the "powers that be," and is therefore a very sacral chakra orientation, because of the sacral chakra's emphasis on power and control, whether self-control, or externally-oriented control.

Following the rules or laws in a literal sense represents the more masculine functional energies of the sacral chakra, because of the energy of self-discipline and self-control. Acting according to the spirit of the law represents the feminine energies, because one pays more attention to the impact on other human beings than to the law itself. The balance of feminine and masculine energies allows one wisely to decide when to follow the letter of the law and when to follow the spirit of the law, because one respects the rule of law, but one also acts according to its ideal expression in each situation and with regard to each individual person.

An underdeveloped, fear-based sacral chakra will emphasize meting out punishment for those who do not follow the letter of the law. Because anyone who breaks the law violates the balance of power, they are typically rendered powerless by being thrown in jail.

A more mature and loving sacral chakra with fully developed feminine energies will be more interested in reforming and developing the potential of those who have broken the law, rather than merely punishing them. From a mature sacral chakra worldview, everyone is redeemable, and prison is less than ideal until it primarily entails avenues for reform and redemption. Reform and redemption can occur because of the invitation to exercise self-control and to be aware of exercising fairness toward others.

Interestingly, the sacral chakra is also the seat of one's sense of personal power in the very basic sense of "I can do this," whatever "this" might be. It is the ability and personal power to achieve in this world, over against a sense of helplessness and self-doubt. The expression of this power can be very physical, as in athletic achievement, or it can be very practical as in having the ability to "get things done," or even to achieve a lot of success through hard work and self-discipline.

Generally, this personal power of the sacral chakra is expressed physically or materially, whether from a secular or a spiritual orientation. The sacral chakra power also energizes physical healing and wellbeing,

> **For an underdeveloped, fear-based, and masculine-energy-only sacral chakra, empathizing with and empowering others is seen as being weak and giving away one's power.**
>
> **Because a fear-based understanding of the universe does not realize that love is powerful, it sees loving kindness as unnecessary, because kindness does not build one's power relative to the other person.**
>
> **Yet a mature sacral chakra knows that empowering *everyone* exponentially increases the power of loving-kindness the more that empowerment is shared and the broader it is spread.**

both through physiological processes and through subtle energy.

The down-side to this energy is that it can also be used very selfishly and exploitatively when energized with fear, by those who therefore value their own power and wellbeing but who do not respect or care for the power, needs, or desires of others. When lacking the feminine energy, the sacral chakra can lead to relating to others by exercising power *over* them, rather than sharing power with them, especially as this power has a need for control, which can extend from healthy self-control to unhealthy domination of others.

For an underdeveloped, fear-based, and masculine-energy-only sacral chakra, empathizing with and empowering others is seen as being weak and giving away one's power. Because a fear-based understanding of the universe does not realize that love is powerful, it sees loving kindness as unnecessary, because kindness does not build one's power relative to the other person.[112]

Being kind is thus seen as a waste of time and energy unless it can be used to manipulate someone and thereby increase one's own power. Empowering others is seen as win-lose instead of win-win. Yet a mature sacral chakra knows that empowering everyone exponentially increases the power of loving-kindness the more that empowerment is shared and the broader it is spread.

---

[112] As I edit this on April 12, 2017, we have just witnessed the violent removal of a passenger from a United Airlines jet. Apparently, kindness was not perceived as being necessary in this situation, despite the passenger identifying himself as a doctor who had patients to see the next day. Without kindness, that is, feminine root and sacral chakra energies, we may have power over others, but we exercise it in very inhumane ways.

Combining fear and lack of sacred feminine energy, we can develop a very self-centered orientation in the sacral chakra. A self-centered sacral chakra orientation can lead not only to being a bully or a master manipulator, but also to being a sociopath. Such people may seem very social if what they love most in life is their own personal power, because they may become very adept at manipulating others. A self-centered person who lacks the sacred feminine but who loves their own personal power may go ahead and cheat on tests or cheat in business simply because they can.

The approach to principled living which is energized by a balance of masculine and feminine energies in the sacral chakra is very concrete and focused on material and relational wellbeing. Rather than being abstract like the principles of the intellect, which are more fully energized by the throat chakra and the brow chakra, the principles of the sacral chakra are practical and oriented to "getting organized," "getting the job done," "doing one's duty," etc. At this level, then, in a healthy sense, we are concerned with rules and fairness for very practical and ethical applications like not cheating at games, not cheating in business, doing "what's right," and so on.

At this level, truth is very practical. Without a practical application, truth is perceived as having little or no value. For instance, ideas about God at this level primarily involve God as a law-giver, with rules we are supposed to obey, and which make decisions about how to live life clearer and simpler for us. The rites and practices of a religion are viewed as extremely important from the sacral chakra worldview. More abstract ideas about God such as notions of how to explain the relationship of science and theology are of little interest, because they only complicate life, rather than solving the day-to-day challenges of "real life."

One typical view of theology from a sacral chakra view would be: God rules, and that's it, so science just follows God's rules. Anything that disagrees with God's rules as written in God's rulebook, whether that rulebook is the Torah, Bible, or Koran, (etc.) is therefore untrue.

> **As far as religious worldviews of the sacral chakra are concerned, there tends to be a strong sense of dividing everything in life into dualistic categories such as black and white, right and wrong, rules vs. breaking the rules, and often even heaven and hell.**

As far as religious worldviews of the sacral chakra are concerned, there tends to be a strong sense of dividing everything in life into dualistic categories such as black and white, right and wrong, rules vs. breaking the rules, and often even heaven and hell. Religious rule books tend to be seen as being perfectly accurate because they were written by some infallible (hear powerful) source, and anything that does not fit this system of right and wrong as taught by the religious rule books cannot be true. There is a high need for control here, and the more fear that is present, the higher is the need for control over what is "true" and "right" and "good."

This type of dualistic sacral chakra worldview tends to arise with the oppression of the sacred feminine – that feminine energy of the sacral chakra that emphasizes sharing power with others, rather than exercising power over others. When fear is added, then the religious rules become our sense of salvation, for we can control whether or not we obey the rules (theoretically – anyway!). With fear, the religious institutions become power centers exercising control over people's lives, with "truth" residing in the hands of the powerful leaders of the religious institutions.

Beyond religion, one develops a fully-energized and healthy sacral chakra when one energizes both the feminine relational, connecting energy with the masculine purifying and organizing energy, so that one loves self and others in very practical, tangible ways. From a more loving and balanced sacral chakra perspective, truth is sensed according to whether or not it feels fair, just, and/or orderly. Truth is seen as leading to organization rather than to chaos. Truth at this level is also seen as purifying: whether physically purifying by presenting a system for cleaning and organizing, or mentally purifying by analyzing, sorting, and organizing ideas, or spiritually purifying by fulfilling one's duty, acting fairly, and standing for justice.

If a concept or approach to life does not help us organize ourselves, our lives, or the "stuff" of our lives smoothly and harmoniously, it is seen as lacking value. If an idea causes conflict with or greater chaos in our current understanding or our way of living life, it is seen as most likely false.

If we are energizing the sacral chakra with love, we will see things like cheating as the opposite of truth, and to be avoided as signs of personal weakness, or of having a weak character which can be harmful to others. However, if we are energizing the sacral chakra with fear, it may lead us to focus first and foremost on our own need for power. From a place of fear and desire to enhance our own personal power, we may see cheating and lying as not a big deal, because "everybody does it" in order to accomplish our survival-get-ahead-win-at-all-costs goals in life.

When energized by fear and a sense of "us vs. them" worldview hanging over from the root chakra, this duty-oriented, power-over way of relating to others arising from the sacral chakra explains a lot of domination in the world, from police brutality to the atrocities committed by loyal members of Hitler's SS. In a fear-based, sacral chakra "us vs. them" system, loyalty is to people in power. Exercising one's own power aggressively becomes "legitimated" when it is seen as doing one's duty or as acting out of loyalty to one's government. As long as one is protecting those in power, that loyalty then "excuses" otherwise inhumanely violent treatment, including rape, torture, and execution.

Energized with fear rather than love, the "truths" of the sacral chakra reflect merely the truths of those in power – that is, the truths that maintain their power, as well as the truths that go along with following one's "duty" and remaining loyal to those in power. Thus, power-over-based "truths" that supposedly justify extreme violence and injustice can include a variety of unjust views. This is evidenced by some American leaders' thoughts on the legitimacy of torture. In addition, a fear-based worldview of the sacral chakra that lacks sacred feminine energy can include the idea that some people are less valuable than others, whether Jews or people of color, the indigenous people of Standing Rock, farmworkers, or "illegal" immigrants (undocumented workers).

So, rather than focusing on principled living with a focus on practical results which tend to benefit everyone, at the level of the sacral chakra, the lack of feminine energy can lead to a sense of not only personal prowess, but also personal entitlement. This appeals to those of us who would rather win than lose, fight and kill the enemy rather than negotiate and find diplomatic solutions, and succeed in business, even when it means cheating and exploiting others in order to "succeed."

Here, in the sacral chakra as energized with fear, we find the seat of the zero-sum game, where our survival feels threatened if we do not feel in control, and where we see others as a threat to our personal power and ability to win or to get what we want or need in life. Through the sacral chakra's fearful worldview, there is a sense that, either my personal power wins, or yours does, and if yours wins, I might not survive, so I need to do everything I can do to survive, even if that means not letting you survive.

Please notice that this competitive personal power is enhanced by denying the sacred feminine: that feminine sense of connectedness with others in which we cannot define ourselves as just existing for ourselves, but rather we understand ourselves as necessarily defined and expressed through existing *with and for others* as well as for ourselves. Without this balance of the sacred feminine, we cannot balance the power of the sacral chakra in favor of a greater good, because the personal power is seen as just a way of getting what "I" want.

> **This lack of sacred feminine connection, tied to the energy of fear, leads the power base of the sacral chakra to become the seat of exercising power over others, rather than sharing power with others.**

This lack of sacred feminine connection, tied to the energy of fear, leads the power base of the sacral chakra to become the seat of exercising power over others, rather than sharing power with others. Only by understanding ourselves as in part defined through the ways we exist with and for others can we face the inadequacy of exercising power over others.

Often, our lack of development here may stem from a period in childhood when we felt powerless to get what we want, and so we shifted away from considering the needs or wants of others, because it seemed to us that we could not both consider their needs and attain our own needs and wants at the same time.

This is a painful experience, when, as children, we experience powerful others taking away or preventing us from receiving what we want and need in life. Such childhood experiences can lead to a sense of powerlessness, or victimhood. If one remains in this energy-consciousness of victimhood, the full potential of one's personal power will fail to develop in the sacral chakra. We may fail to cooperate and empathize with others because we feel excessive jealousy, seeing ourselves as weak and powerless in relation to others.

Alternatively, the powerful others who exercised excessive power over us during childhood may then become our model for how to interact with others by exercising power over them rather than empathizing and cooperating with them. This use of personal power as power over others can be lived out dysfunctionally in adulthood in many ways, chief of which would be through narcissism and sociopathic tendencies. The political version of this is empire-building, dictatorship, hoarding of wealth and consolidation of power, and tyranny in all forms.

This is the fear-based root of the abuse of personal power as it arises in the sacral chakra. This leads to limits on the sense of truth, because whatever threatens our personal power, whether to do business, or to exploit others, is seen as not true, because it limits our "freedom," which is largely understood as personal power devoid of responsibility for the wellbeing of others.

Expressed through government, in the fear-based expression of the sacral chakra, the zero-sum game prevails, and people see budgets as limited, taxes as a detraction from personal power, and whatever empowers the ability of individuals to succeed in power-based endeavors is perceived as holding the highest values. Therefore, all programs that empower those who are perceived as "powerless," such as single moms, families on welfare, and low-income children, are seen as a "waste of tax-payer dollars" because it is empowering the powerless rather than the powerful, which is all that makes sense in this fear-based "winner takes all" mentality.

Only "hard-working people who support themselves" are seen as worthy, because only such people are deemed acceptable. Acceptability is based on one's power to be financially productive. This is how corporate welfare is justified: corporations have the power to be financially productive; therefore, giving corporations tax breaks, bail-outs, tax incentives, and outright financial support with government funds becomes acceptable, because they have the "power" to create more financial power. Taxes and budgets are not based on human needs but rather on which humans have power.

Truth, here in the masculine, fear-based sacral chakra worldview, is not seen as relative so much as black-and-white in terms of who has power, who doesn't have power, and who "should" have power. Usually, because personal power is such a high value in the fear-based version of the sacral chakra, those who "should" have power are those human beings who are a lot like ourselves, because we perceive people who are like us as less threatening.

From the fear-based sacral chakra view, people who are powerless are subconsciously perceived as threatening, because the last thing we want is to be powerless like them. So, if we have money, an education, a great job, a nice house, a happy marriage, or all of those things, we don't want to hang out with the people who don't have those things, because they subconsciously make us feel vulnerable by reminding us that we, too, could lose those things. We are also less likely to want to give money to those less fortunate, lest we end up like them. We protect our personal sacral-chakra-based power by protecting the resources that we perceive as maintaining our power. Money tends to be chief among those resources we hoard and protect.

The more fear-based our views are from the sacral chakra perspective, the higher is our need for control, from either a religious perspective or a materialistic perspective. Religious people who are both fear-based and sacral-chakra-based tend to view our religious scriptures and leaders and our deity as being the powerful ones, so truth is based on what these power figures teach.

For instance, if one has a male, father-figure God who is powerful and who ultimately has control over us, then one will also be likely to see this God as having power and control over people, especially women, and over nature. This male God will also have the power to define what is true and not true, and if people with fear-based sacral chakra worldviews believe this God inerrantly wrote a book full of this God's truths, then no one else's religious book can be speaking the truth, and no other religious institution can be teaching the truth. Therefore, to be in alignment with this God is to be male, to exercise power over women and nature, and to exercise power over anyone who is perceived as not in alignment with this God's version of truth as expressed in this powerful book.[113]

From a materialistic perspective, a fear-based sacral chakra view also leads to a strong desire for control, in order to increase both personal power and "safety" by every means possible. Truth therefore aligns with whatever enables people to control their own sphere of influence, and to protect themselves adequately in business, family, nation, and life.

From a materialistic and fear-based sacral chakra worldview, the rest of the world is only a place to acquire control and resources, while protecting ourselves from its threats. We see this in the politics of war, as well as in the exploitation of indigenous peoples around the world by multinational corporations which exploitatively extract mineral wealth and other

---

[113] I know this sounds harsh, and I do intend to point out the harshness of some religious views, for indeed, the colonialization of many nations occurred simultaneously with the conversion or genocide of "heathens." Please know that I am not objecting to the concept of God, per se, for I dearly love God. What I question is the understandings of God and of religious texts which arise from fear-based lower chakra worldviews. Love-based understandings of God from the heart chakra, brow chakra, and crown chakra create beautiful blessings for the whole world. These love-based understandings of God are ones which I embrace and endorse in my spiritual teachings.

resources, while forcing low-cost labor with no rights or protections.

Material wellbeing tends to be a priority for a sacral chakra worldview, whether from a material worldview, a fear-based religious worldview, or a loving spiritual worldview. From a loving spiritual sense, organizing the world based on laws or on rules and fairness leads to material wellbeing not only for ourselves but also for others. The rule of law is in part a sacral chakra worldview, which harmonizes the world to the degree that the laws are also designed with more love than fear.

From a loving perspective, then, the sacral chakra can also be about organizing the material and concrete aspects of life for good purposes, for oneself and others. With the sacral chakra's tendency to prefer order and organization, material wellbeing and concrete values, people who are strongly energized at this chakra level make great accountants, bookkeepers, financial advisors, store clerks who can organize and beautify the displays, cooks, housekeepers, groundskeepers, lab technicians, administrators, nurses, or anyone who organizes, quantifies, protects, or beautifies the world around us for practical and helpful purposes.

The spiritually healthy and fully mature version of the sacral chakra moves from rigid rules to a sense of fairness. This sense of fairness develops from the feminine energies of empathy and compassion in the sacral chakra.[114] The sense of fairness is developed by

---

[114] I love that Jesus Christ, as a man and as a spiritual teacher, both taught and modeled this approach with his emphasis on living by the "spirit of the law," rather than by the "letter of the law." I am also grateful to my late mother, Joy

learning to listen to diverse perspectives, which requires the feminine energies of connection and valuing relationships. A spiritually mature sacral chakra will also lead us to sharing concern for the greater good of the entire family of humanity. This sense of fairness then guides the sense of "right and wrong" to shape rules that empower and protect everyone equally.

A sense of fairness guides the sense of what is true or untrue, so if something is unjust, it is perceived as false. From a fully-developed sacral chakra worldview, the religious rule books are interpreted not as inerrant, but by standards of fairness, justice, and a higher good for all. As one reads religious texts from a spiritually mature sacral chakra that is balanced with both feminine and masculine energies and energized primarily by love, then only the verses that meet the principles of fairness and equality for all humanity are perceived as true.

From a spiritually mature sacral chakra worldview, the good "stuff" of life is meant to be shared, not hoarded. This would be the origin of the concept of "the commons," "the commonwealth," and the "common good." People are not controlled, but rather power is shared on a more equal basis, with authority respected to the degree that it represents fairness, liberty, and justice for all. Organizations are structured for functional fairness, rather than mere hierarchy and control. This leads to fair and just work schedules, pay

---

Dodson, who originally taught me this concept as she learned it from the Biblical witness to Christ.

structures, and respect for sick leave and family leave time.

From a spiritually mature sacral chakra view, religious institutions exist to empower humanity rather than to control, as well as to educate spiritual seekers rather than to dictate truths to obedient children. Truth is tested for fairness, justice, and equality. What is not empowering of all life is either not true, or is not the final answer. As a sacral chakra virtue, truth is fair for all.

In this fully-developed sacral chakra view, then, sin is whatever creates unfairness and blocks physical and material wellbeing for anyone and everyone. Sin is injustice and disempowerment, inequality, and lack of sharing resources for the common good.

For an underdeveloped sacral chakra, though, sin is weakness, cowardice, and failing to seize power when it is available. "Sin," for an underdeveloped sacral chakra, is seen as being out of control, disobeying the rules, and disloyalty to those in power.

The concept of "Our God is one God" is understood by the underdeveloped sacral chakra as conveying that God is the source of our power, and therefore God is to be feared, because God can render us powerless. God, for the underdeveloped sacral chakra is more likely to be the "golden calf," or source of all good things for life, materially and physically speaking. An underdeveloped sacral chakra may view God as the "Santa Claus" god who rewards people who do what is right, and who punishes those who do wrong. A more spiritual and less religious person with a sacral chakra worldview may be focused on god as our "errand-boy"[115] who answers our prayers and helps us manifest our desires.

For the spiritually-mature sacral chakra, the concept of "Our God is one God," also implies that God is the source of the power of life, and that therefore God is to be worshiped as the One who keeps us alive, and as the One who sustains life. Fully energized with love, the spiritually mature sacral chakra understands the One God as the one who calls us to relate to others around the planet in ways that sustain life for all, justly and fairly, for God is the One God of everyone.

Mentally, the sacral chakra focuses on concrete ideas and the certainties of life: controlling physical and material aspects of life, maintaining safety, organizing things and ideas in practical, logical, and orderly ways, creating reliable rules and laws, and governing with power so that the status quo can be maintained. The focus of mental energy in the sacral chakra is on providing reliability and certainty in life.

Because the sacral chakra focuses on the security that comes from power, for the masculine energies of the sacral chakra: Truth Is Powerful. Because the sacral chakra focuses on harmonizing human relationships, for the feminine energies of the sacral chakra: Truth Is Justice.

---

[115] I am indebted to the Rev. Marianne Williamson for this term and expressing this view in somewhat different words at the Sister Giant Conference in Arlington, VA, February 2017.

CHAPTER NINE

The Solar Plexus Chakra: Worldview, Values, and Truths

"You have your way. I have my way. As for the right way, the correct way, and the only way, it does not exist." [116]
— *Friedrich Nietzsche*

The solar plexus chakra is located directly above the navel, in the solar plexus region of the body. The glands associated with the solar plexus chakra are the adrenal glands, which respond to stress and threats, causing the fight-flight-freeze-fold response that most promises survival in cases of physical danger. The adrenal glands produce a variety of hormones that control blood pressure, convert fats and proteins into energy, affect how we think and feel, reduce inflammation, affect blood sugar levels, and more.

The masculine energies of the solar plexus chakra relate to the physical excitability of the adrenal glands, and focus on responding to what's "out there." The feminine energies of the solar plexus chakra relate to the emotional excitability of the adrenal glands, and focus on experiencing what's going on "inside us."

---

[116] http://www.goodreads.com/quotes/9213-you-have-your-way-i-have-my-way-as-for

Most of us may already be well-acquainted with some of the energetic and intuitive experiences of the solar plexus chakra. That "butterflies in the stomach" feeling that we sometimes get during times of excitement is a feeling generated by the solar plexus chakra. When we feel that "gut feeling" telling us that something just feels wrong or right, we are receiving an intuitive message from the third chakra. Some of us may also be aware of that experience of feeling emotionally "punched in the gut," which is caused by the energetic openness and sensitivity of the solar plexus chakra.

With the excitability of the adrenal glands, the third chakra is more emotional and creative in its expression. The solar plexus chakra reflects that teenage stage of development when we want to express ourselves freely, without being told what to do, but rather insisting on doing things our own way. With the third chakra, we want to find our own voice and express ourselves artistically and emotionally.

> **The solar plexus chakra reflects that teenage stage of development when we want to express ourselves freely, without being told what to do, but rather insisting on doing things our own way.**

The solar plexus chakra is also the drama chakra. We can feel an emotional tug-of-war in relationships through our third chakra. If our relationships are codependent, we can feel energetically drained as we subconsciously "open" our solar plexus chakras while connecting with others, and perhaps unconsciously allow others to usurp our energy.

Because we are developing emotionally, until the third chakra is fully developed, we may experience a lot of emotional and energetic codependence. We can end up feeling drained until we build the self-confidence that is part of the task of the solar plexus chakra. Having the freedom and emotional support to develop our self-confidence as we begin to express ourselves and experience new accomplishments is essential for the fulfillment of the third chakra.

This need for self-confidence particularly relates to the solar plexus chakra because its sense of purpose entails our self-development. At the solar plexus chakra level of personal growth, we develop a dependable sense of personhood and an expressive personality. In fact, the sense of purpose of the solar plexus chakra entails personal emotional fulfillment and both the development and expression of ourselves as unique individuals.

When we experience plenty of love, including the kind of love that gives us the liberty just to be ourselves, we can more easily develop the emotional wisdom and independence we need to succeed at whatever interests us in life. This emotional wisdom and self-reliant confidence energizes the solar plexus chakra to begin to give us a sense of self in life, as well as a safe emotional foundation for being ourselves. A fully energized third chakra creates an abundance of self-confidence, a feeling of being "on top of the world" and able to overcome all fears, as well as sheer joy in being ourselves and doing what we love to do.

From this space of independent self-confidence, in the third chakra worldview, truth is relative, and our sense of right and wrong can be different from someone else's sense of right and wrong, and that's okay. There's no need to be right for someone else, only to be right for ourselves. Truth is seen as something that does not merely get handed down from authority figures, but is questioned and experienced as either true by the validation of our life experiences, or as false by whatever life has taught us thus far.

> **Truth is seen as something that does not merely get handed down from authority figures, but is questioned and experienced as either true by the validation of our life experiences, or as false by whatever life has taught us thus far.**

For the solar plexus chakra worldview, life is a delightful teacher when we have the freedom to choose, think, create, and believe for ourselves. We feel open to exploring new experiences – yes, sometimes unwisely such as teenagers experimenting with drugs and alcohol. Yet, we may wisely explore new areas of knowledge or spend a semester of study abroad, or try out for a new sport or other extracurricular activity. As adults, we may try a new, even risky venture for a career, or finally follow our dreams.

On the other hand, with the adrenal glands activating the fight-or-flight/fold-or-freeze response, we may become addicted to adventure and risk-taking, always seeking the next emotional and energetic "high." This occurs when we only energize the third chakra with masculine energies which move us out of ourselves and into the world boldly. However, a balanced level of masculine energy with feminine energy in the solar plexus chakra enables us to move out into the world confidently, taking only wise or measured risks, considering the longer impact on ourselves, on others, and on the world around us.

The feminine energy of the third chakra harmonizes our emotional wellbeing through feelings of emotional self-confidence, affirmation, and self-acceptance. The feminine energy of the solar plexus chakra also more fully develops the empathy which began to be energized in the sacral chakra, along developing a greater acceptance of others.

With only feminine energy and less masculine energy, we may overly express our emotions, and dwell on them without necessarily moving outside of ourselves to be brave enough to connect with others or brave enough to accomplish anything. Yet, a balance of strong feminine energy with masculine energy will lead us to be more empathetic and connected with others in active and productive ways, being able to work well with others when needed.[117]

---

[117] Ambika Wauters wrote an excellent book, *Chakras and Their Archetypes: Uniting Energy Awareness and Spiritual Growth*, (Berkeley: Crossing Press), 1997, which compares the servant archetype and the warrior archetype of the

People who are primarily energizing the solar plexus chakra may be good artists, actors, teachers, as well as managers who have to deal with a diverse group of people. Managers with fully-developed solar plexus chakras are gifted at tuning into the unique personalities and motivations of each employee and seek to empower each one with their unique strengths, while respecting their individuality and uniqueness.

Solar plexus-oriented people can inspire others with a love for and acceptance of diverse individuals, diverse cultures, and diverse points-of-view. If we are energizing our solar plexus with feminine energies, we can often make other people feel good and motivate them by affirming their own worth and value.

The personal power of the solar plexus chakra is the power to be ourselves as unique individuals, alone and in relationships. The solar plexus gives us the power to define ourselves, to be creative, as well as to express our emotions, desires, and goals.

In the solar plexus chakra worldview, truth is seen as personal and relative. Therefore, one person's "truth" can be "false" for someone else, because freedom of thought and self-expression are paramount values. A certain equality tends to exist in this view, at least until one person threatens another person's freedom of self-expression.

---

solar plexus chakra, emphasizing the development of self-esteem. Here, in *Truth and Illusion,* I would express the servant energies as feminine and the warrior energies as masculine for the solar plexus chakra. I recommend Wauters' book for assisting with greater emotional development along the chakra system.

"Live and let live" is the appropriate motto for the solar plexus chakra.

Fear can change this motto to disdain for those who seek to dominate others in any way. Our "truth" will be seen as more accurate than their "truth" if they (whoever "they" are) seek to impose their truth on us. Truth and freedom are so correlated, that we cannot accept someone else's truth if it threatens our own. So, if someone else is trying to dominate us or coerce us into believing their truth, we will reject their truth as "untrustworthy" and "untrue." As long as there is no threat, no hierarchy, and no coercion, then everyone is entitled to their "truth."

This dynamic of truth and freedom is felt at a visceral, emotional level. We see this dynamic lived out by people who see all religions as sharing some truth, but who remain aloof from religions because of the tendencies of many religious people to impose religious rules on others. For the solar plexus chakra worldview, truth is an individual matter, not necessarily a collective experience, except perhaps as truth relates to the dramatic events, relationships, and emotions of life.

In politics, a solar plexus chakra view, minus feminine energy and with a dose of fear leads to libertarian views, as in "Don't tell me what to do, don't interfere with my freedom, don't let government regulate my business or my life." The feminine energy here is lacking, because there is no balance to consider the impact on someone else's life of not having regulations. There also tends to be no consideration of the impact on life on this planet in general, sort of a lack of maternal instinct to care for those around her. The attitude rather seems to be: just don't impinge on my freedoms, regardless of whether or not a lack of regulations results in others getting to live freely and sustainably.

The underdeveloped solar plexus chakra lacking the masculine energies of self-discipline and self-responsibility from the sacral chakra can result in a bohemian lifestyle. This freedom-loving lifestyle is more concerned with the freedom to avoid responsibility and may result in excess drinking or drug use.

We see a unique dynamic played out by people who have developed a third chakra level of emotional development and love freedom, but who have a sacral chakra worldview of religious truth, and who operate from the energy of fear rather than love as well as more masculine energy than feminine energy.

As one example, some of us may still have second chakra beliefs that our religious rulebooks absolutely declare homosexuality to be immoral, but we are emotionally developing our own sense of freedom and individual empowerment so that we will question civil laws which restrict us. We will therefore object to having any legal infringement of our expression of our religion in order legally to protect the rights of gays and lesbians to live freely themselves. Because we live in fear rather than love and with very little feminine energy of empathy and compassion, our freedom is essential to us, but their freedom is not.

So then, instead of accepting civil laws that protect homosexual rights, we will object and refuse to do our job or carry out our business with gays and lesbians if we are expected to do something that contradicts our beliefs such as cater homosexual weddings or sign marriage licenses for gays and lesbians. We will only do this out of fear, rather than love, along with a desire for our personal freedom, without the feminine empathy to feel concern for the freedom of others who are different from us.

A lack of feminine energy in the solar plexus chakra leads to a lack of empathy, especially a lack of empathy with and acceptance of people who are perceived as different from us, and only by lacking such empathy will we demand our freedom from oppressive laws without caring about other people being protected from oppressive laws, as in the case of failing to empathize with gays and lesbians. Clearly, we will only protect our own freedoms at the expense of the freedoms of others if we lack these feminine qualities of empathy with and acceptance of others through the solar plexus chakra.[118]

> **Clearly, we will only protect our own freedoms at the expense of the freedoms of others if we lack these feminine qualities of empathy with and acceptance of others through the solar plexus chakra.**

---

[118] I must apologize that, as I am endeavoring to use "we" and "us" language everywhere possible to affirm our oneness, this issue appears to set up an "us"

This is a combination of sacral chakra and solar plexus chakra worldview, because a person who believes this way feels the need to act on their own beliefs without limitations by anyone else, and yet still holds dualistic sacral chakra views of the "rightness" of their religious rulebook.

Someone who operates from a strictly sacral chakra view will also object to civil laws that violate his or her religious rulebook, but may defer to civil authorities because civil authorities have the power. For individuals with the sacral chakra dualism and respect for powerful authorities, along with a solar plexus chakra desire for freedom, the only recourse to faithfulness to the religious rulebooks is to try to undermine civil authority by giving more power to one's own religious authorities than to civil authorities. Of course, one desires this for one's own religious authorities without also granting that power to other religious authorities whose views oppose one's own beliefs, especially from other religions.

We see this sacral chakra worldview among Christians who desire a fundamentalist Christian worldview to dominate American laws and government, and believe that the country was founded as a "Christian nation," despite evidence to the contrary, as in the separation of church and state. We also see this view among Muslims who desire to impose Sharia law over against secular laws and who desire Islamic rule rather than a secular government. Both the fundamentalist Christian views

---

vs. "them" paradigm, making it difficult for me to express our oneness, since I do not hold these views of excluding the LGBTQ community from equal rights.

and the fundamentalist Muslim views derive from fear-based sacral chakra worldviews that lack feminine energy, and that have a rebellious, self-expressive solar plexus chakra energy that desires its liberty as well as its power over everything else.

At the level of the third chakra, if we are primarily loving rather than fear-based, we will question the lack of love expressed by the judgments in our religious rulebooks. A person with a fully-developed solar plexus chakra will most likely reject judgmental religious rulebooks for the limitations they often place "unfairly" on some people while still sanctioning the activities of others.

> **At the level of the third chakra, if we are primarily loving rather than fear-based, we will question the lack of love expressed by the judgments in our religious rulebooks.**

The still-developing third chakra view will emphasize liberty only for our own view. If we energize the feminine energies and love energies of the third chakra, we will emphasize liberty for everyone, as long as no one is causing anyone else harm. If someone is causing someone else harm, whether physically or emotionally, they are clearly seen as infringing on another person's autonomy through a lack of respect for the person as an equal.

Because freedom and individual expression are primary values of the solar plexus, equality is also a primary value, understood more complexly through both the feminine energies of empathy and the masculine energies of self-expression and self-worth. The spiritually and emotionally balanced and well-energized solar plexus chakra helps us develop and maintain true democracy by equally valuing the self-worth of everyone.

If we are well-developed emotionally and spiritually in the third chakra, we will empathize with everyone's desire for freedom. Therefore, out of the feminine energies of empathy, we will emphasize liberty for everyone to express themselves and their religion (or lack thereof) in a civil society that protects such freedoms.

> **A healthy solar plexus grants liberty to all.**

In the mature solar plexus chakra, then, we develop the view that freedom and equality are essential for everyone, so that everyone is free to explore and to discover truth on their own spiritual path, living that truth in their own way. A healthy solar plexus grants liberty to all. The solar plexus chakra affirms everyone's right to believe according to what is right and true for them.

Please notice that religions that deny women the same freedom and equality as men are generally acting out of first or second chakra worldviews. Men with these lower chakra worldviews dismiss the rights of women because they have not yet fully developed the feminine energy of empathy and they value the power-based dualistic and patriarchal religions more than they value fairness, equality, and empathy, all of which are energetically feminine. With the feminine energy of empathy, men recognize that women generally desire to be just as free and self-directed as men desire to be.

Of course, women operating out of these first three chakras may not have developed their masculine energies for each chakra, and therefore may feel emotionally and financially "safe" when taken care of by a more powerful male. That view begins to break down with the desire for individual freedom that comes with the solar plexus chakra.[119] At that point, co-dependent relationships may still exist, until one feels fully and lovingly empowered as oneself. Only with balanced feminine and masculine energies are we able to move beyond codependence, whether the codependence is based on sexism or any other emotional or spiritual dependency issues or addictions.

Only when both men and women develop the masculine and feminine energies of the solar plexus chakra within ourselves can we then create relationships as equals who are interdependent with one another without any unhealthy dependence, codependence, or addiction.[120]

---

[119] As a woman, I add my gratitude for us women experiencing the freedom to develop masculine solar plexus energies: I thank God for our freedom and independence! Nonetheless, I highly value feminine energies of each chakra, and I see such a great need for us to be cultivating feminine energies across all strata of society and culture on a global scale. Because of 5,000 years of patriarchal religion, the development of feminine energies in each chakra seems much more commonly to be lacking than the development of masculine energies in each chakra.

[120] Please understand that I address this issue from a primarily heterosexual position because I need to clarify healthy ways of relating over against patriarchal stereotypes. One of the spiritual gifts of the LGBTQ community is the invitation to understand ourselves beyond gender and sexual stereotypes,

Because the solar plexus chakra is about experiencing and expressing one's unique self, truth is experienced as relative. Therefore, truth is perceived primarily intuitively and emotionally. When truth is experienced intellectually from a solar plexus chakra worldview, it is from a place of free-flowing ideas or stream of consciousness rather than from logic or systematic thinking.

Truth in the solar plexus chakra is primarily perceived through that "gut feeling" that something is right. Sometimes we just sense that something feels wrong to us, and that is our gut (solar plexus chakra) giving us an intuitive alert that something here is not right for us, or is not the truth. A peaceful feeling can be a sign of truth and what is right for us at the level of the solar plexus.

Please notice that the intuitive information of the solar plexus chakra is usually a measure of what is true for us, rather than necessarily what is true for others. We may cause issues for others, in effect denying them liberty, if we assume that our gut feeling is telling us what is also "right" for them.

This is one aspect where parents may have considerable difficulty discerning whether their gut feeling is just for themselves, or for their children as well, especially teenagers. For instance, we may have excessive fears for our children's safety, to the point that we feel our own fear in our gut, and that fear may overrule our

---

showing us that what is important is developing both the masculine and feminine energies in ourselves rather than merely seeing ourselves as biologically masculine or feminine.

reasonable allowance for the freedoms a teenager may typically enjoy safely and responsibly. On the other hand, if our solar plexus chakra is signaling danger to us, that may be a true signal for everyone around us, especially teenagers!

Teenagers are more likely to be developing the solar plexus chakra, at least emotionally and energetically along the lines of their own gender. Also, teenagers may be more likely to get themselves into risky situations, so listening to their own gut is really important, especially when experiencing peer pressure. That gut level feeling that something may be wrong is a particularly important form of intuition for teenagers to learn to listen to.

In the teenage years, a personal sense of truth is a necessary developmental phase in order to achieve adult levels of independence, confidence, and self-sufficiency. Truth and the freedom to express our truths need to be tasks that educators, coaches, and parents support the development of in teens. If individual self-expression is not encouraged and supported, teenage rebellion is likely to ensue, especially as teens develop both the feminine and masculine energies of the solar plexus chakra.

Autocratic rule of the teenager who is developing the solar plexus chakra results not only in rebellion, but also the stunting of the movement from fear to love energy. Because authoritarian rule is unloving, it generally gives rise to fear and/or rebellion, rather than to personal growth and healthy self-expression. By contrast, loving empowerment assists the full and unique self-expression of feminine and masculine energies in each individual.

Let's consider the concepts of sin and evil from the solar plexus chakra's spiritual worldview. For the solar plexus chakra, sin and evil relate to denial of the right of self-determination and the freedom to be oneself and to express oneself freely. Therefore, anything that infringes upon one's freedom is likely to be considered sinful or evil. When one has fully energized the solar plexus chakra, it becomes the sacred guardian of freedom as essential in our quest for truth.

The right to free speech typifies the kind of law that honors the truths of the solar plexus chakra, as does also the freedom to practice the religion of one's own choosing. So, from a solar plexus perspective, the enactment of laws that guarantee freedom of religion and free speech become sacred guardians of humanity's individual and shared experiences of truth. Only those who have not yet fully energized the solar plexus chakra will question and detract from these freedoms. For a fully energized solar plexus chakra, free speech and freedom of religion are sacrosanct.

> **From a solar plexus perspective, the enactment of laws that guarantee freedom of religion and free speech become sacred guardians of humanity's individual and shared experiences of truth.**

From a personal, individual perspective, for the solar plexus chakra, sin means not being true to yourself and your god. Sin can also arise as emotional or interpersonal betrayal, where one person usurps a relationship's benefits at the expense of the other person. Sin generally results from a lack of empathy.

The spiritual/emotional dysfunctions related to the solar plexus chakra include: codependence, fear, anxiety, lack of faith, self-doubt, low self-esteem, devaluing one's worth and value,[121] and a lack of trust in the universe (or one's understanding of God).

As for the idea that "our God is one," for the developing solar plexus chakra, this statement must be questioned, starting with, "What do you mean by 'God'?" Also, the main truth about God for the developing solar plexus chakra is: "my god is just as important and real as your god, or my questioning the existence of god is just as important as your belief in god."

For the fully developed solar plexus chakra, "the only true God (or true principle of the universe) is the one who accepts us all just as we are, and gives us the freedom to be ourselves."

From the solar plexus chakra's spiritual worldview, my God is the only God that makes sense for me, but we all have our own gods, therefore God is something or someone big enough to be everybody's God somehow. The solar plexus chakra is not particularly interested in pursuing the intellectual and logical explanation of how

---

[121] I am indebted to Ambika Wauters for including these aspects of low self-esteem in her book, *Chakras and Their Archetypes*.

this can be true, but accepts that every person's god is equally important for their own self-expression.

The solar plexus chakra gives us the freedom to question, to engage in exploration, and to experience the truths of life and spirituality as each of us is uniquely able to experience them in our lifetimes. From this place of uniqueness and freedom, we express our truths to the world.

Ultimately, the solar plexus chakra teaches us that "truth" is never our "own" unless we have questioned it, felt it, understood it, experienced it, and lived it as our own truth. This was also one of Buddha's teachings: that we cannot simply learn the truth, or dharma, from a teacher or a book, we must learn it for ourselves. When we have fully developed the solar plexus chakra, we fall in love with a truth that we can live with great love and joy, and we can enjoy sharing the freedom this brings us with others.

As Christ said, "You will know the truth, and the truth will make you free."[122] In the fully-spiritually-developed solar plexus chakra, the truth yields perfect freedom:

- freedom from fear,
- freedom from ignorance,
- freedom from lack,
- freedom to love unconditionally,[123]

---

[122] John 8:32, *NRSV*.
[123] Loving unconditionally as opposed to codependently or conditionally. There is no emotional tug-of-war or being bound by social or relationship expectations. Instead, true love simply sets one free to love others both freed from their expectations as well as without expectations of them. This does not mean that we love without empathy and compassion, for true love empathizes

- freedom from attachment to the world of form,[124]
- freedom from judgment,
- and finally, the freedom to be one's true, higher Self.

For the masculine energies of the solar plexus chakra, Truth Is Freedom, and for the feminine energies of the solar plexus chakra, Truth Is Relative.

---

and loves the other as they need to be loved, from a spiritual standpoint rather than an emotionally codependent standpoint.

[124] The "world of form" refers to the material aspect of the universe as devoid of Spirit. This freedom comes when we live as one with Spirit, which leaves us free from material wants and needs at the level of true mastery.

CHAPTER TEN

The Heart Chakra: Worldview, Values, and "Truths"

> *Oh, Lord, who may abide in your tent?*
> *Who may dwell on your holy hill?*
> *Those who walk blamelessly*
> *And do what is right,*
> *And speak the truth from their heart.*[125]

The heart chakra offers the first full opportunity for each human being to transcend the limited self to achieving a sense of oneness with the Higher Self through the power and consciousness of unconditional love.[126] The ancients knew the wisdom of the heart. In the tradition of ancient Judaism, the heart was considered not only the seat of emotions, but also the seat of the intellect.

Recently, researchers have begun to find many links between the heart and the brain. In the 1980's, researchers discovered that the heart creates a hormone, atrial natriuretic peptide (ANP, also called ANF), which helps lower blood pressure. As a result of this discovery, the heart became reclassified as an endocrine gland.

---

[125] *Psalm 15:1-2, The Bible – New Revised Standard Version*
[126] The fully developed solar plexus chakra that experiences the freedom to love unconditionally can only do so when the heart chakra has also developed to a necessary degree for us to love unconditionally.

Since then, the influence of the heart has begun to be better understood as going far beyond the pumping of blood throughout the body. Indeed, communication occurs from the heart to the brain via the vagus nerve and other mechanisms, even resulting in alterations of perception and cognitive processing. According to the Heartmath Institute, the heart communicates with the brain four ways: via hormones, through the nervous system, through pulse waves, and via electromagnetic fields.[127]

As part of the chakra system of the body, the heart chakra is associated with not only the heart, but also the thymus as its primary gland. The thymus secretes a hormone that helps T-cells develop, but then the thymus atrophies with age. The thymus thus functions importantly as part of both the endocrine system and the lymph system, providing important immune system defenses, even long after it ceases to be active.[128]

Metaphorically paralleling the atrophying of the thymus gland, as we mature, we can shift from developing our defenses to developing our spiritual and emotional strengths, as we energize the heart chakra more fully. In other words, with maturation, we can move from being defensive and reactive to being responsive and proactive. Rather than focusing on protecting our sense of vulnerability and ego-based defenses, we can mature into a generosity of loving, giving, and serving.

---

[127] Research compiled by the Heartmath Institute:
https://www.heartmath.org/research/science-of-the-heart/heart-brain-communication/
[128] https://www.endocrineweb.com/endocrinology/overview-thymus

For the developing heart chakra, we still love others conditionally, though perhaps less for what they can do for us, and more for who they are as themselves. As our heart chakra matures emotionally and spiritually, we discover that we are able to love others for who they are as soul selves, regardless of the appearance of potentially hurtful and limited ego in and through them. With a fully developed heart chakra, we can love others not only unconditionally, and no longer out of self-interest, but also selflessly, as in the highest essence of a mother's love, or a hero's willingness to die to save someone's life.

The feminine energies of the heart chakra are the energies of compassion and understanding. Here, understanding goes one step beyond empathy in order to understand conceptually as well as to feel what another person experiences and needs. Thus, feminine heart energies lead to:

- empathizing,
- serving, including servant-leadership
- connecting with others either selflessly or for mutual benefit and personal growth,
- reaching out to empower all life, especially those who are in need,
- organizing families, institutions, and governments in ways that empower everyone to receive what they need in life for their personal growth, education, and health, as well as for fulfilling personal and communal potential, (not just jobs)

- and ultimately, creating communities where everyone shares love and respect.

Those of us who have not yet fully developed the chakras up through energizing the feminine energies of the heart may describe heart chakra individuals as "bleeding hearts."

The masculine energies of the heart consist of the mental strength and determination to overcome and to heal all emotional wounds, as well as the inner courage and emotional strength and determination to overcome all obstacles in life, especially for the benefit of others. Indeed, the root of the word "courage" is the Latin word for "heart."

The masculine energies of the heart chakra reflect the immense power and strength of the subtle energy of love. The masculine energies of the heart chakra thus potentially lead to heroic actions, whether fighting fires, pulling someone out of a car that's about to explode, or saving others in the middle of war.

> **For the heart chakra, we arrive at truth through empathy and compassion, and truth is inseparable from unconditional love.**

For the heart chakra, we arrive at truth through empathy and compassion, and truth is inseparable from unconditional love. In other words, for the mature heart chakra, truth arises through awareness of the needs of others, not just self-serving narcissistic awareness. Truth that is limited to self is only partially true and not the whole truth. The whole truth considers the wellbeing of all of humanity, not just a single nation, nor a single culture, nor a single religion. Furthermore, the whole truth considers compassion for all life, and for the planet which supports life.

The mature heart chakra approaches truth as universal, but focuses instead on the unconditional love that makes truth possible, for without love, truth is seen as lacking virtue. The heart chakra wisely knows that truthfulness cannot be virtuous without love, and what is truth, if it is not also virtuous? How can moral excellence, or the quality of any virtue, be moral or excellent without truth? The spiritually-developed heart chakra knows the interconnections of truth with virtues such as love and courage, wisdom and understanding, patience and fortitude.

From the perspective of the heart chakra, love and truth are inseparable; there is no truth without love. So, until the heart chakra is fully developed energetically, the simple ego version of this heart energy is "it is only true if it feels and seems loving to me." The healthy spiritual understanding of truth in a fully-developed heart chakra is that "truth heals us through love, empowers us to be our best selves, and unites us in love, peace, and harmony."

The main spiritual energies of the fully-blossomed heart chakra are compassion, courage and unconditional love. Unconditional love entails both feminine energies of connection, compassion, and understanding, as well as the masculine energies of courage and independence, because unconditional love stands in its own strength and asks nothing in return.

People who relate to others primarily from the heart chakra relate out of empathic concern and loving connections. Such an individual may be called a "Connected knower," a term used in the book *Women's Ways of Knowing*, a truly insightful book about a variety of human ways of experiencing, understanding, and relating to life.

A connected knower "learns through empathy," following what the writers call an "experiential logic," which recognizes that people learn and reason within the context of human life.[129] This is indeed a feminine way of knowing: not reasoning merely on the basis of logic, but understanding logic within the context of human experience and as part of it, not as something that denies human subjective experience but rather draws from it.

I am indebted to that book for helping me realize that Jesus Christ was a connected knower, not a claim the authors made, but an observation I made when discovering the sacred nature of knowing reality through our connections with others and their needs and desires, not just our own narcissistic, self-centered perspectives on life. Connected knowers share power with others, and understand that truth is multi-faceted based on the varieties of human experience. Both the Buddha and Mahatma Gandhi would be considered

---

[129] Mary Field Belenky, et al, *Women's Ways of Knowing, The Development of Self, Voice, and Mind,* Basic Books, Inc., 1986, pp. 114-115.

connected knowers as well, because they placed compassion at the heart of human interactions, just as Christ also did.

Compassion and sharing power are indeed primary values of the heart chakra; equality is at the core of the heart chakra worldview as well. Truth only resonates when it serves the needs of humanity, for anything that disempowers life and dishonors the nurturing of human beings cannot be true in any ultimate and virtuous sense, only in a temporary and exigent sense.

Connected knowers and heart chakra people don't have to be gay or lesbian or transgender to understand that another person's self-understanding is an equally valid way of being human. In fact, people whose heart chakras are well-energized as wise, connected knowers will seek to understand other people's ways of viewing themselves and life, rather than shutting them out and labeling them as "inferior," "sinful," or "mentally ill." Connected knowers love to learn from the different experiences of people with unique or particularly different lives, understanding that we are not so separate or different from each other when we connect and realize that we are all connected by life.

The heart chakra's way of learning and perceiving truth is expansive, interpersonal, and wise. Therefore, those of us with fully energized heart chakras understand that everyone deserves to have their basic needs met in life, and that we are all accountable to ourselves and one another to make sure that happens. Heart chakra people give generously, and trust that we will receive what we need in return.

Heart chakra people trust others in their own moral decision-making processes, and therefore legislate for individual freedoms that cannot be overridden by others unless one person's practice of individual freedoms infringes on the rights and wellbeing of others. For instance, heart chakra people may very much personally reject abortion, and yet we will unconditionally love and trust others to make their own choices.

As a matter of fact, both as a minister, and as an intuitive life coach, I have listened as women have shared with me the agonizing decision of choosing an abortion. As a minister and as a life coach, I would be failing to love a woman if I judged her for her choice, yet sometimes, I found myself thinking I probably would not have chosen to get an abortion in those circumstances. Yet, as I listened with the deepest empathy, I always realized that each and every woman made that agonizing choice from a place of love, believing that she made the most loving choice she possibly could. How can I judge anyone who makes a choice based on their utmost effort to be loving?

A fully developed heart chakra world view has no room for judgment, and certainly no room for condemnation. However, those of us with fully mature heart chakras also understand that sometimes we need to experience the consequences of our choices, and that holding ourselves and others accountable for our choices is generally the most loving and responsible way to interact with each other and with life. Accountability does not necessitate punishment, but it can include drawing healthy boundaries, setting limits, and allowing natural consequences.

Even so, the most spiritually developed heart chakra believes in grace, and forgiveness is exercised as though the heart muscle was designed for stretching expansively with forgiveness for all. The mature heart chakra sees no enemies, only people who need to be loved.

The purpose the heart chakra teaches us is simply to love and be loved. Ultimately, when all the chakras are developed, the purpose the heart chakra accomplishes in us is to live in a constant flow of love and to become the very presence of love for others.

> **The mature heart chakra sees no enemies, only people who need to be loved.**

A heart chakra that is partially developed, with only masculine energy but not feminine energy, may be action-oriented, courageous, and bold. The masculine heart chakra minus the feminine energy may strongly serve a higher good, but may also lack sensitivity, and avoid feelings. If there is only masculine energy and some remnants of fear, then denial of feelings, denial of love, and shallow commitments or even a fear of commitment may occur.

A heart chakra that is partially developed, with only feminine energy but not masculine energy, may be focused on empathizing with others, discussing feelings, yet pre-occupied with feelings over intellect and action. The strength of a heart chakra world view with feminine energy is the emphasis on cultivating healthy relationships, keeping commitments, and following through with responsibilities. If there is only feminine energy and some remnants of fear, then avoidance of courageous activity relating to the larger world may occur, such as failing to work for a larger cause of justice, fearing that the world will not change even if we do something.

The undeveloped heart chakra results from not yet being fully energized by love, and fears still remain, whether from a lack of feminine energy, masculine energy, or a lack of both. As a result, an underdeveloped heart chakra struggles to forgive, holds a grudge, and loves conditionally. Fear can still block the flow of love, both to oneself, and to others, in the undeveloped heart chakra.

Ultimately, with fully mature chakras all the way up through the crown chakra, the heart chakra enables us to know and to live the truth that Love Is Infinite, and that Source is Infinite Love. At the mystical level of religions, the Divine is experienced as Infinite Love and Light.

We can heal and fully energize our heart chakras by affirming a blessing that intuitively came to me for one of my clients. What I intuitively heard for the client, and I trust it applies for many of us, is:

> "I am Infinite Love,
> and you are created in my image.
> The only thing blocking you

> from becoming one with Infinite Love
> is not loving yourself infinitely.
> I am Infinite Love; you are created in my image,
> and I love you *infinitely*."

While we are all "created in the image" of Infinite Love, most of us probably do not yet love ourselves with an infinite love. To love ourselves and others with Infinite Love, we need to heal our heart chakras. To heal our heart chakras, we can follow a simple process:

> First, sit quietly and use deep breathing and, if you like, other meditative techniques to find your own inner calm.

> Second, as you breathe in, think the word "love," and as you breathe out, think the word "peace." As you continue breathing in-and-out, continue thinking "love" on the in-breath, and "peace" on the out-breath.

> Next, think of someone who loves you, or think of yourself, if no one else comes to mind. Think of the love you feel when you contemplate the other person hugging you, or contemplate loving yourself. Work at this if you need to, by *choosing* to love yourself, and by *choosing* to feel loved. If you need to make it easier, you might try placing your hand on your chest with the intention of "putting love into" your own heart. Then, seek to feel the love, from the other person, or from yourself.

> Next, let this love expand outward around you, growing until it feels like a universe full of love –

Infinite Love. Feel this Infinite Love loving you. Then, feel how much *you* love this Infinite Love, for Infinite Love loves you infinitely – this Love loves you unconditionally and with no limits.

Feel your own love for this love, a love which you can trust implicitly to love you at all times, even in the midst of difficulties and danger. Feel this Infinite Love loving you, feel your heart filled with and warmed by this love. Love the Love, and feel the love, allowing yourself to become aware that you are loving yourself with this love.

When you feel full of this love, become aware that you can now share this love with others, for you have no reason to fear them, and no reason to judge them. From this place of Infinite Love, we are able to love ourselves, and we are able to love others.

As part of this process, we also may need to forgive ourselves or others. The heart chakra energy, when energized with love, is what enables us to forgive others. When our heart chakra is filled with love, we also find it easier to forgive ourselves.

For the heart chakra, sin is the failure to love, the failure to forgive, and the failure to act lovingly and courageously. Sin consists of conditionally loving rather than unconditionally loving. Sin entails fearing rather than loving. The heart chakra teaches us of the loving nature of ultimate truth. Ultimate truth entails love and forgiveness, courage and strength, for ultimate and eternal truths heal people and relationships.

The heart chakra begins to teach us that ultimate truths heal all of the false dichotomies, so that, through ultimate, unconditional love, we begin to experience the oneness of divinity and humanity, of humanity and nature, as well as the oneness of all life. Only a fully mature heart chakra, full of love, can lead us to experiencing our ultimate oneness.

> **The heart chakra empowers us to experience our Oneness in Love, as well as our Oneness *as* Love.**

For the developing heart chakra, the One God of everyone is Love. For the fully developed heart chakra, that great, Divine Love is unconditional and unites us all. The masculine energy of the heart chakra teaches us: Truth is Love, and this Divine Love is infinitely powerful. The feminine energy of the heart chakra teaches us: Truth is Holistic, for Truth is Connected, and Truth Connects All as One, which makes us whole.[130]

As we begin to understand that ultimate Truth is Unconditional Love and that Truth Connects all that exists, we may begin to experience our oneness with others and with God as Love. The heart chakra

---

[130] One might go on to assert: Truth is Holographic. I am indebted to a friend long ago who taught me the concept of the holographic universe, based on Michael Talbot's book by that title. I have not yet read the book, *The Holographic Universe* (Harper Perennial, 2011), but I do believe that the true nature of the universe is holographic. The wisdom of feminine energies senses our interconnectivity at all levels of being, and this interconnectivity may well be holographic.

empowers us to experience our Oneness in Love, as well as our Oneness *as* Love.

For the fully developed heart chakra, then, Truth is the Love that Connects us all.

CHAPTER ELEVEN

The Throat Chakra: Worldview, Values, And "Truths"

*I feel safe in the midst of my enemies,
For the truth is all powerful and will prevail.* [131]
– Sojourner Truth

Technically, the throat chakra's purpose relates more to seeking and speaking the truth than any of the other chakras. The throat chakra is also the seat of the will, initially in the sense of a person's sense of self and self-will. As the throat chakra becomes fully energized, this sense of self-will matures into seeking divine will and speaking divine truth, not just one's own will and one's own convictions.

The gland associated with the throat chakra is the thyroid gland. The thyroid's main function is to create two hormones that regulate metabolism, breathing, heart rate, as well as the central and peripheral nervous systems. Essentially, the thyroid hormones metabolically affect every cell in the body. The thyroid has two wings, like a butterfly, balanced equally on both sides of the throat.

Just like the thyroid gland, the essential quest for truth represented by the throat chakra forms the basis for health on all levels of human life. Just as the two thyroid hormones have to be kept in balance, the quest

---

[131] http://www.azquotes.com/author/14828-Sojourner_Truth

for truth cannot be either simply intellectual or simply intuitive; it must be both. For the throat chakra, the quest for truth is both intellectual and personal. The throat chakra's quest for truth relates to what makes empirical and logical sense, but also relates to a personal sense of purpose in life.

The energies of the throat chakra relate not only to a person's will, but also to our intentions and our sense of purpose in life. At the sacral chakra level, that sense of purpose can either relate to a mental world often devoid of the Divine, or an intuitive world filled with sacredness and/or spirits.

If our sense of purpose is mental, we will willfully focus on the intellect, and if our sense of purpose is more intuitive, we will seek a higher purpose and a higher guidance. If our sense of will is merely personal, we will focus on what we need to be doing in life, until we discover a larger sense of purpose in life. Generally, a more universal sense of purpose does not show up until the brow chakra is also well-energized.

The throat chakra is the seat of clairaudience, or being able to hear higher guidance. This is an audio version of intuition instead of the feeling-based intuitions that each chakra has been sensing up to this point. The throat chakra's intuitive ability arises through language and the ability to hear our own inner guidance. Clairaudience evolves all the way from our basic ability to hear the voice of our own conscience,[132] to psychic

---

[132] The voice of our own conscience depends on our level of chakra development, which determines to a large degree our level of vibration in terms of spiritual or subtle energy. Our level of vibration determines the

abilities, to the ability to hear divine guidance through higher beings (angels, for example) all the way to being able to hear "the voice of God."

The intuitive ability of the throat chakra advances as we advance spiritually. One can, instead, become schizophrenic either through drug use or through an experience of emotional trauma, either of which can energetically blow open the chakras, as mentioned before.[133] In the case of the throat chakra, blowing it open leaves one vulnerable to hearing the voices of disembodied spirits, and unless one has very pure intentions, one may draw unsavory spirits to oneself, and hear "crazy" voices.[134] The murderer known as

---

morality with which we resonate or fail to resonate, and thus determines what we are "able to hear" as moral guidance. Our own conscience will only tell us what we are able to hear, and that is usually only at our current vibratory level or perhaps one vibratory level higher. (The chakras represent our vibratory levels as well.)

[133] I fully realize that this is neither a medical nor a psychiatric etiology for psychopathology. However, energetic sensitivity through and excessive openness of the chakras can lead to hearing other voices, as well as to the negative influence of other energies including excessive psychic control by other people. Ultimately, I agree with the teaching that I learned through my Progressive Counselling training in England: all mental illness is a form or spiritual cop-out (giving up), or, I would add, occurs because of a spiritual crisis. The physiological and chemical expressions follow the energetic patterns of the person's spiritual state, which can also be created through karma, whether past-life, or otherwise. When karmic patterns come through past-life carry-overs, modern science generally labels these "genetic predispositions." I would suggest that both are true: karma and genetics are intertwined.

[134] For those of us who do not believe in disembodied spirits, I simply invite us to practice multiple spiritual disciplines, especially pure meditation, until we have fully developed all seven chakras, and attained full enlightenment. At the level of mature throat or brow chakra development, we can begin to encounter higher consciousness more clearly. Our sense of truth, and therefore of what is real, evolves with our chakra development, including our experiences of higher beings, as well as of souls who have passed on. I speak from my experiences

"Son of Sam," who believed that he heard a demon in his neighbor's dog tell him to kill people, would most likely be one example of this.

The reason that we so often do not trust people who say that they heard God speak to them is that so very few of us are emotionally, mentally, and spiritually evolved enough to do so! In other words, few of us are so evolved that our throat chakras are completely energized with both masculine and feminine energies, and also purely and potently energized with love rather than fear. To arrive at this point where we have achieved the true spiritual maturity to hear the voice of God is rare indeed. Until that point, we hear the voice of our own conscience, which may often reflect only the very best of our own chakra development, because it can be so hard for us to understand any truth higher than our current level.

> **To arrive at this point where we have achieved the true spiritual maturity to hear the voice of God is rare indeed. Until that point, we hear the voice of our own conscience, which may reflect only the very best of our own chakra development.**

Signs that one truthfully hears the voice of God would include the mature, loving worldview of each preceding chakra:

---

working with people in ministry as well as working with clients. (Pure meditation refers to two specific techniques in Raja Yoga Meditation.)

- Root: all of humanity is part of one big family in which everyone is worthy of being loved, protected, and supported in life;
- Sacral: justice, equality, fairness, self-discipline, and self-reliance balanced with cooperative sharing of both power and resources are all paramount virtues for human life;
- Solar Plexus: freedom of individual self-expression, personal responsibility, and interdependence are foundational for healthy human relationships;
- Heart: unconditional love, non-judgment, compassion, and generosity are fundamental qualities of Divine Love.

Any "truth" attributed to the "voice of God" that does not inherently resonate with all these chakra characteristics would not reflect the highest spiritual understandings of the "voice of God." Until one develops through the chakra system, the teachings one perceives as coming from God simply resonate with the "truths" that one is ready to hear based on one's own level of chakra development.

Let's return to the throat chakra's own development. Like every other chakra, the throat chakra develops over time emotionally, mentally, and spiritually. The full development of the throat chakra also depends on fully energizing its masculine and feminine energies as well as fully energizing love rather than fear. The throat chakra's sense of purpose in life entails a full development of each person's sense of self as a unique person, not necessarily as we relate to divinity, although it will ideally include that as well, but primarily from a sense of separateness rather than union.

The sense of self in the throat chakra is very personally understood, not as the creative, and a-rational self-expression of the solar plexus chakra, but as personal, logical, and intuitive expressions of selfhood in relation to other people. This throat chakra sense of self also entails a sense of personal priorities, values, and logic.

The masculine energy of the throat chakra is logical and intellectual. I do not mean that the throat chakra is the seat of the intellect, but that the masculine energy of the throat chakra chooses reason and logic as the primary means for making sense of the purpose of life.

Here, in the throat chakra, the emphasis is on the *choice* of intellect, rather than its full functioning. One might ask: why am I placing the intellect in the throat chakra? Others surely place intellect in the brow chakra's purview, and indeed, the brow chakra enables the full flowering of intellect.

However, the throat chakra spiritually energizes the intellect, just as the carotid arteries in the throat feed the blood supply to the brain. The function here is energizing consciousness, both intellectual and intuitive, left brain and right brain, just as there are left and right carotid arteries.

The power of personal will in the throat chakra energizes our intellect and/or our intuition. This choice, empowered in the throat chakra, relates to our spiritual evolution, as to whether our soul chooses to energize intellect or intuition, or both, at a given time and in a given lifetime.

The emphasis here in the throat chakra is not on the intellect itself, but on the motivation or will to choose intellect and logic. The full development of intellect and intuition occur in the brow chakra. Here, it is the energy of desire, will, or motive that chooses intellect or chooses intuition as a means of arriving at truth.

> **From the masculine energy perspective of the throat chakra, even relationships are considered from the point of view of what seems logical.**

For instance, a person with a lot of masculine energy in the throat chakra may become very rigidly logical in our thinking, or focused merely on the logical ways that things make sense in life, without considering higher consciousness or the interconnectedness of intuition with intellect. From the masculine energy perspective of the throat chakra, even relationships are considered from the point of view of what seems logical.

This masculine throat chakra worldview can end up with a strong sense of duality (think of the thyroid's two wings), in which everything is either logical or nonsensical, right or wrong, true or false, worthwhile or a waste of time, "should be done," or "shouldn't be done," and so on.

There's a strong judgmentalism to this dualistic thinking, particularly if a person lives with more fear than love, with a still-underdeveloped heart chakra. However, this judgmental dualism is more intellectual than religious, though it may also express itself moralistically or ethically, based on an expected set of "logical," ethical, or practical rules for behavior. The thinking of a throat-chakra based intellectual can become very rigid, whether our rigid thinking concerns ethics or science. This intellectual rigidity tends to develop only if our sense of self has not fully developed with love and feminine energies to match the rigorous masculine intellectual energy.

> **Our quest for truth in the throat chakra, when energized by feminine energy plus love, becomes highly intuitive, often receiving higher verbal guidance, including internal, auditory divine or angelic messages.**

The feminine energy of the throat chakra is personal and intuitive. Our quest for truth in the throat chakra, when energized by feminine energy plus love, becomes highly intuitive, often receiving higher verbal guidance, including internal, auditory divine or angelic messages. This level of development can entail developing psychic abilities as well.

With feminine energies in the throat chakra, our sense of will can be driven from very interpersonal thinking. If also energized with fear, we can, at this level, have very precarious self-esteem, if we have not yet become strongly developed in our own personal sense of self, and if we believe others to be better or more important than ourselves.

With feminine energies and fear in the throat chakra, we may become preoccupied with what other people think of us, with what our own image and reputation are, and with doing what other people think we "should" do rather than what feels right to us. This fear-based throat chakra view leads to a lack of truly knowing and being ourselves, because we neither want to speak nor act in ways of which others might disapprove. I have felt these energy patterns in the throat chakras of many of my clients.

If the throat chakra is energized with feminine energy, masculine energy, and love rather than fear, the quest for truth expands to become not only logical but also intuitive. Logic and intuition are not mutually exclusive; in the throat chakra, we discover that truth is logical, and can also be accessed intuitively. One may then become more gracious in one's approach to the intellect, understanding that fulfilling a higher function through intellect is the goal.

If the feminine energies of the throat chakra are developed with love rather than fear, we might prefer working with people and intuition rather than with logic and ideas. The loving and personal focus of the throat chakra yields intuitive guidance to help us live our lives authentically as ourselves, rather than projecting an artificial image into the world.

The simple version of this fear-based image projection entails motivating ourselves by what we think we "should" do, or by what others think we "should" do. When we motivate ourselves and others on the basis of the concepts of "should" and "ought to," then we often dismiss or deny feelings and parts of ourselves that we feel we need to hide from others.

I often feel the energy pattern of this throat chakra view as an up-and-down motion during healing, as though their own will is driving them to "keep their chin up." Often, the "should" pattern occurs because people need to maintain incredibly high standards of expectations set by others, especially Western professional culture. This leads to relegating the soul-self to the back seat, and energizing the will to drive ourselves to act in ways that culture deems "appropriate."

Image projection becomes part of the fear-based myth of the "successful" sense of self that can arise in the throat chakra. For the underdeveloped throat chakra, we are successful if we achieve wonderful reputations due to our wealth or great accomplishments on the material plane, without regard to the spiritual plane. The only nod to spirituality might be a view of religious "success" if one's religiosity gains one wealth and/or favor in the eyes of others. Fear often drives the throat chakra worldview's desire *to appear to be* successful and sane to the outside world.

When focused outward, a fear-based throat chakra worldview leads one to believe that the dualistic world of Western science and of the five senses is all there is. From a fear-based throat chakra, one often feels a need to wear a mask to hide one's real feelings and authentic self. If one is beginning to suspect that the dualistic, scientific view of the world doesn't explain everything, and yet fears expressing one's spirituality, then one may "hide" oneself if one lives in a culture that believes only in "rational" science.

Rather than being concerned with what other people think, a mature throat chakra worldview will lead us to be concerned with what we think of ourselves, and to begin to be more self-directed mentally and in terms of how we define "success." A fully mature throat chakra will lead us to a deeper sense of spirituality. With this mature spirituality, we will become more interested in pleasing the Divine with our thoughts, words, and actions, or with modeling ourselves after spiritual teachers from our religious tradition, or both.

We hear ourselves in the throat chakra, then, exploring the truth of the self, often creating illusions of the self, while also seeing the self primarily as separate from others and from the universe, and ultimately separate from our Source.

The throat chakra fulfills the ego's mental journey of separation, believing that we are an individual self, separate from all other selves. As ego consciousness, the throat chakra believes that it can create meaningful lies and illusions, because ego is a master of truth and illusion derived from a mental intelligence and an a-moral personhood that exists for itself. The fear-based, underdeveloped throat chakra's ego-consciousness believes that it is all there is; that no higher consciousness exists. This ego consciousness in the throat chakra represents an extremely underdeveloped spiritual worldview.

As our soul self develops in the throat chakra through increasing levels of love, we begin to expand beyond the ego's limited sense of self to a greater sense of connection with the Divine and with others. Developing with the mature throat chakra, this expansive view of self understands the interconnectedness of life along with the multi-dimensional nature of reality.

To an expansive throat chakra worldview, life begins to be more mystical, intuitive, and connected beyond what meets the eye. Knowledge begins to become more intuitive, and intellect and intuition begin to create connections unknown before. Music from the throat chakra elevates, inspires, and challenges us to move beyond expected dualities to ecstasies of hope and faith that the ego-mind cannot grasp. Yes, the mature throat chakra can lead us to be creative, especially with words and music, but also with ideas and mental constructs. Abstract thought arises and reigns in the throat chakra worldview. Poetry speaks, and truth finds richer tones and melodies, connecting self and world more intuitively and with abstract beauty.

Even when considering the universal truths, the developing throat chakra worldview will wonder how this impacts our own selves. The more mentally focused throat chakra worldview will prefer the intellect and the world of ideas to the world of spirit, until it develops spiritually and matures through becoming fully energized. When it becomes mature, the throat chakra finds a faith that opens intuitive doors that were unopened before.

One of the many tasks of the throat chakra is to express one's sense of will. When the throat chakra is still underdeveloped, one's sense of will and intentions will remain egocentric and self-serving. As the throat chakra becomes mature and fully energized with love, we will desire to turn our will over to Divine will, and seek to do "the will of God." We will seek to speak truth,

> **As the throat chakra becomes mature and fully energized with love, we will desire to turn our will over to Divine will, and seek to do "the will of God." We will seek to speak truth, and as we mature spiritually in the throat chakra, we will seek purer and purer intentions as well as to be increasingly honest and of integrity.**

and as we mature spiritually in the throat chakra, we will seek purer and purer intentions as well as to be increasingly honest and of integrity.

While the throat chakra is still developing, the throat chakra worldview can at first be very focused on facts and an objectively verifiable truth. Truth is initially sensed as being factual. From the ego's perspective in the throat chakra, the only truths we can know are those that we empirically verify through logic as well as through the five senses and through Western-style scientific studies. As we develop our throat chakras, we begin to see truth as fulfilling a higher purpose, an ideal, or a virtue.

The throat chakra offers us the last vestige of dualism: right or wrong; logical or illogical; true vs. false.[135] In the throat chakra, we perceive ourselves as a sense of self in relation to the world from a more mental, analytical view, and less an emotional view. We tend to motivate ourselves by what we think we "ought to do" or "should do." In an under-developed throat chakra, this sense of "should" and "ought to" guides our motivations, like a last vestige of dualistic judgmentalism, though often based on ideas of what is "reasonable" and what could be argued for by logic. Our will thus becomes captive to judgmental motivations based on either logic and reason, or ethical and personal imperatives.

Unlike the sacral chakra, this judgmentalism does not primarily seek to amass worldly power. However, with this judgmental throat chakra energy, we can engage in verbal struggles for power over who is "right" and who is "wrong." Winning mentally or intellectually can be important with underdeveloped throat chakra energy, and again, one may become overly concerned if one's reputation is at stake.

This judgmental approach to motivating ourselves will guide us until we fully develop our sense of self beyond the ego's judgment of "right and wrong." With a mature and loving throat chakra, we will simply make our choices consistently with who we are and what we think

---

[135] My initial title for this book reflected an appeal to the popularity of the throat chakra's intellectual worldview: *Truth vs. Illusion*. When I soon realized that the duality was not the ultimate message of the book, I changed the title, invoking the higher consciousness of the brow chakra and above.

or believe, rather than what others may expect. We will no longer shame and judge ourselves and others based on a rigid set of expectations of what people "should" do, but rather seek intuitively to understand people's motivations, as well as our own, through exercising understanding rather than judgment.

(Please notice, here, the feeling-state of empathy doesn't function as much as it does in the solar plexus chakra, nor the mere awareness of connection that arises in the sacral chakra, but rather, the mental reasoning which leads to understanding.)

Wisdom arises out of this ability to be understanding. Wisdom exists at each chakra level, with the masculine and feminine, love-based energies of each chakra, but it arises noticeably with this more mental ability to reason our way to understanding, such as leads to making peace with one another, or to hearing and honoring diverse points-of-view, despite intellectual differences.

With feminine and masculine energies and strong energies of love, a well-developed throat chakra will help us develop a healthier spiritual worldview. From a healthy spiritual perspective, we sense truth intuitively, aware of whether or not it brings love, peace, justice, and a higher good.

Through the mature throat chakra, we will also sense whether a given truth is real in the sense that it brings connection with higher wisdom, and with Source Consciousness (i.e., God). This mental experience of intuitive truth is common among mystics, and may be replicated through the practice of spiritual disciplines. From the throat chakra-up, spiritual disciplines become both more desired and more necessary for fully energizing the intuitive "truths" of each chakra.

In her book, *Anatomy of the Spirit,* Caroline Myss associates the Catholic sacrament of confession with the throat chakra.[136] Protestants also recognize confession as essential in our relationship with God, but Protestants believe confession happens between a person and God, not through a priest as an intercessor.

> **From the throat chakra-up, spiritual disciplines become both more desired and more necessary for fully energizing the intuitive "truths" of each chakra.**

The concept of confession in the broader Christian tradition entails the concept of sin and guilt, which call for judgment and which create the possibility of condemnation. To alleviate sin and guilt, one engages in confession and repentance (and in the Catholic tradition, penance). These practices restore the individual to God's grace. For Protestants, the restoration to a state of grace happens because of Christ's sacrifice through death on the cross; his grace is sufficient for all humanity for all time.

Yet, all Christian traditions, (as far as I have experienced them in 58 years of being a Christian,

---

[136] Myss, Caroline, *Anatomy of the Spirit: The Seven Stages of Power and Healing.* (Three Rivers Press: New York), 1996, p. 220.

including at Vanderbilt Divinity School and serving churches as a minister), seem to leave lingering vestiges of negative consciousness through judgment of both the sin and the sinner, as well as some sense of condemnation. Confession, in the Christian tradition, seems laden with negative energy, and a negative consciousness that shames, blames, and judges ourselves and others when we "fall" from the spiritual ideal in our behavior, our beliefs, or our thoughts, words, and religious practices.

This negativity associated with confession in the Christian tradition is something that, ideally, we can live without. The more I experience a higher consciousness within me, the more I experience the Divine calling me to recognize the Divine Self in myself and others; indeed, focusing on the positive is the way I continually experience myself as called to see all of humanity, even those whom I feel tempted to judge, blame, shame, resist, or reject. The fact that I have felt such temptations really stems from my Christian background!

Intuitively, the guidance I receive now is that confession functions, not as an avenue of judgment and guilt, nor blame and shame, but much more positively in an interfaith, higher consciousness sense. From the mystical perspective, confession merely entails recognizing that we have gotten ourselves out of alignment with the pure Divine energy of blessing, and then admitting that misalignment inwardly or outwardly, whichever is appropriate (or both).

This combination of recognition and acceptance of responsibility for our lowered vibration through misalignment with Divine Will in effect enables us to release or let go of the lower vibration. Letting go of the lower vibration through acceptance of responsibility in essence also entails letting go of some attachment to the world of form, which means we are "repenting" (turning away from) the world of form and choosing (turning towards) the world of Spirit. The act of letting go of form and choosing Spirit then empowers us to be raised to a higher energy state and a higher consciousness. Such higher consciousness will better enable us to be blessed, as well as to be a blessing to others.

Please allow me to give a simple example that applies to so many of us, particularly urban dwellers. We may, from time to time, while driving, resent other drivers pulling in front of us, slowing us down, getting ahead of us in line at a light, forcing in front of us in narrow spaces, and so on. We might also find ourselves driving aggressively to be first in line and so on. We will only do these things if we feel attached to being first. As soon as we realize that we are attaching our desires to something other than unconditional love, we are confessing our out-of-alignment, releasing the need to be first, and re-energizing ourselves with energies of blessing which will enable us to drive in ways that are considerate of (blessing) others.

Confession simply entails admitting our lack of alignment with higher energies, and recognizing that we seek and ask for assistance or guidance in aligning ourselves and our consciousness with higher energies once more.

There is no guilt, there is no blame, there is no shame, there is no condemnation, there is no need for an intercessor, and there is no need for penance, because suffering penance would just lower our energies again. The penance occurs quite naturally by letting go of whatever attachment we held that prevented us from seeking only to serve the higher energy consciousness of Divine Blessing in this world and for this world.

> **In true confession, there is certainly no condemnation, only a restoration to the higher consciousness that the Divine knows we can manage to embody at this stage of our spiritual journey.**

In true confession, there is certainly no condemnation, only a restoration to the higher consciousness that the Divine knows we can manage to embody at this stage of our spiritual journey. There is no expectation, only invitation to be in alignment with the energies that love, heal, and bless us with peace, joy, and bliss. In turn, these energies empower us to be a blessing to others.

Properly understood, confession is the restoration of blessing through raising our energy/consciousness to a state in which we bless the world. The simple version of this entails making amends and causing no further harm. The mystical version of this entails seeking to be a blessing every way possible to everyone possible.

For the underdeveloped throat chakra, "sin" is being "wrong," "mistaken," "incorrect," or "unpopular," "misfit," or "uncool." For the well-developed throat chakra, sin is being dishonest, out of integrity, or out-of-alignment with our own higher purposes, that is, not seeking and doing Divine Will.

For the throat chakra, confessing faith in one God who is "our God" is an act of intellect, an act of will, and a commitment to seeing the world a certain way. The world then becomes the purview of a God who is rational and who makes sense, thus leaving room for science and intellect. For a fully-developed throat chakra, this God's universe also leaves room for intuitive, miraculous, and mystical experiences.

Throat chakra individuals often have systematic mystical understandings of the universe, which may include practical applications, such as psychic experiences, energy healing, astrology, and the like. Throat chakra individuals may be particularly drawn to mystical and spiritual tools like astrology, Tarot, crystals, tools of divination, Kabbalah, praying the Rosary, mantra meditation, and any orderly, especially any language-based, mystical approach to discerning and connecting with divinity.

The fully developed throat chakra rejoices in uniting mind and spirit, fulfilling one's own purpose through fulfilling divine purposes, being part of the divine or universal "plan" of life, and speaking truth into being. For the masculine energies of the throat chakra, Truth is Logical. For the feminine energies of the throat chakra, Truth is Personal.

CHAPTER TWELVE

The Brow Chakra – Worldview, Values, and "Truths"

What we think, we become.
~ Buddha[137]

In so far as the mind sees things in their eternal aspect, it participates in eternity.
~ Baruch Spinoza[138]

The brow chakra, or Third Eye, is located between the eyes and just above the nose. The gland associated with the brow chakra is the pituitary gland, which lies midway between the back of the brow chakra at the base skull, and the Third Eye itself, located energetically on the forehead. Although others have associated the pineal gland[139] with the brow chakra, we will understand the placement of the pituitary gland as

---

[137] As quoted here, accessed on March 16, 2017:
https://www.brainyquote.com/slideshow/authors/top_10_buddha_quotes.html
[138] *Spinoza in der europäischen Geistesgeschichte*, as accessed here: https://www.goodreads.com/author/quotes/122092.Baruch_Spinoza on March 16, 2917.
[139] Primarily Madame Blavatsky of the Theosophical Society. However, not only did my training in England teach me the pituitary gland is associated with this gland, but also the placement of the pituitary argues in its favor. Further, if the pineal gland is the "seat of the soul," as claimed by René Descartes, https://en.wikipedia.org/wiki/Pineal_gland then the pineal gland surely must be associated with the crown chakra, which functions as the seat of the soul as well. The person as an incarnation of their soul is what I feel energetically when feeding healing energy into their crown chakra.

energetically significant for its link to the brow chakra, because it falls along the line of energy flow between the front and back openings of the brow chakra.

The pituitary gland is the "Master Gland" of the endocrine system.[140] Influenced itself by the hypothalamus, the pituitary in turn influences all the other endocrine glands, and thus has a highly central role in the optimal functioning of our bodies. Metaphorically, the pituitary thus resonates with the Third Eye, which is central to influencing our complete spiritual health, centering us and attuning us with higher consciousness.

> **The brow chakra is the seat of enlightenment. For Christians, the Third Eye is the seat of Christ-Consciousness. For Buddhists, the Third Eye is the seat of Buddha-Consciousness, or the Buddha mind.**

The brow chakra is the seat of enlightenment. It is also the seat of clairvoyance. Here, clairvoyance can refer either to the ability to foresee the future, or to have mystical visions which are true experiences, or both. For Christians, the Third Eye is the seat of Christ-Consciousness. For Buddhists, the Third Eye is the seat of Buddha-Consciousness, or the Buddha mind. In Hinduism, it is the seat of higher consciousness that enables us to pierce the veil of

---

[140] https://www.endocrineweb.com/endocrinology/overview-pituitary-gland Accessed March 16, 2017.

illusion, or Maya, to perceive the true reality beyond this world of form.

The higher consciousness of the brow chakra leads us to let go of concerns with "things of this world," by practicing non-attachment to things, people, and events in this world. The brow chakra thus raises our consciousness beyond the motivations of self-interest and consistently motivates us to put others first, seeking above all to bless others.

Not only is this selfless approach to living what was taught and modeled by Christ and Buddha, but is evidenced by the lives of all true saints, from Mother Teresa, to Gandhi, to Lady Kwan Yin, who is also known as the Bodhisattva of compassion. The brow chakra life is the life of a Bodhisattva, as expressed in Buddhist thought and practice for a Bodhisattva serves others compassionately and selflessly.

At the brow chakra level, truth is seen from a longer-term perspective, whether that perspective is intellectual or spiritual. This multi-generational perspective on truth is reflected in Native American teachings of considering the impact of our decisions on the seventh generation.

The wisdom of the Third Eye is focused on the present moment, knowing that "now" is all we have. And yet, this Third Eye level of truth takes account of the past and its rich learning while also being visionary, looking towards the future and how truth impacts the common good in the long run. The Third Eye brings the quality of being a visionary, whether mentally or spiritually.

The more well-developed the brow chakra is, the more these visionary qualities are available. Fully-energized, the brow chakra also maintains a constant awareness in the present, focusing on the breath if need be, but flowering with mindfulness, peace, and compassion.

The truths of the brow chakra are about the larger issues of life and the good of everyone, whether pursued mentally and intellectually, or from one's sense of purpose in life, or from a spiritual perspective focused on bringing through spiritual truths and practices. Any "truth" perceived through the brow chakra relates to higher consciousness and higher purposes, serving a greater good.

The ego aspect of the brow chakra generally remains focused on mental and intellectual analysis and awareness, which can result in great good on the material plane, for the life and well-being of many. Or, intellect and mind can be subsumed into service for lower chakra, ego-based interests, which do not necessarily serve a higher good. This only occurs if we have not yet fully developed the lower chakras, and fear remains a significant factor in one's life.

The masculine energies of the brow chakra are mental and intellectual, and can be roughly associated with left-brain tendencies. The feminine energies of the brow chakra are intuitive and artistic, and can be largely associated with the right side of the brain. Just as the brain continues to develop the executive functions of the prefrontal cortex (right behind the Third Eye), until around age 26, so also the Third Eye chakra reflects a certain degree of maturity and wisdom, as though only the insightfulness of an old soul can be found here.

Until one fully develops the lower chakras with both feminine and masculine energies and with love rather than fear, their underdeveloped qualities can continue to diminish the potential of the brow chakra for expansive consciousness. As a way of distinguishing between developing 6th chakra energies and fully-developed 6th chakra energies, I will refer to the brow chakra as still developing, and the Third Eye as fully-developed 6th chakra consciousness.

The brow chakra is also the seat of principled-knowing and scientific worldviews. By scientific, here I refer to the sense of reliability, verifiability, and replicability that are the hallmarks of both Western academic science, and also Eastern yogic science, or spiritual science.

Both Western science and spiritual science study nature, but from different viewpoints. Both rational science and spiritual science consist of standards of excellence which entail principles, integrity, systems of thought, record-keeping, and precise processes. The primary difference between the two is that one believes that human beings can only "know" anything in a rational sense, and the other understands that humans can know "things" both intuitively and rationally.

The Third Eye also knows that only what we can know intuitively is *really* real. As the Rev. Dr. Martin Luther King, Jr. once wrote: "Everything that we see is a shadow cast by that which we do not see." So, for this higher consciousness, whether we are discussing, objects, stars, planets, or ourselves, the only reality is the spiritual truth of Being as it is embodied in each aspect of being, or how each aspect of being expresses the nature of Source.

The understanding of the "self" may distinguish Western science and yogic science, because the approaches to consciousness are so different. For the intellectual mind, consciousness and therefore the self are products of the brain, which is now generally studied from a neurochemical and neuroprocessing perspective. For the spiritual mind, consciousness is intertwined with energy, and consists of the energy field of the soul as well as of the mind. This combined energy field extends outside the brain, all through the body, as well as outside the body in the aura and etheric body as well.[141] The "self" is therefore a conscious field of energy, residing temporarily in a body.

For the spiritual mind, the separate sense of "self" begins to be recognized as just part of the illusions of this world of form. The conscious awareness of the Third Eye becomes expanded to an understanding of patterns of energy and consciousness, recognizing that

---

[141] The aura entails the subtle energy around the physical body. The aura is affected by the level of vibration of the mind, the soul, and the current thoughts and emotions of the person, as well as their physical state of wellbeing. The etheric body is the soul's imprint for our physical manifestation in a given lifetime. All of this is part of the science of subtle energy, or spiritual science, which has been studied by practitioners of yoga for many thousands of years. Other Asian practices draw on the science of subtle energy, particularly including most martial arts, Qi Gong, Tai Chi, and acupuncture. I must also note that consciousness and the Self, extend beyond our physical being to connect with the Infinite, with the Eternal, or God.

"we" arise from waves of energy/consciousness. Yes, we can, to some degree, direct these patterns of consciousness, but who is the "we" who directs these patterns? For the Third Eye's expanded awareness, there is no separation between our "self" and the greater Self that is both Source of all that is, and also One with all that is.

With a fully-developed Third Eye consciousness, we no longer live for ourselves. There not only is no more "self" to live for, but also, we live so that others can begin to experience higher consciousness, compassion, love, and becoming one with others through spiritual community.

This is why Buddha left his life of privilege, and also why he founded sanghas: not only to spread enlightenment and to live in ways that diminish the separate sense of self, but also so that people could experience our oneness through the communal aspects of sangha; for when we lose our sense of individual self, we find ourselves in the All. For Buddha, there was no "self" with a small "s," only the larger oneness found in compassion and peacefulness.

> **With a fully-developed Third Eye consciousness, we no longer live for ourselves.**

Of course, Buddha's original motivation was to find a way to end suffering. When one lets go of self, and form, and tunes into higher consciousness through the Third Eye, one begins to laugh in the face of suffering, for it is not real, and laughing diminishes the power of suffering. Yes, the "Laughing Buddha" reflects this truth.[142]

The Third Eye consciousness entails living not for oneself, but for the larger principles of life, that is enlightened principles, divine purposes, the Tao, or call it what you will. To live at this level appears to require great sacrifice to those who do not yet live at this level, but the Third Eye brings great peace through non-attachment to worldly pleasures, desires, and so on. The sense of inner peace, compassion, and truth far outweigh earthly delights.

Meditation, more than anything else, hastens the development of such higher consciousness. Fasting and other spiritual disciplines, including simplicity, generosity, and prayer, can all contribute to such higher consciousness. One cannot simultaneously hold onto desire for something earthly and maintain this higher consciousness. Even a desire to be treated a certain way, or to receive some kind of comfort diminishes the vibration and "drops" one down from this higher consciousness.

Mystics are generally very energized in the Third Eye, and visions at this level can take many forms. Often, one is able to perceive higher planes of existence, higher beings, including angels and Ascended Masters, or even loved ones who have passed on. One may begin to experience "inexplicable" spiritual gifts, including healing miracles.

---

[142] I have personally had mystical experiences of the laughing Buddha getting me to laugh at myself and my problems!

One form of meditation actually serves to focus on and energize the Third Eye. Personally, I believe that Jesus Christ practiced this technique, not only because Paramahansa Yogananda wrote in his book, *Autobiography of a Yogi*, that Christ knew this technique, but also because there is a verse in the New Testament which suggests this truth. The verse which testifies to this claim really makes very little sense any other way, and yet makes beautifully profound sense when understood as meditating on the Third Eye chakra.

The verse in question is Matthew 6:22: "If thine eye be single, thy whole body will be full of light." (KJV). Newer scholarship fails to render the Greek adequately (in my opinion based on a translation once made by a clergy colleague), and also fails to render the true depth of spiritual meaning. I believe the reference to the single eye is to the Third Eye, because focusing on it can enable one to experience God as Light, and this light fills one's whole being.

I could worry about how people react as they read this, for I did once fail to convince a New Testament scholar of this idea, or I can simply know the truths that I have experienced in my own mystical visions, and live from my own inner contentment. Please note, that I am consciously choosing this latter path!

A true mystic need not please anyone, even oneself, for the only Self a mystic seeks to please is God. This level of development only happens after fully energizing the brow chakra with love and both feminine and masculine energies, because then one begins to sense or even to hear truths that no one else may be "getting."

This can feel like such a difficult stage of spiritual development, because all of a sudden, what makes sense to a mystic doesn't make sense to anyone else around them, unless they are surrounded by people engaged in the same spiritual practices. Becoming a mystic can feel a bit like going crazy, until we get used to it. Eventually, the joy and peace of "knowing" make a very great difference in life.

In the meantime, doubts can creep into our brow chakra awareness. At this level, we may be less effected by outright visceral fears as in the solar plexus chakra. We may, however, become preoccupied with worries, if we have not yet fully healed our lower chakras. For the brow chakra, though, doubt and worries not only arise from fear, but also maintain and even increase the energy of fear in our whole being.

In the brow chakra, we may doubt ourselves, we may doubt life, we may doubt spiritual teachings, we may doubt God. Any and all doubts can hinder our access to truth, unless we are engaging in healthy doubts about teachings and things that are not true.

Again, until our brow chakra is fully energized, the measure by which we can believe or doubt ideas, thoughts, experiences, or teachings comes from the truths that we have already learned through our lower five chakras. Just like the throat chakra, we will only believe truths that have passed the tests of truth for all the lower chakras. Here is a reminder of these truths:

WE ARE ONE

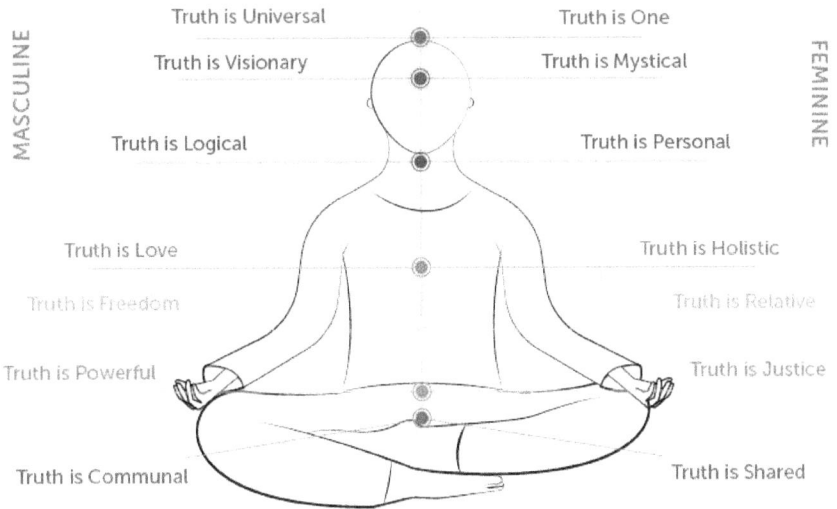

Masculine (left) and Feminine (right) Aspects of Truth for Each Chakra (*Artwork by Davonne Flanagan*)

If we find ourselves doubting ourselves or our Divine Source, it lowers our vibration, which in turn creates a sense of disconnect between us and God. At the level of the brow chakra, full faith is required in order for us to develop into the truth of our own being. The fully energized Third Eye fortunately leads us to the truth of our self as higher consciousness.

From the Third Eye, we become aware of our own direct connection with that "one God" who has been primarily conceptual, that is, just a Being about whom we have had thoughts and ideas. At the level of the Third Eye, contact with God begins to be experiential, through actual perception of God. Through the Third Eye, one begins to move from mere conceptions of God to direct perceptions of God.

For the brow chakra, sin consists of doubting, worrying, putting self before others, and focusing on form (earthly stuff) in order to live as form and to enjoy form, rather than focusing on and living from pure Spirit.

For the masculine awareness of the Third Eye, Truth is Visionary. For the feminine consciousness of the Third Eye, Truth is Mystical.

CHAPTER THIRTEEN

Crown Chakra: Worldview, Values, and Truths

"When you feel a peaceful joy, that's when you are near truth."
— *Jalaluddin Rumi*[143]

The crown chakra is the pinnacle of our body-based chakra system. The crown represents the fulfillment of our spiritual path, evolving through the chakras over many lifetimes. It is through the crown chakra that we are restored to union with God.

The gland associated with the crown chakra is the pineal gland. The pineal gland is not yet fully understood according to Western science, but it is located near the center of the brain, and is stimulated by light. During dark periods, it releases melatonin, and during the daylight, it stops melatonin production. In this way, the pineal gland regulates our sleeping and waking cycles, or our circadian rhythms. The pineal gland's secretion of melatonin causes a reduction in the production of gonadotropins, which are essential for the healthy functioning of the testes and ovaries.[144]

The location of the pineal gland is significant, because it actually sits between the two hemispheres, as its own

---

[143] https://www.goodreads.com/author/quotes/875661.Jalaluddin_Rumi?page=4 Accessed November 28, 2016.

[144] https://www.endocrineweb.com/endocrinology/overview-pineal-gland Accessed on March 19, 2017.

entity. The centrality and independence of the pineal gland metaphorically represent the centrality and uniqueness of the higher consciousness of the crown chakra. The sensitivity to light represents the crown chakra's openness to "The Light of God." The pineal gland's contributions to the regulation of sleeping and waking represent the crown chakra's significance in our evolution of consciousness from an unawakened state of being to being fully conscious and fully awake spiritually speaking.

Energizing the crown chakra leads to intuitive knowing that arises from an expanded consciousness within this world of form, so that we may "know" things that are true or are going to be "true" without needing the tangible evidence for us to know that it is so. This gift needs to be carefully nurtured so that it is neither abused, nor mistaken for projection of our own thoughts and beliefs.

The crown chakra also leads to intuitive knowing that comes to us from a higher spiritual plane beyond this world of form. This higher and expanded sense of truth serves the highest good not only in an earthbound sense, but also in an eternal, or timeless sense. The truths of the crown chakra serve to connect us more fully with our soul's truths and the truths that we are called to live by in this lifetime, in order to fulfill our soul's purpose, as well as to accomplish higher spiritual goods for others.

Through the Crown Chakra's full energization, we achieve what is called Self-Realization, or becoming one with our own soul's Higher Self. From this union, we progress to the truly God-Realized state of Union with the Divine Self. At that stage, we are liberated from the cycle of rebirth, and no longer depend upon returning to earth in human form for making spiritual progress. This state of liberation has been called "moksha" in the ancient Himalayan traditions.

In May 2010, I experienced a transcendental state during meditation, and received an extended visionary experience which I refer to as my "Enlightenment Vision."[145] After this vision, my consciousness changed, and I became aware, incredulous though I was, that my crown chakra had opened. Clearly, I had attained some level of enlightened consciousness, but a few months later, after my father's death, I dropped down from that elevated state.

Ever since that time, I have "bobbled up-and-down," into and out of that higher consciousness. Meditation and a couple of pranayama techniques both help raise my consciousness. Learning to remain in a high state is still a goal, requiring that I give up other attachments first!

Although I have not yet attained full Self-Realization, I have received this remarkable ability simply to "know" spiritual truths, especially through simply asking, and

---

[145] For the full description of this amazing vision, a discussion of my spiritual journey, and the amazing teachings I learned from higher consciousness, as well as from Ascended Masters including Jesus Christ and Buddha, please see my book *Mornings with the Masters: Mystical Journeys in a Postmodern World*. *Mornings with the Masters* is available in both Kindle and paperback versions on Amazon.com. Or, you may go here:
https://selfrealizationtherapy.wordpress.com/2013/12/01/the-original-enlightenment-vision-i-experienced-in-2010/

receiving answers. I take no credit for this ability; it simply seems to arrive with the opening of the crown chakra. For instance, a friend once asked, "What is Self-Realization?" and the answer I immediately received was: "Self-Realization occurs when we cease to struggle with that which is not."

That answer is perfect. When we cease to struggle with our lower selves, and when we cease to struggle with circumstances in which we find ourselves; that is Self-Realization, because we live in the true reality beyond this limited reality of form. I have not yet found myself in that consciousness, except perhaps in a moment here or there.

What I observe here, at the level of still energizing the crown chakra, is that, as we let go of everything else, including the breath, then higher consciousness comes to us, or we are already there, with no separation. Bliss occurs.

I first "went into bliss" (as is the only way I know how to describe it), while meditating during the fall of 2013. I experienced an out-of-body awareness of "seeing" my own crown chakra, and the Bindu (or 8th) chakra, which is beyond the body and above the head. This awareness was energized by a feeling/intention of utter non-attachment to anything in this world.

The mystical experience was fulfilled by hearing the voice of Jesus Christ saying, "Behold, the pearl of great price," as I was seeing, from above and behind my own head, a beautiful pearl above my head and above the lotus blossom of the crown chakra. I realized Jesus was telling me that this experience of non-attachment is the "pearl of great price," which was also a Biblical reference (in some translations) to the kingdom of God. The "kingdom of God" is clearly a higher state of consciousness that we reach only through pure non-attachment!

At any rate, that energy of bliss remained with me for hours, and was palpable to others in the huge aura that surrounded me. Occasionally, I have felt bliss, especially during times when I have taught meditation classes and channeled higher consciousness "answers" for the class.

What has most likely held me back from complete Realization has been my earthly desires, fears, and attachments, which have also often led me to minimize my meditation practice. When I do meditate for longer periods, and when I have made significant choices of non-attachment, my consciousness has notably raised.

More importantly, I have met a couple of completely God-realized individuals: Amma, the hugging saint, although I have not yet gotten to converse with her, and Dada (J.P.) Vaswani, the wonderful guru of the Vaswani Mission in Pune, India, whom I met in May 2015.

When I met Dada Vaswani, we were in New Jersey at the home of one of his followers. I was privileged to speak with Dada one-on-one because some of his followers were hoping I would persuade him to let me write his biography. (He had, up to that point, refused all biographies of himself.) Dada still refused to have a biography written of him, but we had the most remarkable conversation I have ever had in my entire life.

When I asked Dada if I could write his biography, this dear, God-Realized, and at that time 97-year-old man replied: "I am nothing." One might rationally object that he was a physicist, a philosopher, and not only that, he was a saint!

At the time, I did not fully understand this answer, "I am nothing," although now, I realize that in order to become God-Realized, we must understand our own nothingness, for we do not exist apart from the Divine Self. Furthermore, and most importantly, we must empty ourselves of all that is not God in order to become filled with God.

> **In order to become God-Realized, we must understand our own nothingness, for we do not exist apart from the Divine Self. Furthermore, and most importantly, we must empty ourselves of all that is not God in order to become filled with God.**

At the time when I met Dada Vaswani, I knew that I needed answers to three questions on my spiritual path (personal answers that I would not be able to find in a book). I had even thought about asking Dada one of the questions as I drove to meet him. I did not, however, end up thinking to ask Dada any of the three questions when I was in his presence. I asked him nothing that I had really wanted to know beforehand, except would he let me write his biography.

Without my ever asking Dada the three questions I most needed to have answered, he nonetheless answered every single one of them and also taught me what I truly needed to know at that stage on my spiritual path. A truly God-Realized master, Dada Vaswani did not need me to ask anything in order for him, as one with the mind of God, to know what I truly needed to hear that day. Ultimately, he reminded me to stop identifying with the body as myself (I'm still working on that!), and told me to "live the truth."

Well, I do wonder if living the truth would be easy if we knew the truth. So, knowing the truth and living the truth are my current quest. What does this mean for our quest that we not only seek Truth, but also seek to live the Truth?

Could the Truth simply be that we are nothing and that God is All? I am beginning to believe that this is so, and that living by this Truth just might be the answer to everything! This seems especially to be so when one becomes familiar with enlightened consciousness, and also becomes self-aware of one's own thoughts as to whether or not they are rising to enlightened consciousness, or dropping down with ego fears, attachments, or desires, to a lesser mode of being. This lesser mode of being is ego-based, and therefore illusory, or not the truth!

The one other time I have clearly experienced Ultimate Truth was while I was meditating one morning in March of 2016. I had meditated to a state of incredibly beautiful, and I mean *exquisite*, peace. There was not one vibration inside me or outside me that was not of perfect peace. It felt like one big, golden bubble of peace filling me and surrounding me.

In this state of perfect peace, I then heard what I call the Teacher Voice in my head announce, "This ... Is ... God." I felt that truth for about a second, and then my ego-mind, which had been theologically trained by reading lots of words about God, hearing lots of words about God, and writing and speaking lots of words about God, immediately objected with the thought, "No! I want words!" How ludicrous that was.

I realized it was a ludicrous thought, and went back to experiencing this incredible and perfect peace. Then, I realized, "If this is God, everyone will fall in love with God."

The truths that I experience with the crown chakra may thus be able to be said to go beyond words, to a feeling state of peace and bliss. I have recently learned to reach for connection with God as love, so that a beautiful feeling of love fills my heart chakra. So, then, crown chakra awareness, as far as I can tell, leads to a state of being in which we are one with wordless love, peace, and bliss. This state of being is somehow our ultimate truth, despite its lack of words!

So, if you don't like the word "God," or don't believe in God, all I can say is, that's okay, but Love, Peace, and

Bliss, now *they* Are Real. Love, peace, and bliss are Heavenly, and they are what "I" would call "God."[146]

> Love, peace, and bliss are Heavenly, and they are what "I" would call "God."

To equate love, peace, and bliss with God or with truth may seem a bit confusing, until we realize that there is a consciousness as well as an energy that goes with each one. The state of consciousness that creates love, peace, and bliss surely is the wisest consciousness we can imagine. That consciousness which is wise and which gives rise to love, peace, and bliss could also be called "God."

The truth of God may therefore be that there is a wise consciousness that creates love, peace, and bliss, and out of this infinitely wise consciousness and its infinite energy, the entire universe was created. I am aware that this sounds like speculation, yet I am inviting us to conceive of a higher consciousness than most of us have yet attained.

The conclusion I invite us to agree on is that, without being in a state of loving, peaceful, bliss, we will be unable to access ultimate Truth. On the other hand, as we attain a state of loving, peaceful bliss, we will open our limited minds to Universal Truth, which might also be called "God."

---

[146] There technically is no separate "me" to call anyone anything! Perhaps you can hear Buddha laughing?!

With the crown chakra open, clearly, from my own experience, we can nonetheless be drawn back down to the consciousness of lower chakras, and still feel fear, until we just let go of all that is not love. For if we do not choose to go up, we regress to lower vibrations, and those are so much less fulfilling!

Some of my mystical experiences during meditation have included connecting with and being guided by Buddha. A book on truth and illusion from a spiritual perspective would be lacking if I did not include what Buddha taught me about the fundamental nature of reality. What Buddha taught me is that the fundamental nature of reality is: "All Is Well." In other words, the Divine consciousness that exists as love, peace, and bliss, and that creates the universe exists in a constant state of being in which all is well.

Even when the situations in which we find ourselves do not appear to be all that great or even appear to be awful, the truth hidden in-and-through and beyond what the world of form is presenting to us is that all is well. We may not see it, and we may not feel it, until we transform our consciousness into this higher plane.

So, then, if we would like to access ultimate and universal Truth, we need to transform our everyday consciousness into a continual consciousness that "All Is Well." This is the Divine Consciousness in every moment: "All Is Well." Until we maintain that consciousness, we will only continue perceiving illusions as if they are real. Only God, as "All Is Well," is real in the ultimate and eternal sense.

We can only achieve this implicit trust in the "All Is Well" through raising the kundalini through the central sushumna, or energy channel, that rises up the etheric (energetic) spine, to feed all the chakras. This central energy channel carries kundalini, which is powerful because it is faithful and trust-filled. It can only safely be raised all the way to the crown chakra when we are spiritually, mentally, and emotionally evolved enough to handle the power of the energy, and the truth it entails, which is implicit trust in the Divine.

> **Letting go of all that is not Love
> is the key to rising to new heights!
> With every breath,
> we can focus on feeling peace.
> With every thought,
> we can let go of attachment.
> With every intention, we can choose love.
> With every situation,
> we can choose gratitude and joy.**

When the kundalini rises, we live in complete and utter trust in God in all things, as well as in complete and utter trust in our Higher Selves, and every person and situation presenting themselves to us, because we know all leads us back to the state of being, "All Is Well."

How bad could that be to claim that only a state of being which entails love/peace/bliss is eternal? If we stop being afraid of finding out who God really is, and open ourselves to discovering that maybe we really would fall in love with God, in part because love/peace/bliss just feels so fantastic, then we can truly and finally open ourselves up to the very Love which loves us so very much – the Love which loves us completely, and which invites us to be part of that immense, powerful, and everlasting Love.

Letting go of all that is not Love is the key to rising to new heights! With every breath, we can focus on feeling peace. With every thought, we can let go of attachment. With every intention, we can choose love. With every situation, we can choose gratitude and joy.

For the crown chakra, sin is attachment to anything that is not God. (Understanding God as this wordless, formless, love/peace/bliss, rather than as a projection of our human minds.) Holding onto anything that exists in the world of form as a replacement for the Divine rather than merely honoring it as an expression of the Divine is a sin. This preference for *form* over the *Source of form* includes holding thoughts that separate us from being One with the heavenly energy of love/peace/bliss.

Meditation, especially pure forms of meditation designed to open the brow and crown chakras, offers the surest key for unlocking this higher state of consciousness which is beyond thought and beyond mind. This consciousness is a pure soul awareness in a state of love and peace and bliss.

In this state, Truth is beyond words, and yet Truth is Ultimate, and Truth is real beyond our imagining. Truth, for the crown chakra, is where we know and experience ourselves as One with the Divine, and One with one another. For the crown chakra, the Truth is that We Are One.

CHAPTER FOURTEEN

Truth as Wisdom to Heal Humanity – a Universal Dharma

I have found the paradox,
that if you love until it hurts, there can be no more hurt,
only more love. [147]
– Mother Teresa

We must learn to live together as brothers,
Or perish together as fools.[148]
– Rev. Dr. Martin Luther King, Jr.

Let us consider truth as embodying the wisdom we need to heal humanity. If you notice, I am inviting us to consider truth almost as a verb. If truth has any value, is it not something that will heal humanity?

If truth is both ideal and potential, as well as realized and existential, and if truth also holds universal value, then it will be a reality that has the potential to heal humanity. Healing humanity in this sense has to be universal as well as personal. Truth as wisdom in a universal sense will heal us politically, globally, environmentally, communally, and individually. This truth as personal truth entails the possibility of mental healing, emotional healing, physical healing, relational

---

[147] https://www.brainyquote.com/quotes/authors/m/mother_teresa.html
[148] As quoted here:
https://www.brainyquote.com/quotes/authors/m/martin_luther_king_jr.html
Accessed March 22, 2017.

healing, and spiritual healing, not just for one individual, but for all human beings.

This may seem incredibly idealistic, but we are questing for truth. In this quest for truth, does it not make sense to quest for ideal truth? Does it not make sense to quest for a truth that is universal, has active implications, operates at a personal level, and also heals?

> Truth as wisdom in a universal sense will heal us politically, globally, environmentally, communally, and individually.

As a healer, I would suggest that truth is the ultimate source of healing. When we are out of alignment with truth on any level of our being, this lack of alignment with truth can be felt energetically.[149]

In many religions, there is a concept often referred to in English as "salvation." Salvation and the means to it are usually considered aspects of ultimate truth in religions. Regardless of the details of how each religion may define it, "salvation" refers to an ultimate state of being. Salvation, in its root, thus refers to our restoration to wholeness and ultimate wellbeing.

If we seek to discover what is our ultimate wholeness as well as the ultimate source and state of our wellbeing,

---

[149] As an intuitive, mystic healer, I usually feel this sort of out-of-alignment in the throat chakra, which is, of course, energized by speaking the truth. By the time our chakra energy has been thrown off into an unhealthy flow pattern, we have begun to affect the body's state of wellbeing.

will we also find this universal truth? I believe it is so. This is why I suggest that the ultimate, universal truth heals humanity: any ultimate and universal truth will restore our ultimate wholeness and wellbeing.

In practical everyday terms, truth here is of no value unless it recognizes the essential unity and goodness of all of humanity, for this is where truth starts at the level of higher consciousness, from the brow chakra and the crown chakra. Truth is founded on the inherent goodness, potential, equality, and importance of all human beings, as well as the inherent value and dignity of life and all living beings.

From a spiritual perspective, the truth of oneness informs all else. This is the primary truth that forms the basis of reality and gives rise to understanding all other truths.

> **From a spiritual perspective, the truth of oneness informs all else.**

What contributes to the wellbeing of life as one inseparable whole forms the basis of tests of truth at the crown chakra level. Whether objectively verifiable or not, truth, as revealed through higher consciousness, must be grounded in the sense of the priority of oneness, equality, and sanctity of life – every life.

Let us start this quest for a Universal Truth that restores humanity to health and wholeness on all levels by addressing the false dichotomies that block us from perceiving the truth of oneness that leads to wholeness. These false dichotomies are: humanity and nature as separate; divinity and humanity as separate; we human beings as separate from one another; and ego as separate from soul. We cannot necessarily address these in "logical" sequence, because they are holistic and possibly even holographic; unity just works that way.

We will also address this Universal level of Truth as a Universal dharma. The way I use the word dharma entails two aspects of meaning: a spiritual teaching, as well as the fundamental nature of reality.[150]

What do we mean in this case, then, that Universal Truth reflects a Universal Dharma? First, the teaching is that, in the Divine aspect of what is really real, we experience the truth of Divine Being: All Is Well. If you think about it, the Divine Source, as the Source of life, love, peace, joy, kindness, and so on, must exist as a state of being in which all is well. That is the heavenly state of being that flows from our Divine Source. This is the fundamental nature of reality: All Is Well.

Secondly, this Universal Dharma teaches us that we must share this fundamental nature of reality with all of life. For example, I recently realized that our tendency in America is to define the term "holistic health" as something very individualistic. We tend to think of achieving holistic health as individuals through diet, exercise, supplements, yoga, and the like.

---

[150] I am indebted to Karen Armstrong and her book, *Buddha,* for a helpful definition of dharma (or dhamma) in the glossary of this book. Her definition confirmed what I had just received intuitively via a mystical experience during meditation. It is from this mystical understanding that I employ the word dharma.

However, "holistic" health is not holistic unless it includes the consciousness of our unity with nature, other human beings, and the Divine Self.

In other words, holistic health requires maintaining a healthy environment, a healthy planet, healthy cultures, healthy economies, as well as healthy food,

> **Holistic health requires maintaining a healthy environment, a healthy planet, healthy cultures, healthy economies, as well as healthy food, healthy relationships, healthy communities, global peace, and the holistic health of all humans, not just some of us. That is the Universal Dharma.**

healthy relationships, healthy communities, global peace, and the holistic health of all humans, not just some of us. That is the Universal Dharma; not individualistic, though it may be personal, but rather universally understood as encouraging wellness and wholeness for all life.

From this understanding of a Universal Dharma which seeks the "All Is Well" as a state of being for all life, let us reflect on overcoming false dichotomies.

The first is, of course, the false dichotomy that we are separate from nature. As long as humanity survived as hunter-gatherers, we were part of the ecosystem without substantially altering it. Once we began to engage in extensive agriculture, we began to change our ecosystems.[151] As nomads, we could exist as part of the ecosystem unless we were also shepherds who drove large herds of animals who consumed most of the available vegetation. Once we began to build permanent homes, we also altered local ecosystems.

The question becomes: how can we restore ourselves as part of ecosystems? There are some innovative plans and designs; efforts to restore significant green spaces in the city of Paris set one example of the potential. Restoring green spaces, however, also needs to take account of the original animal inhabitants of the land, in order to give them a chance to revive their populations. This calls for large green spaces such as preserves, wetlands, forests, and so on, where the wildlife are empowered to exist as just that – wildlife.

Why is this important? This is important first because humanity is one with nature, not separate from it. Secondly, as we have moved away from our sense of unity with nature, we have lost some of the higher consciousness of what it means to be human as well as spiritual. Higher consciousness is uniting and empowering, not divisive nor destructive.

When we have defined ourselves as separate from nature, we have then sought to dominate nature. As we have dominated nature, we have formed significant attachments to our own power, as well as excessive

---

[151] I am familiar, from childhood memories in Africa, with the concept that indigenous people have practiced agriculture in harmony with ecosystems. I remember discovering, while traveling through a rainforest, that local people had planted their "garden" plants in and among the trees of the rainforest, not separate from, but part of the overall ecosystem.

attachments to the material wellbeing that our power over nature has enabled us to attain. These attachments to power and materialism have influenced us to move from humility and gratitude to domination and greed. Obviously, domination and greed are neither healing, nor unifying, nor do they reflect higher consciousness.

In terms of our economies, we need to restore the harmony of ecosystems as well. If we think about it, the environment itself is not only the basis of our economies, for all resources come from nature, but also the environment is the very real limit of the potential of our economies, because once we use resources and destroy ecosystems, they no longer exist for anyone's benefit. Basing our economies on ecosystems just recognizes the truth that already exists, and works *with* the environmental foundations of our economies rather than *against* the environmental foundations of our economies.

> **Basing our economies on ecosystems just recognizes the truth that already exists, and works *with* the environmental foundations of our economies rather than *against* the environmental foundations of our economies.**

To create economies based on ecosystems, we need to restore local communal control, such that every good and service produced within each community is seen as part of the local ecosystem, and the local community can therefore decide whether or not that good or service enhances the local ecosystem, or needs to be moved or produced differently so that the local ecosystem remains intact.

I know this sounds perhaps simplistic and overly idealistic, but we are speaking of higher consciousness, oneness, and healing humanity. Nothing is more important than that we attain this degree of higher consciousness for the healing of all humanity. For those of us who think I may be completely unrealistic, excessively idealistic, and out-of-touch with "reality," I defer to the wisdom of Frederick Douglass: "I prefer to be true to myself, even at the hazard of incurring the ridicule of others, rather than to be false, and to incur my own abhorrence."[152]

Because patriarchy is part and parcel of the value system of capitalism, it is time for women's voices to be heard. What sounds unrealistic to patriarchal capitalism is, I would suggest, sanity. To have such wealth disparities is, I would suggest, collective insanity. The time has come for women's voices, and those with a balance of feminine and masculine energies, to speak up for what might be called "sacred sanity." Sacred sanity protects all of humanity as equals; anything else is just bully economics.

As the Rev. Dr. Martin Luther King, Jr. once wrote: "Capitalism does not permit an even flow of economic

---

[152] Frederick Douglass, as quoted here:
http://www.goodreads.com/author/show/18943.Frederick_Douglass
Accessed on March 25, 2017.

resources. With this system, a small privileged few are rich beyond conscience, and almost all others are doomed to be poor at some level. That's the way the system works. And since we know that the system will not change the rules, we are going to have to change the system."[153] Though one might argue with some of Dr. King's words, there is visionary truth in them. Basing our economies on the economies of nature is a step in the right direction.

In addition to attempting to change "the system," we need to learn to change our focus. If we focus on oneness, both the community and the individual will be empowered. If we focus on ecosystems, we will focus on sustainability rather than exploitation. A shift in focus empowers all, not just some, to attain economic and social empowerment.

For instance, a shift in focus would entail actually engaging with the townspeople of local mines in indigenous communities around the world. In the Democratic Republic of the Congo (yes, where I was born), that would entail engaging local communities in discerning solutions to their problems, and flowing money to the community itself, not just the owners of the mine nor to the local warlords. That would mean paying sustainable wages to the adults who mine, so that children will not also have to engage in exploitative labor in unsafe mining conditions.

---

[153] Martin Luther King, Jr., https://www.brainyquote.com/quotes/quotes/m/martinluth691624.html Accessed on March 22, 2017.

A shift in focus would mean working directly with workers in places like Pakistan, to focus on what is needed for workplace safety, adequate wages, and union representation, if possible. Microloans to empower workers to form their own businesses could help shift the current systems of exploitation.

One possibility would be for states to require corporations to be chartered only as "benefit corporations," that is, as corporations that pledge to benefit communities, workers, and the environment. The design of corporate boards could be mandated to include people from communities in which the corporation operates, as well as those where it derives resources and employs workers, both directly and indirectly.

A shift in focus could mean teaching vertical ocean farming which has been developed by a few entrepreneurial individuals off the Eastern seaboard, where vertical farms in the ocean can produce greater quantities of a variety of sea life, primarily kelp, other seaweed, and shellfish.[154]

Though my knowledge of this is limited, I recognize the potential of vertical farming along coasts for transforming and developing fishing industries in ways that work with ecosystems and ocean populations rather than against them. For instance, as described by the heroic ocean entrepreneur, Bren Smith, "3D

---

[154] See, for instance, this inspirational story of the development of vertical ocean farming: https://medium.com/invironment/an-army-of-ocean-farmers-on-the-frontlines-of-the-blue-green-economic-revolution-d5ae171285a3#.xb1hmlz7m Accessed on March 25, 2017.

ocean farming" requires no inputs of fertilizer, feed, fresh water, or arable land. The farmed kelp of these vertical ocean farms "soaks up to five times more carbon than land based plants," and the oysters "filter up to 50 gallons of water a day, pulling nitrogen – the cause of our oceans' spreading dead zones – from the water column ... seaweeds could be a powerful source of zero-input biofuel .... If you were to create a network of our ocean farms totaling the size of Washington state, you could feed the planet."[155]

As evidenced by this very exciting prospect of 3D ocean farming, it is possible to save ourselves and the planet. Many of the concepts called for through vertical ocean farming reform the system based on the oneness of us all in this situation of changing economies leading to economic hardships for so many people around the world.

With regard to international trade, a shift of focus that achieves greater oneness could occur through temporary exchanges of families with children, in order for people to understand that disparities arise in part because of our ignorance of each other's needs and advantages.

While this sounds idealistic, what I am suggesting could be accomplished either through local communities or corporations, taking the idea of a "sister city" one step further, and engaging cities from developing nations. In this approach, a small percentage of families from each

---

[155] Bren Smith, https://medium.com/invironment/an-army-of-ocean-farmers-on-the-frontlines-of-the-blue-green-economic-revolution-d5ae171285a3#.xb1hmlz7m Accessed on March 25, 2017.

community and/or each corporation involved with international trade would move to the places around the world affected by mineral extraction, cheap labor, polluting factories, and so on, and families from those communities would exchange places with them.

When exchanging places, people from exploited communities would take their children and live in the countries where their goods and services have created wealth and wellbeing. Only by forming temporary exchanges of families and discovering the impact of international corporate activity on the local families, will we be able to discover the truths we need which will enable all people to thrive economically.

> **Children are born into different circumstances, and equality dictates that we change the disparity of those circumstances, otherwise, inequality rules.**

In other words, only by living each other's lives will we be able to learn the truths of the world we have created. Only by learning the truths that we have created together will we be able to transform them.

This is also why "ag-gag" laws prohibiting the taking of photos of the various meat industry's cruelties to animals must be reversed. Only when we know the truth, will we be able to set ourselves free from it. The truths of what we do, via our economic systems, to children, animals, and the ecosystems around the world need to be front-and-center in our daily lives.

More specifically, only by putting children first, by focusing on the oneness and equality of all children, will we be able to effect lasting economic change. It would be most wonderful if we took turns taking care of one another's children. I would love for us to find ways to do that.

Children are born into different circumstances, and equality dictates that we change the disparity of those circumstances, otherwise, inequality rules. For many of us, the oneness of children may be our guide to

> **Oneness is the foundation for economic advancement; not capital, not profit, not military might, and not political domination. Only oneness will enable us to accomplish world peace. Oneness is the source of the consciousness that will lead to peace and prosperity for all. Oneness is therefore the Truth we seek in order to attain world peace**.

experiencing and attaining our adult sense of oneness.

Frederick Douglass once taught us: "It is easier to build strong children than to repair broken men."[156] And yet, by empowering children through equality and oneness, we will heal and strengthen ourselves – all of us, adults and children alike.

---

[156] Frederick Douglass, as quoted here:
http://www.goodreads.com/author/show/18943.Frederick_Douglass Accessed on March 25, 2017.

Oneness is the foundation for economic advancement; not capital, not profit, not military might, and not political domination. Only oneness will enable us to accomplish world peace. Oneness is the source of the consciousness that will lead to peace and prosperity for all. Oneness is therefore the Truth we seek in order to attain world peace.

Prioritizing oneness in our quest for truth therefore entails overcoming the third dichotomy of believing that we are separate individuals. Discovering the higher consciousness Truth that we are all One on the soul level leads to realizing that how I treat you is also how I am treating myself. To quote the Rev. Dr. Martin Luther King, Jr:

"Injustice anywhere is a threat to justice everywhere …. Whatever affects one directly, affects all indirectly. I can never be what I ought to be until you are what you ought to be. This is the interrelated structure of reality."[157]

The truth of our oneness as souls on a human journey reflects this interwoven nature of reality. Our souls evolve, and to some degree, our own evolution affects the soul evolution of everyone else. When we vibrate with and embody unconditional love and peace, we directly affect everyone else around us. Our souls are intertwined on this journey in which we are all returning to Love.

---

[157] Martin Luther King, Jr., Accessed here: https://www.brainyquote.com/quotes/quotes/m/martinluth122559.html and here https://www.brainyquote.com/quotes/quotes/m/martinluth403521.html on March 22, 2017.

The Syracuse Cultural Workers have a beautiful teaching called, "How To Build Global Community." Many years ago, I purchased a postcard expressing their advice on building global community, and I love the sense of oneness it conveys. The beautiful advice from the Syracuse Cultural Workers on how to build global community begins with these three lines:

> *Think of no one as "them"*
> *Don't confuse your comfort with your safety*
> *.... Talk with strangers*[158]

We must begin to form such local efforts, as in Syracuse, New York, to create local economies based on our oneness as well as the ecosystems of which we are part. We need to work at this together with our neighbors, and with people who may be different from us, including refugees and people on disability,[159] who are so often overlooked and undervalued in our culture.

In order to increase our sense of oneness, the second false dichotomy we must further address is the idea that humanity and divinity are separate. Many religions speak of the sacredness of life, especially human life. What is sacred is divine. Beyond duality, at the mystical levels of virtually all religions, one discovers, through mystical experiences, the truth of our oneness

---

[158] Syracuse Cultural Workers, postcard: "How To Build Global Community," 2002. The more recent versions of the postcards, posters, and so much more can be purchased and more inspiring information is available here: https://www.syracuseculturalworkers.com/ Accessed on March 25, 2017.
[159] If you are a refugee or on disability and reading this line, please understand that I know we are one with one another; I speak to we who have forgotten.

with divinity. However, as soon as we discover our oneness with divinity, we know that this oneness with divinity is true of all humanity, and we can no longer see ourselves as separate from one another.

Spiritual disciplines, especially the practice of meditation, are what lead us to this truth of oneness of ourselves with the Divine and with one another. So, for the healing of humanity, both personally and universally, the practice of meditation becomes necessary to help us discover our own inner sacredness of being. Inside ourselves, we can discover peace. Inside ourselves, we can discover love and compassion. Inside ourselves, we can discover an inner knowing and inner wisdom which can guide us to better lives.

Truth lies within. When we discover the truth that lies within, we also may discover that Truth exists beyond

> **Truth lies within. When we discover the truth that lies within, we also may discover that Truth exists beyond this universe. From this perspective of Ultimate Truth, the universe is like a single breath of God, singular, yet pregnant with everything that ever was, is, and will be.**

this universe. From this perspective of Ultimate Truth, the universe is like a single breath of God, singular, yet pregnant with everything that ever was, is, and will be.

We may believe that our search for truth is outside ourselves, but it is not until we discover our own inner truths within our own deep, inner peace, that we can share truths outside ourselves that are healing for others. All truth lies within, and ultimately the wisdom we need lies within as well.

Nature can show us and teach us wise ways of being, but even observing these does not increase our own wisdom unless we listen with our hearts, and intuitively learn nature's ways, for her ways are the truths spoken in our own hearts and minds. We experience ultimate truths as truths of the heart which also bring us peace of mind. But peace of mind alone is not enough of a measure of ultimate truth, for ultimate truth serves Life and the wellbeing of others as well. Ultimate truth sings forth from hearts of compassion, and brings joy to ourselves and others.

Ultimate truth heals humanity personally and universally, because it resonates with love, peace, and great joy.

In order to be able to discern ultimate truth, we must overcome a fifth false dichotomy, which is that the soul is separate from the ego. The truth is that the ego self is not real; ego is an illusion that merely appears to be real, like everything else that derives from the world of form. Where one part of a dichotomy is unreal, there is no dichotomy. Ego just wishes us to believe in the duality of soul and ego, and we generally do, until we realize that ego is one of the biggest expressions of nothingness there is, because ego arises from fear and a sense of separation from our Divine Source.[160]

We exist as souls in human bodies, which generally develop a low-vibration consciousness that we may call ego. Ego is the part of body-consciousness that feels separate from God, separate from other human beings, and separate from nature. Experiencing itself as separate from love, ego constantly seeks to protect itself and its own sense of existence as a body.

Ego believes it thinks separately from God, and ego thinks of itself as being separate from Source/God/Spirit/Higher Power. Yet ego is part of our experience of self on this earth. Ego is the part that we have to "love enough to let go of," as I was taught during my spiritual training in England.

In believing itself/ourselves to be separate from Source Energy, the ego lowers its vibration, from which we derive the sense of a "fall" from a heavenly state, or a "fall from grace." When living from our ego consciousness, we experience reality as anything but heavenly, and as anything but grace.

Egos don't believe in grace. For the ego, everything has to be earned. For the ego, fear reigns far more often than love, and love is conditional and focuses on getting

---

[160] I would also suggest that money is the biggest "nothingness" there is in life, for money is simply a medium of exchange which represents something else, that is, the relative value of goods and services. Money is part of the illusion of this world, and as such, it can either serve divine purposes or the ego's purposes based on fear and separation. Ultimately, as Paramahansa Yogananda wrote: "Money is God's slave." *Autobiography of a Yogi,* p. 112, Thirteenth edition, printed in 1999.

what we want and need for ourselves, and for our own "loved ones." For the ego, the main answers in life are material, practical, and "rational," devoid of any spiritual understanding.

I place "rational" in quotes because the ego believes that it is rational to understand ourselves as separate, and to look out for our own self-interests first. This form of "rationality" is, in fact, irrational in its consequences for humanity in the long run. We are currently seeing the consequences of this "rationality" in rampant environmental destruction of wildlife and ecosystems, in climate change's destructive effects, in the destruction of healthy food and healthy soil through GMO's and pesticides,[161] as well as through rampant greed and a failure to support the rights of all

> **Ego believes that it is rational to understand ourselves as separate, and to look out for our own self-interests first. This form of "rationality" is, in fact, irrational in its consequences for humanity in the long run.**

---

[161] In addition to pesticides drastically reducing populations of beneficial or desirable insects such as monarch butterflies, honey bees, and (I believe) fireflies, pesticides kill the microorganisms in soil that break down dirt, making nutrients available for plants to absorb them. GMOs are avoided by racoons and deer when they encounter GMO and non-GMO crops side-by-side; they will eat only non-GMO crops. See, for example:
http://blogs.webmd.com/health-ehome/2009/07/animals-dont-want-to-eat-gmos-so-why-are-we.html   Accessed on April 14, 2017.
Who is smarter than whom? Us or a racoon?

workers to a living wage. These consequences are not rational; they are merely short-sighted and greedy.

What *is* rational is living life based on the harmonious qualities that come with higher consciousness. These harmonious qualities are love, peace, compassion, empathy, gratitude, and joy. These harmonious qualities derive from the four harmony principles of oneness: humanity and nature are one; humanity and divinity are one; divinity and nature are one; and we are all one.

By contrast, the "rationality" of the ego arises from a belief in separation, which belief allows people to treat other people and the environment destructively, because we believe we can survive at the expense of others. Because the ego approaches life from a lower vibration of fear and separation rather than the higher vibrations of unconditional love, harmony, peace, joy, and bliss, the ego tends both to experience, and to create, a lot of emotional, physical, and psychic pain.

As a healer, life coach, and human being working with clients and also contemplating these things from my own life experience, I have become deeply aware of our inner need for healing. Our ego selves have existed in this culture that believes in separation for so long, that many of us have experienced deep psychic woundedness. The very belief in separation inflicts a degree of psychic pain, because it denies the grandness of our own inner being as well as our interconnectedness with Source and life in this universe. This sense of disconnection evokes fear and anxiety, which leads to self-protection, often at others' expense.

The emotional wounds and "psychic/mental" wounds of life do not necessarily show clearly on the outside, but lie often hidden within us, needing to heal in order for us fully to love ourselves. If we would like to "love our ego enough to let it go," then we need to love the hurt, anxious, and wounded parts of ourselves deep inside. When we love our inner wounded parts, we heal the lower vibration, thus raising it to a higher vibration through the power of love.

Once we begin to love and heal all the inner, hurting parts of ourselves, we can safely discover that these parts served us in some way, showing us the truths of our own inner need for healing, but just as importantly helping us understand the needs of others for healing as well. Discovering our own inner emotional wounds helps us to realize the truth that emotionally or verbally wounding ourselves and one another does not help humanity live well together.

Loving our inner wounded child self helps us gain emotional strength. Once we begin to find our strength, we will find our sense of voice. When we get really good at loving ourselves, we will raise our subtle vibration.

When we raise our subtle vibration, we may discover that ego was not separate from ourselves, it was just a lowering of our own vibration to the world of form, which is not real. When we lower the vibration of our own subtle energy, then we lower our consciousness from the consciousness of our soul, to the consciousness of ego.

So then, ego is not separate from soul, ego, as an illusion of self, is just a lower vibratory expression of the soul's pure essence. As such, it often does not look or sound much like our soul self, but it does carry the essence of intending love as a form of protecting itself, even though it goes about it in ways that tend to inflict pain on others as well as ourselves. It is these lower intentions of inflicting pain, whether on ourselves or others, that are unreal, for only the world of form can give rise to harmful intentions. Only fear gives rise to the intention to harm anyone, or to the lack of care which allows harm to occur to others. Ego is merely the voice of fear giving rise to personal protectionism.

Ego believes it needs protection because ego never feels completely safe.

Ego is just a distortion of our soul's pure energy and consciousness. When we see ego that way, we can love it, heal it, and let go of its low vibration and its low-frequency thoughts, fears, and intentions. When we love ego enough to let it go, we raise our vibration to that pure awareness of being one with our soul Self, one with Source, and one with one another on the level of our souls.

From this place of Oneness, we see that the ego is not real. Only then can we begin to know our True Self.

This returns us to our second false dichotomy: the separation between humanity and divinity. The truth is that our souls are one with God. All souls come from

God, and are an extension of the Divine, existing in human form. We all return to God; this is our ultimate healing as well as our Ultimate Truth. The journey through the chakra system of human development is really a spiritual evolution of the soul in its apparent separation from, and ultimate return to God, via free will, living in this world of form.

Therefore, the teaching from the text which refers to "our God" and "God is one," refers, at its highest and most mystical level, to the oneness of humanity in and with God. The highest spiritual evolvement of the spiritual teaching of one God is: God is all there is and everything else is existential illusion or Maya.

We awaken spiritually when we realize the truth that God is One and we are one with God and with one another. In other words, the ultimate truth of this view is in alignment with what Christ taught: "Those who worship God must worship God in Spirit and in Truth." For when we realize our true nature as Spirit, and that all are One in Spirit, then we realize that there is no truth that is separate from our spiritual Source.

> **When we realize our true nature as Spirit, and that all are One in Spirit, then we realize that there is no truth that is separate from our spiritual Source.**

The world of form is then recognized as a temporary illusion, and only Spirit and the qualities of spirit are ultimately true. In other words, what is really "real" consists not of form, but of higher consciousness, which might be conceived of as pure Spirit, or pure mind. Furthermore, pure Spirit entails the qualities of being of unconditional love, peace, bliss, and the energetic state of being in which All Is Well.[162]

This enables us to overcome our fourth false dichotomy: that we are separate from each other. Only when we understand that we are all created by the energy-consciousness of love, peace, wisdom, compassion, and bliss can we know that all of life, the earth, and the entire universe is comprised of this energy of love-peace-bliss. Wherever the vibration lowers itself from love-peace-bliss, illusion has occurred.

Because all of creation, that is, the entire universe, is imbued with divine energy-consciousness, divinity and nature are also one. This understanding overcomes the third false dichotomy, the idea that God and nature are separate. Beauty in nature is part of the expression of this energy-consciousness of love-peace-bliss and All Is Well.

Wherever we see beauty in nature, we perceive signs of the presence of beautiful Source energy. Beauty, wisdom, compassion, empathy, love, peace, kindness, patience, trust, and joy are all energies that testify to the presence of Source energy. Of course, inner beauty, such as loving-kindness and thoughtfulness, far more accurately reflects the true nature of Source than does external beauty alone. It is important to acknowledge that non-human animals often evidence many of these

---

[162] This concept of "All Is Well" was explained in chapter .

inner qualities just as human animals do, for animals are capable of love, trust, kindness, and even empathy and compassion.

Love is everywhere; if only we will perceive it through the eyes of unity-consciousness. Unity consciousness leads us to living in a state of Oneness.

Oneness is the healing we seek. There is not only great wisdom in this oneness, there is also great love in this oneness. When we become more consistently able to feel the love, peace, and joy of oneness, then we have begun not only to discover, but also to experience and to live Ultimate Truth.

> **Oneness is the healing we seek. When we become more consistently able to feel the love, peace, and joy of oneness, then we have begun not only to discover, but also to experience and to live Ultimate Truth.**

Discovering, experiencing, and living Ultimate Truth is entirely possible, for it simply means living the truth of a greater Presence which is love, patience, kindness, peace, compassion, and inexpressible joy. We have a choice to believe that this is our ultimate nature. The more we discover ourselves as love, peace, and joyfulness, the more we discover ultimate Truth within ourselves.

The more we maintain this love-peace-bliss state of being, the more love, peace, and joy we are able to share with others. When we all discover this inner healing wisdom, it will bring us all into a state of peace, in which we are one. When we fully discover and live our oneness, then love will rule, peace will prevail, and joy will become a natural way of life.

The final key for entering this state of love, peace, and joy is the realization that the Ultimate Truth of Life is that "All Is Well." The nature of Source is a state of being in which all is well on a continuous basis. To enter into oneness with Ultimate Truth, we must enter into the trusting state in which we believe, and even know, that everything is somehow working towards the state in which all is well, even when the worldly appearance around us suggests otherwise.

Ultimate truth entails not only love, peace, and bliss, but also this fundamental nature of reality in which all is well. When we are able to trust this state of being, which might also be called Divine, miracles can occur. Trusting that all is well changes our experience of life.

It is almost as Einstein said, that the theory with which we observe things determines what we are able to observe. Just so, what theory we apply to the state of our lives also determines that very state of being in which we find ourselves. If we believe life is hard, indeed it will be so. If we believe that all is well, life will work itself out so that all goes well because we believe all is well.

The reason that our beliefs shape our lives is that freedom and free will are part of the ultimate truths of this universe. This includes the free will to believe that things are a certain way. So, those who believe there is no god are free to experience that there is no god. Those who believe in miracles are free to experience miracles.

Since the universe is made up of energy-consciousness, everything is affected by the energy-consciousness of everything else, at least to some degree. So then, even our thoughts and beliefs affect our reality. Because free will holistically affects every level of energy-consciousness in life, our own consciousness determines our experience of reality to a large degree. If we have a bad attitude, we are far more likely to have a bad day. Free will at the level of consciousness in this universe just works that way; that we generally manifest what we believe, except when there are karmic blocks to that manifestation.[163]

The highest and most universal expression of the concept of "All Is Well," is the extension of it to others, indeed, the extension of "All Is Well" to life on earth. If we simply believe that "All Is Well" for ourselves, we still remain in a lower vibration until we understand that we are to embody the energy-consciousness of "All Is Well" for everyone else also.

Embodying the energy-consciousness of "All Is Well"[164] turns this state of being into a verb, in which we must

---

[163] This is the principle underlying the movie and the book, "The Secret," as well as other approaches to manifestation. Karmic blocks occur because they are consequences of previous choices and beliefs, the energy-consciousness of which is still present to affect and shape our lives. Such karmic blocks can be either positive or negative in the appearance of their effects.

[164] In case it has not become obvious at this point near the end of the book, I capitalize concepts which, to me, express the Divine nature, out of reverence for the sacredness of these concepts as Divine.

actively seek wellness and wholeness and a happy, healthy state of being for everyone. Just as a mother embodies her unborn child for its wellbeing, so also we must all become, to some degree, the Universal Mother who holds the wellbeing of others within her sphere of care and concern. If we would discover the fullness of Ultimate Truth, we must embody this wellbeing through the consciousness of "All Is Well" for everyone else as much as we are able.

Ultimate Truth is never just about ourselves, even though it is both personal and universal. Ultimate Truth cannot just heal one part of humanity. Ultimate Truth is a state of being in which all is well for everyone, and so we must do our part to align with the gift of love, peace, joy, and wellness for *all* life.

> **Ultimate Truth is a state of being in which all is well for everyone.**

When we align ourselves with the gifts of love, peace, joy and wellness for everyone, then we become an actual expression of Ultimate Truth. The Ultimate Truth of who we are is the truth that we *are* Love; we *are* peace, we *are* bliss, we *are* wellbeing and blessing for everyone.

When we come to know ourselves as the Ultimate Truth of blessing the Oneness of all life, then we become part of the healing or salvation of humanity. We become one with God when we learn to live as God, the One who imparts wellbeing (blesses), the One who heals, and the One who loves without limit.

May we find this universal dharma, the truth that we are Love. When enough of us do so, the world will be healed, and humanity will be restored to our original state of Oneness, in wholeness, peace, joy, and love. May it be so, and thank you to all of us for doing our part!

ABOUT THE AUTHOR

Rev. Carol Richardson, M.Div., MPH, was born on the equator in what was then the Belgian Congo, now the Democratic Republic of the Congo. Raised on two continents, in four countries, and in three states in the USA, she feels most at home in Maryland and the greater Washington, DC area.

With a BS in psychology, a Master of Public Health degree, and a Master of Divinity degree, she loves caring about people mind, body, and soul. Widowed at the age of 28 when her 34-year-old husband died suddenly of a cerebral aneurysm, she was left to raise a 22-month-old daughter and a 7-month-old son. Decades later, they are now well-educated, high-achieving, happily married young adults.

In 1996, Carol learned Raja Yoga meditation, and started on an Eastern path of spirituality, combining this science of yoga with her Christianity. She traveled to a spiritual centre in England for four years in a row to study intuitive forms of life coaching and energy healing, as well as Kriya yoga, and more. She also studied animal healing and Reiki. In May 2010, she had what she calls an "Enlightenment Vision," in which she met and was blessed by various Ascended Masters, including Jesus Christ, Buddha, Mother Mary, Paramhansa Yogananda, High Priest Melchizedek, and Lady Kwan Yin. Since then, her healing work has been blessed and guided by archangels and Ascended Masters.

Ordained in the Christian Church (Disciples of Christ), she has served churches for over 15 years. She has lived in the greater Washington, DC area since July 2011, working a variety of jobs and also seeing clients as an intuitive life coach, energy healer, and hypnotherapist. She offers stress reduction workshops, teaches meditation and lightworker training, offers motivational talks, and hosts meditation circles.

Carol, also known as "Anandi," (meaning "bliss"), is a leading expert in accessing higher consciousness, empowering you to discover your core self, heal yourself, and find your bliss. She delights in helping others find themselves more fully healed and transformed on their spiritual paths.

Rev. Richardson is available for speaking engagements, meditation retreats, and more. Please go to the book website or the Highest Harmony Healing & Coaching website for more information:

http://www.truthandillusionbook.com/

http://www.highestharmony.guru/

www.ingramcontent.com/pod-product-compliance
Lightning Source LLC
Chambersburg PA
CBHW071854290426
44110CB00013B/1148